The Adventurous Life of Amelia B. Edwards

The Adventurous Life of Amelia B. Edwards

Egyptologist, Novelist, Activist

Margaret C. Jones

BLOOMSBURY ACADEMIC
LONDON · NEW YORK · OXFORD · NEW DELHI · SYDNEY

BLOOMSBURY ACADEMIC
Bloomsbury Publishing Plc
50 Bedford Square, London, WC1B 3DP, UK
1385 Broadway, New York, NY 10018, USA
29 Earlsfort Terrace, Dublin 2, Ireland

BLOOMSBURY, BLOOMSBURY ACADEMIC and the Diana logo are
trademarks of Bloomsbury Publishing Plc

First published in Great Britain 2022

Cover design: Rebecca Heselton
Cover images: Amelia Edwards by August Weger, after Elliott & Fry, line and stipple
engraving, after 1876 © National Portrait Gallery, London. The Giza pyramid complex,
greater Cairo © Marti Bug Catcher/ Shutterstock. Symbols of ancient Egypt © Liudmila
Klymenko/ Shutterstock. Desert sand, temples and camels © unsplash.

Bloomsbury Publishing Plc does not have any control over, or responsibility for, any
third-party websites referred to or in this book. All internet addresses given in this book
were correct at the time of going to press. The author and publisher regret any
inconvenience caused if addresses have changed or sites have ceased to exist, but can
accept no responsibility for any such changes.

A catalogue record for this book is available from the British Library.

A catalog record for this book is available from the Library of Congress.

ISBN: HB: 978-1-3502-9396-0
         PB: 978-1-3502-9395-3
         ePDF: 978-1-3502-9399-1
         eBook: 978-1-3502-9397-7

Typeset by RefineCatch Limited, Bungay, Suffolk
Printed and bound in India

To find out more about our authors and books visit www.bloomsbury.com
and sign up for our newsletters.

To the memory of Sophia Hughes – the best listener

CONTENTS

ILLUSTRATIONS

PREFACE

On an upper landing of the Egypt Exploration Society's offices in Doughty Mews, London, an elegantly dressed woman with neatly backswept, grey hair and a serious, intelligent gaze, presides from her portrait over the scholars and archivists toiling up and down the iron spiral staircase.

They are all here, in this building crammed with books, manuscripts and priceless artefacts, thanks to the woman in the picture. And, at this same moment, while the Exploration Society carries on its work of deciphering and classifying at the London headquarters, a select band of archaeologists is out, digging under the broiling Egyptian sun, to enrich our knowledge of the past. They, too, are able to carry on their work, owing to the organization Amelia Edwards founded, nearly a century and a half ago.

If you had shaken hands with her in some Victorian drawing room, or passed her, walking briskly on an errand up Bristol's Park Street, you would have met with the same pleasant-faced, dignified woman, dressed simply but elegantly, in long skirt and jacket. You would have noticed little about her that was obviously remarkable at first sight – only her upright walk, her impeccable neatness, her unfailing good manners. How could you know that the polite spinster lady had done things most women, and some men in her day, had never even dreamed of?

This was a woman who never glanced sideways to check with anyone else whether she was 'doing it right'. Nor, for that matter, did she make any unseemly fuss. In all she did, Miss Edwards was highly discreet. Yet – simply by how she lived her life – she challenged many of the normally unquestioned assumptions of her age.

The multi-talented Miss Edwards was an adventurous traveller, who wrote lively accounts of what she did and saw for the stay-at-homes back in England. She travelled by mule through the Dolomite mountains, at a time when few outsiders knew of their existence. In her account of a voyage from Cairo to Nubia, *A Thousand Miles Up the Nile*, she brought an appreciation of the wonders of ancient Egypt to fascinated audiences in Britain and America, while rescuing and preserving that country's treasures for posterity. And she left money in her will to endow a Chair of Egyptology at London University, that for the first time established Egyptology as a serious academic discipline.

Outwardly conservative, in her personal life Edwards remained independent and unconventional. There were passionate same-sex relationships, in one of which she privately married her partner at the church altar.

As the best-selling and critically acclaimed author of eight popular novels and dozens of short stories, she wrote about unusual subjects for a Victorian woman writer – a battlefield in Italy; blockade-running in the American Civil War; the bohemian lives of male students in Paris. She supported feminist causes and animal rights, and had republican sympathies.

For all her independence, Amelia Edwards had a deceptively quiet way of going about the world, that concealed a relentless drive to accomplish whatever she set out to do.

She was also full of contradictions.

Fascinated by ancestry and drawn to the cultivation of 'celebrities' in the arts, she yet was a democrat at heart. She deplored social snobbery based on class and satirized it mercilessly in her novels. Daughter of an army officer who earned his medals fighting in the Napoleonic wars, and whom she greatly admired, towards the end of her life she came to denounce war as 'the great crime'. She opposed vivisection; she campaigned for the protection of birds. Yet she admired skill in shooting for game, and in her youth owned a gun. She praised rebels but always with an uneasy awareness that their quest for freedom might involve curtailing that of others.

Even Edwards' many career achievements are hard to pigeonhole. How is she best to be remembered? Is she mainly a novelist? Or mainly a writer of travel books? Or is she better celebrated as the distinguished Egyptologist she became in the last decade of her life, who furthered the discipline of Egyptology for generations to come?

When she died in 1892, those who wrote her obituaries faced the same conundrum. For some, her death came mainly as 'a severe blow to the interests of Egyptology', while others cherished memories of her best-selling novels, that were said to have 'amused a generation'.[1] One point the obituaries could agree on, however: hers had been a distinguished career. 'England', said one of them, 'has lost one of her foremost daughters'.[2]

Edwards' lifelong involvement in campaigns and causes is often regarded as only marginal to her main achievements, and hence unworthy of investigation. Press reports of her attendance at suffrage meetings, the evidence of her signature on suffrage and animal rights petitions, her membership of committees, and her own public statements, suggest otherwise. While it would be equally mistaken to overemphasize such commitments, they certainly formed an important background to her life. We fail to appreciate her contributions to progressive movements of her day, if we ignore them.

Her quiet acceptance of her sexual orientation, and the unconventional lifestyle that arose from it, have in recent years made her a figure of interest to the LGBT movement. After one abortive attempt to 'fit in' as a young woman, by accepting a male friend's offer of marriage, all her close emotional attachments were to other women.

She made her mark in fiction. Edwards' novels were never out of print in her lifetime, went through multiple editions not only in England but in America, Australia and New Zealand, were translated into several European languages and appreciatively reviewed in the British press. A reductive focus on her early mass-market fiction, and on her popular ghost stories for magazines, has tended to obscure both the satiric wit and the originality of her mature work. This is particularly true of her fictional explorations of English people's involvement in conflicts overseas – the independence struggle in Italy, or the American Civil War. It is something the present book aims to set right. In discussion both of her life and of her writings, I have revisited some of the contradictions Edwards encountered – not least in relation to the conventions of her day. She was always preoccupied with the predicament of women – particularly creative women – caught as they were in a web of obligations and conventions regarding marriage, sex and property. I am also interested in what seems to be the mainspring of her personality – the compulsive, passionate nature that would not let her rest, but drove her on to complete one challenging task after another. Why could she not remain content with a career that would have satisfied many people, as an acclaimed writer of fiction? Why, when already in her fifties, did she let go of that and sacrifice her career as a novelist, her time, income, energies, even her health, for the work that came almost to possess her – that of discovering and preserving the treasures of Ancient Egypt?

Abandoning her novel writing when at the height of her popular success, she devoted herself to a new vocation, and left an enduring legacy in that field. The enigma of the choice she made then will always fascinate.

In case all this sounds too solemn, it must be said that Amelia Edwards is entertaining company. In her witty dialogues, biting satire and dry observations on life, readers of her fiction and nonfiction will find a great deal to enjoy.

Because different aspects of her many-faceted life and work will appeal to different readers, it has seemed useful here to follow a mainly thematic approach, rather than telling the details of her life in strict chronological order. Readers will thus be able to focus on what interests them most. There are only a few exceptions to this rule, for the sake of continuity. So, the first chapter, 'Young Amelia', traces significant incidents in Edwards' childhood and early life, as she built her writing career during the 1850s.

The next two chapters focus on her relationships with other women, and her experiences as a traveller. In chapter 2, love and loss in her personal life are discussed in connection with a winter and spring spent in Rome – her passionate affair with Anne Brewster, and with her newfound love, Lucy Renshaw. The chapter which follows deals with her decision to make the journey by mule through the Dolomite mountains, in company with Lucy. Chapter 4 explores Edwards' encounters with the world of Egypt – that of the nineteenth-century present, and of the ancient past, on a voyage that would transform her life. Her vivid word-paintings of places, and her lively accounts of interactions with people met along the way, have made both her travel books, *Unfrequented Peaks* and *A Thousand Miles Up the Nile*, perennial favourites down the generations. The writings and talks on Egyptology that were the fruits of her Nile journey are discussed next, as the vivid imagination of a novelist is deployed to bring to life the ancient past. (Chapter 5, 'Inventing Egypt'.) 'Founding the Fund', the following chapter, tells of Edwards' struggles to establish the Egypt Exploration Fund, with inevitable personality clashes among the often eccentric men involved with nineteenth-century Egyptology.

Chapter 7, 'A Very Private Life', discusses the personal world of this reticent woman. Her letters, and the occasional magazine article, give some idea of her strategies for keeping outsiders at a distance.

Chapter 8 offers the serious appraisal of Edwards' achievements as a novelist that I believe her work deserves.

Edwards' triumphant speaking tour of the United States, with its attendant ominous accidents, merits a chapter 9 to itself. 'America' also describes her interventions during the tour, in the cause of women's rights. Chapter 10, 'A Quiet Activist', challenges the notion, first advanced by earlier biographers, that Edwards was, if not apolitical, at least passive with regard to causes she supported in theory. The chapter traces her active involvement in what today would be called 'single issue politics', with campaigns for female suffrage and the protection of animals.

'Reputation', the final chapter, deals with public perceptions of Edwards, in her own times, when she was a central cultural figure with an international reputation – and in the years after her death. It assesses her contributions to literature and to Egyptology, ending with an appraisal of her status today. While she is best known for her founding of the Egypt Exploration Society, she is also enjoying a revival of interest in her writings.

The Adventurous Life is my tribute to this gifted, original woman.

ACKNOWLEDGEMENTS

Warmest thanks are due to all those who took time from their busy schedules to assist with my work on this book; not least, those erudite, helpful people who guided me through their archives. Dr Brigitte Balanda of the Egypt Exploration Society sat with me in the EES library through a most enjoyable and illuminating day, as we worked together through voluminous collections of Edwards' letters. The Society's director, Carl Graves, and other members of his staff have also been most supportive. I am indebted to the Exploration Society, too, for permission to reproduce in my illustrations an engraving of the original seal of the Egypt Exploration Fund.

I am most grateful to Dr Francisco Bosch-Puche and his welcoming staff at the Griffith Institute in Oxford, who showed me their Edwards memorabilia, and enabled me to study the Kate Bradbury *Journal*. At Somerville College, likewise, archivist Kate O'Donnell guided me to the rich store of manuscripts and photographs in the Edwards collection there. William Joy, the encyclopaedically knowledgeable curator of the Peggy Joy Egyptology Library in Michigan, a real enthusiast for everything relating to Amelia Edwards, most generously shared with me previously unknown letters from his abundant store. Alan and Susan Boyle, both authorities on Amelia Edwards in the context of her time in the Dolomites, have been kind enough to tell me about their recent discoveries among census records and baptismal certificates.

I also thank the following institutions, for permission to access and cite from material held by them: Bristol Central Library; HathiTrust; the Huntington Library in San Marino, California; the Library Company of Philadelphia; Tameside Family History; University College, London; the University of Minnesota, and Princeton University; Chicago University (the Gerald N. Wachs Collection).

My thanks would be incomplete without mention of Professor Steve Poole, of the University of the West of England, and Dr Rose Wallis, Associate Director of the Regional History Centre at UWE. Last year, with the super-efficient assistance of Karen Garvey, Engagement Officer for Bristol Museums, they enabled me to speak to an audience across Europe and beyond, about Amelia Edwards, and about *The Adventurous Life*. The book itself would not exist at all in its present form, if not for the encouragement of Professor Marie Mulvey-Roberts, who first persuaded me that Amelia's story would be of interest to Bloomsbury.

I am grateful to all those readers, both named and anonymous, who have discussed ideas with me, asked probing questions, drawn my attention to previously overlooked sources – made this a better piece of work in so many ways. Among them are my friend and former colleague Marion Glastonbury; and another dear friend, the late Sophia Hughes, to whose memory *The Adventurous Life* is dedicated.

Finally, I owe an already substantial debt, that no doubt will accumulate over the coming months, to the conscientious, patient and supportive work of the people at Bloomsbury: to editors Ben Doyle and Laura Cope; to Christelle Chamouton, Amy Brownbridge and other administrative staff; to Bloomsbury Project Manager Merv Honeywood; editors Sandra Creaser and Rachel Walker, to the unnamed and unsung cover designers . . . in short, to everyone who has helped steer this book through to the light of day and will see it on its way in future.

1

Young Amelia

The baby girl who came to the world on June 7, 1831, and was christened Amelia Ann Blandford Edwards, arrived fourteen years into her parents' marriage. To childless Alicia and Thomas, who might well have given up any idea of parenthood, the birth of little Amelia must have seemed special indeed.

Alicia, in particular, was proud of her only child, who from an early age showed creative talent. Amelia seems to have inherited her Anglo-Irish mother's intelligence, wit, and facility with words. Tutored at home, the child quickly became an avid reader. Her liberal-minded parents let her read whatever she wished in their well-stocked home library; 'and I do not think I was the worse for my liberty', she said of herself in later life.[1] She loved tales of adventure, especially if they contained mystery and drama, or were set in distant places – Fenimore Cooper, Captain Marryat, Bulwer Lytton, the early Dickens. The description of travels among native peoples and lost Mayan temples, in John Lloyd Stephenson's *Central America,* nourished her lively imagination, and gave her a hunger to visit exotic foreign parts. And, lying dormant, to bear fruit after many years, were the visions conjured up by J. Gardner Wilkinson's *Manners and Customs of the Ancient Egyptians.*[2]

Her father Thomas Edwards, a younger son in a family of Suffolk small landowners – 'gentlemen farmers' – had served as an officer with Wellington's army during the Peninsular campaign against Napoleon, and fought at the Battle of Corunna, in 1809. To Amelia, he would be a lifelong example of self-discipline and serious mental application. Now on half-pay, with a minor management position in a bank, he was a man of almost obsessively regular habits. 'Slight and spare as a man could well be, taciturn, austere and methodical as clockwork', Amelia's cousin Matilda said of him; adding that he was 'exact to punctiliousness': 'I dare aver that my uncle was never a second late for anything in his life.'[3] Every morning, Amelia's father 'rose, read *The Times*, breakfasted, started for the bank, supped and went to bed, by the clock'.[4] Apart from a Sunday afternoon stroll with two elderly female companions, he had practically no social life outside of working hours. He seems to have had little in common, then, with his lively wife, who loved company and conversation. If one believes cousin Matilda, her father's silent manner was troubling to Amelia. '"I fear I shall grow as silent as himself", she used to say.'[5] Amelia need not have worried. In social interaction, as in her writing, she had the gift of eloquence.

She clearly admired and respected her father, however. To the end of her life, she treasured his medal from the Peninsular war, and a ring, a gift from a Frenchman – a prisoner of war, perhaps – with whom in his campaigning days Thomas had struck up an unlikely friendship. Though he had transferred the orderly habits of his army days to civilian life, having been honourably discharged from his regiment on health grounds, Amelia's father still had thoughts of military life. When, in 1853, the Crimean War broke out, although by then in his sixties, he wrote to the War Office, offering to re-enter active service.[6]

Amelia's Anglo-Irish maternal grandfather, Robert Walpole, had been a barrister. She was proud of the connection with the illustrious family, and tried, largely unsuccessfully, to find out more about the Walpole connection.[7] Her novels often show a keen interest in the law, and a knowledge of legal niceties.

The house where Amelia was born, 1 Westmoreland Place, City Road, was in Islington, then a little-known area on the outskirts of London. It was a quiet suburb at that time, divided from the bustle of the city by gardens and meadow, that would by the end of the century be covered with buildings.[8] Later, when Amelia was in her twenties, she and her parents moved to 19 Wharton Street, Islington, a mile from Kings Cross Station. That address now bears a commemorative blue plaque, testimony that Edwards once lived and wrote here.[9]

Islington at that time, then, was a pleasant area, frequented by writers and artists. Charles Dickens, and the playwright Sterling Coyne, lived nearby. Though Amelia's parents sometimes struggled to pay the bills, Alicia, through clever domestic management, saw to it that her family were comfortable in their home. 'First-rate housekeeping and rigid economy gave the home an air almost of opulence', cousin Matilda recalled.[10]

Except for infrequent visits to cousins much younger than herself, in rural Suffolk, the little girl had almost no contact with other children: 'Few children ever lived less with playfellows of their own age', her cousin Matilda said of her.[11] Amelia's chief companion remained her mother. They read together, studied together, and together made frequent trips to the theatre – the only luxury Alicia allowed herself, and which both mother and daughter enjoyed. If the family struggled financially, dependent as they were on Amelia's father's military pension and his small salary from the bank, her mother always found money for this one indulgence.

Exposure to mainly adult conversation encouraged young Amelia to develop her talents early. By the age of four, she was trying her hand at writing poetry. At nine, she won a prize for a 'Temperance' story illustrating the dangers of alcohol, in a competition in a penny magazine. At twelve, she published a children's tale, 'The Story of a Clock'. 'I was always writing', she would recall later in life, 'when other children were playing with dolls'.[12]

Meanwhile, she had begun to paint and draw. In her childhood, she enjoyed drawing cartoons and caricatures. 'I was always drawing', she would recall many years later, 'from the time when I could hold a pencil'. Art was a love that followed her into adulthood, enabling her to produce the evocative sketches and watercolours that adorn her travel books. At Hill Farm in Suffolk, home of her Uncle William and Aunt Maria, Amelia drew a mural, six feet across, on a storeroom wall, of the Romans landing in Britain. Two Britons, clad only in animal skins from the waist down, step over a pile of bodies of their fellow-Celts to confront a helmeted Roman soldier who threatens with a sword. Years later, when cousin Matilda visited the house, the drawing was still there.[13]

One of their neighbours in Islington was George Cruikshank, famous for his illustrations for the novels of Dickens. Alicia and Thomas were startled one day, by a visit from the famous artist; even more so, no doubt, when they learned the visit was about their daughter. Cruikshank, who lived close to Wharton Street, had seen a sketch by Amelia, done on the back of a page in a story she had submitted to a popular magazine. Cruikshank liked the drawing enough to want to meet the artist – and was greatly surprised to find the work had been done by a young girl. Impressed by her precocious talent, Cruikshank offered to take on Amelia as a pupil, free of charge. The parents considered his offer; but felt it necessary to tell the would-be tutor that their daughter had a weak chest (which may actually have been the case). They feared, they told Cruikshank, that the fumes from oil paints would be bad for her lungs. It is possible, too, that they were uncomfortable with the idea of their young daughter being tutored by this older man, especially given the disreputable image of artists at that time. Her parents, Amelia thought, when, as an adult she recalled their refusal of the artist's offer, entertained the 'old prejudice against the artist life'.[14] (It seems she never quite forgot her parents' polite excuse. In her novel, *Barbara's History*, the narrator makes fun of a pretentious lady who tells an aspiring female artist that oil paints are bad for the chest.)[15]

Young Amelia proved quite able to carry on drawing and painting without Cruikshank's help. She taught herself quite a lot of other things besides – history, geography, foreign languages. (Contrary to Matilda's claim that Amelia 'only spoke one language – her own', she learned French before she was out of her teens; and then Italian.)[16] As she once told Matilda, who although five years younger than Amelia, became the one close friend of her adolescence: 'I can never learn from others. I must be my own teacher and acquire in my own way.' All her life, she learned how to do whatever it was by trial and error, seeking the advice of others only as need arose.

An important source of inspiration for Edwards as a writer, would always be her childhood summer visits to her father's relatives in Suffolk. One year, when there was a cholera epidemic in London, Amelia spent whole months in the countryside, where she and her young cousins enjoyed a good deal of freedom to roam. There were visits to Creeting and Baylham, to call on relatives there, and to Gosbeck, where the churchyard held the graves of Amelia's paternal grandparents.

The rural scenes filled the imagination and the memory of this city child – the orchards, dark larch wood, the dusty narrow lanes, their hedgerows crowded in early summer with wildflowers. The old houses, too, built of warm red brick, or yellowing stone – like Westerfield Hall, the Elizabethan manor house where Matilda lived, with a brood of younger siblings. This house would reappear, lovingly evoked, in the early chapters of Edwards' novel *Barbara's History*, published when she was in her early thirties.

Although five years her junior, Matilda would become Amelia's lifelong friend. To the younger girl, Amelia ('Amy'), was at once friend, sister and role model. Amelia called her cousin, 'Middy'. In Suffolk, when not roaming the countryside, they read poetry together, or practised their music. Amelia liked to tutor Middy. As in everything she did, she was a perfectionist, which made her a demanding teacher: 'I well remember', Matilda wrote, in her memories of those days, 'how she sat by my side at the piano, day after day, till I performed certain of Mendelssohn's Songs Without Words to her liking'.[17]

Both women would grow up to be well-known novelists. At which point in their lives, 'a certain amount of reserve', according to Matilda, developed in the cousins' relationship. Also, possibly – although Matilda does not say so explicitly – a certain rivalry. They had an unspoken agreement not to comment or offer advice on one another's work.[18] All the same, Matilda would remember her cousin as a 'staunch friend and brilliant literary confrère'.[19]

One source of irritation in their professional lives, would be the similarities in their names. Amelia B. Edwards and Matilda B. Edwards were constantly confused with one another in the public mind, in ways that proved annoying to both of them. If Matilda's family home in Suffolk was named in the press as the birthplace of Amelia Edwards, that was not so bad; but when one author's work was attributed to the other, that was truly maddening. Matilda urged her cousin to remove the 'B' from her name – which Amelia flatly refused to do. We had 'a bee in our bonnets', Matilda said.[20] All the same, Matilda all her life remained full of ambivalent admiration for her older cousin. She had looked up to Amelia from an early age – even if at times she found her behaviour puzzling.

Matilda's very first memory of Amelia, is of 'a tall girl of twelve or thirteen with regular features, pale, clear complexion and abundance of dark brown hair hanging in pigtails down her back' who burst in upon the younger children, as Matilda and her siblings sat at tea in the nursery at Westerfield. Seizing a half-eaten loaf, Amelia challenged the children: '"Who dares me to throw this out of the window" she cried, undauntedly meeting our aghast gaze.' One of the younger children decided to go one better, took the bread and, to the shocked indignation of their governess, flung the bread out.[21]

The Suffolk relatives, let alone the surrounding community, never quite knew what to make of Amelia, or what to expect next. It was not just her middle-class, 'educated' London accent, that puzzled the locals, and at times made it hard for Suffolk country folk to understand what she said.[22] She was for other reasons 'the pride, the wonder, and . . . the terror, of bachelor uncles and maiden aunts'. She was given to pranks. She once locked her Aunt Maria in the pantry as a practical joke.[23] Once, she frightened her cousins by sending them word that she had had a serious accident. They had to get ready to take care of her, they were told, as she would be carried into the house unable to stand, and wrapped in blankets. On another occasion, she arrived at the front door of Westerfield Hall disguised as a young man, with a letter of introduction from someone in London. The servants, and even some of Amelia's relatives, were completely taken in.[24] Matilda remembers being woken from sleep by Amelia laying a hand on her shoulder and saying loudly in her ear, to test her memory of Keats, 'Oh Milly. What poet was it who said, "Oh sleep, thou comfortable bird?"'[25] In these incidents, we see a certain exhibitionist streak in Amelia; a love of making an impression. Or, perhaps, the actions of a lonely child seeking to be noticed by others. But there is also a love of fun and mischief. Because of her liveliness and intelligence, and her creative gifts, Amelia's eccentric pranks were tolerated.

When not bent on annoying her relations, Amelia could be a great source of entertainment. In a rural world where not much happened to amuse them, she would get up theatricals with the other children, and have them each play a part. Matilda remembered her cousin teaching them to memorize passages from Shakespeare for these entertainments.

For six months, while Matilda was at a boarding school in London, Amelia saw a great deal more of her cousin, and the two young women renewed their interest in amateur theatricals. They became friendly with the family of the playwright Sterling Coyne. They spent long evenings in the Coynes' home, reading and performing scenes from plays. Matilda considered Amelia to have 'dramatic gifts of a high order'. If she had taken to acting a little earlier in life, Matilda thought, and if the prejudice against acting as a career had been less, her cousin might have 'tried her fortunes' with a career in the theatre.[26]

Another cultural influence came into Amelia's life at this time, in the form of cousin Matilda's aunt and godmother, Matilda Betham. The older Matilda was a poet and a well-known painter of miniatures. She had written a biographical dictionary of famous women and had been a close friend of Charles and Mary Lamb.[27] Young Amelia must have found her lively company, with her talk of Madame de Stael, the Romantic intellectual who had supported the 'great French Revolution' in its early days; with readings of her poems, and the copies of intellectual journals and fashionable magazines she brought to the Edwards home. She offered Amelia a new perspective on the wider world beyond the narrow confines of her home life.

With the encouragement of her parents to boost her confidence, Amelia was determined to make her mark in life, in one area of the arts or another. At the age of fourteen, but in what she would later call 'an evil hour', she opted for music as a profession.[28] Coached by a well-known musician and composer, Ann Sheppard Mounsey,[29] while practising for eight hours daily at the keyboard, Amelia became an accomplished pianist and organist. She also composed – on average 'eight or ten pages of music weekly'. Soon, she felt able to start giving music lessons to young pupils, as a means of supplementing the family income and helping her, by now, ageing parents.

Young Amelia's chief ambition, though, was to achieve recognition as a singer. While the role of a professional actress was seen as disreputable, singing in a concert hall, before the right kind of audience, could be socially acceptable even for a woman from a 'respectable' family. A woman might also perform – even for payment – in domestic settings. But Amelia's other dream, of appearing on the stage, was to be realized only as wish-fulfilment, in the portrayal of her heroine Natalie in her early novel, *The Ladder of Life* (1856), where a young woman from a humble background makes a career in opera.

Amelia gave seven years to the pursuit of her musical ambitions. But her hopes of fame as a singer were interrupted when, in November 1849, she contracted typhus and lay bedridden for fourteen weeks. All the same, the summer of the following year saw her still pursuing her goal of singing professionally. After a successful performance at the Guildford Town Hall, she was, she writes, 'intoxicated with success', and 'dreamt dreams of fame and fortune'.[30] Another success eight weeks later, in Brentford, encouraged her to continue her pursuit of a singing career. But then she began to suffer constant colds and sore throats. Another planned appearance, in an oratorio at Exeter Hall, had to be cancelled owing to illness. She would never become a singer.

In September 1850, to further supplement the family income, she took a job as an organist at St Michael's Chapel. The place lay seven miles from London, at Wood Green. Amelia would recall this as a dismal time in her young life. 'I was very miserable. I knew no one and was constantly ill.' The whole experience made her wretched: 'I used to dread the journey to Wood Green so much that I had a nervous attack every Saturday night and diarrhoea every Sunday. At the close of the year for which I was bound by agreement to remain, I resigned the appointment.'[31]

She seems to have been an inspired player, however, if cousin Matilda is to be believed. When, one summer in Suffolk, she filled in as temporary organist at Witnesham church, and played a Bach voluntary as a sign for the worshippers to leave at the end of the service, nobody moved, sitting spellbound 'till the magic notes ceased'. Music of 'this impassioned kind' was something quite new to the rural congregation.[32]

Still resolved on making a career in music of some kind, Amelia decided to focus for a while on her teaching work. It was still a way of helping her parents, in their constant struggle to make ends meet.[33] All the same, she looked for another organist position, writing to several distinguished musicians to seek their support. She managed to secure fifteen 'first-rate testimonials'. One of these, from Sir John Goss, organist of St Paul's Cathedral, has survived: 'Miss Edwards having played a Psalm and fugue of her own composition to me on the organ in a very creditable manner, I have pleasure in stating that I consider her qualified to fill the situation of organist.'[34] By the autumn of 1851, however, Amelia had given up any idea of making a career in music. She now felt certain that the musical profession was not for her. The failure was certainly not due to any lack of effort on her part: 'Although I worked terribly in earnest, I virtually threw away another seven years of my life; for the divine gift of music was not mine, and although I became a thorough contrapuntist, a trained vocalist, pianist and organist, and covered reams of music paper with laboriously studied compositions . . . I never wrote anything worth a second hearing.'[35] The extreme difficulty, for a woman of the nineteenth century, in making a career in music – not least in the wholly male-dominated world of musical composition – does not seem to have occurred to her. Whether or not she did possess any real talent in that regard, we shall never know. In any case, she was inclined to blame her own artistic shortcomings, rather than her cultural environment. She would have to seek other outlets for her multifaceted creative abilities.

It was around this time, that she got engaged to be married. 'I had become engaged to a gentleman whom I had known for years, in the January of 1851 and he came round every Sunday to fetch me home from Church.' Nothing else is known about this fiancé, Mr Bacon, except that he accompanied her back every Sunday from the church where she played the organ; and that his company, and the idea of impending marriage to him, made her increasingly miserable. 'We were ill suited and though he loved me very much I could not really love him. I had accepted him out of regard and esteem, and found that insufficient.' By the end of the year, she had broken off the engagement.[36] Although she was to have many platonic friendships with men in her life – generally highly-educated and intelligent ones – this would be her first and last approach to heterosexual marriage.

Over the summer of 1851, while staying with her cousins in Suffolk, and even as she prepared to find a new organist job, Amelia had returned to the old occupation of her childhood. She began to write in earnest – first a study of English poets; then translations of poems from the Italian, a language she had started to learn that year.

She had often told ghost stories, to entertain her cousins. Now she began to write them down. She wrote 'a tale founded on a dream (one of my best)' called 'The Château Regnier'. *Eliza Cook's Journal* published the story. In 1853 she published two more stories, 'The Brilliant Ring', and 'The Painter of Pisa', in the *Illustrated Magazine of Art*.[37]

Though she went on teaching music all through 1852, and tried, unsuccessfully, to find a new position as a church organist, Amelia was coming to the conclusion that a musical career was not for her. After the success of her short stories – plus 'two or three' novels that she dismissed as 'bosh for the public' and that do not appear in the list of her later fiction – she had decided that her future path would lie not with music but with writing.[38]

By 1852, when she reached twenty-one, Amelia Edwards had, in more senses than one, come of age. She had successfully avoided the trap of what would almost certainly have been an unhappy marriage. She had started to write in earnest, and to publish her work. Although she always would deeply regret the seven years expended on training herself as a musician, other possibilities were opening up for her. Suddenly, her world seemed full of hope and opportunity.

The following year, she received her first substantial payment, for a short story. 'Annette', about a young Frenchwoman seduced by an English aristocrat, appeared in the prestigious *Chambers' Journal*. The receipt of a cheque for £9 marked a turning point for Edwards, giving her confidence that she might actually be able to earn her living as a writer. Over the next three years, she published further work in *Chambers' Journal*, and in *Literary World*; in *Eliza Cook's Journal*, *Illustrated London News*, *The Century*, *Household Words* and *Harper's Monthly*, among others. She had begun working for newspapers, too, helping her parents with the always straitened family budget. She wrote for the *Saturday Review* and the *Morning Post*, covering every branch of the news for these papers except for police and parliamentary reports – topics at that time deemed unsuitable for coverage by a female journalist.

She carried on writing short stories, many with a Gothic element – tales of the supernatural, or of gruesome murder, and revenge, building on her childhood experience of terrifying the Suffolk cousins with her pre-bedtime yarns. The stories proved as popular with an adult readership as they had been with her younger relations. An annual ghost story for the Christmas number of Charles Dickens' *Household Words* became a regular event. Some of these stories, like 'The Phantom Coach', have been reprinted in recent years in anthologies.[39]

There were in London, even for a young woman from an obscure middle-class background like Amelia's, opportunities to take part in the city's intellectual life. For a time, she attended a salon for philosophical and political discussion, frequented by freethinkers and socialists, at the Bayswater home of the painter and radical Samuel Laurence. There, she would have met, among others, the novelist Eliza Lynn Linton, the co-operative socialist and philanthropist Robert Owen (something of a revered 'elder statesman' to the salon's younger participants), the philosopher-critic George Henry Lewes (at that time not yet the partner of the novelist, George Eliot, but in an 'open marriage' with Agnes Jervis); and the novelist and feminist, Matilda Hays. Free love was frankly discussed in the salon, along with utopian ideas for the transformation of society, in an atmosphere of general irreverence towards all received opinions and conventions. The lively mind of Amelia Edwards must have found it all both stimulating and challenging.[40]

European travel gave her still broader scope. In the spring of 1853, she went with one of her cousins, accompanied by a governess, to visit Paris. The following year, she persuaded her father to allow her to visit Belgium in a group of five, cousin Matilda among them.[41] There followed other European trips – with her father to visit the Paris Exhibition of 1855;[42] and to France, Switzerland and Italy. She travelled to Florence, to Venice and to Rome, visiting artists' studios. January 1857 saw her in Europe again, now as a responsible chaperone to Matilda. They travelled by coach to Pisa, and on to Rome – with Edwards keeping a log of their expenditure along the way, and keeping a keen eye on 'Middy', who found the journey physically demanding, and suffered from minor illnesses, and from culture shock.[43] They stayed briefly in Paris at the home of one Emile Stéger, to whom Edwards had a letter of introduction. He introduced her to the Bohemian life of Paris and became a good friend. In 1862 and 1864, she would go to Germany, and to Switzerland.

European travel had become a passion for Amelia and fed her creative imagination. Her novels and travel writings are full of allusions to painting and music, history and archaeology – of scenic descriptions, of meetings with local people, of folk tales and legends – gathered on these journeys.

Amelia was keen to be a true Bohemian intellectual at this time in her life, taking part in activities that challenged gender stereotypes. Along with oil painting – another challenge, perhaps, to her over-cautious parents who had worried about the effect of oils on her lungs – the hobbies of her twenties were fencing, riding, smoking, mathematics, learning German, and pistol-shooting. (She once, she would recall, 'nearly shot one of my friends', while showing off a new pistol.) Although Edwards was outwardly conservative in her dress, and never flouted convention when in polite society, her role models in other respects were women like George Sand, who smoked, had love affairs, and wore trousers.[44]

In the summer of 1854, with the cholera epidemic in London, Edwards and her parents moved out of the city to spend the whole summer with the Suffolk cousins. There, she began work on her first mature novel, *My Brother's Wife*, based on her experiences of travel in Europe. She read it to her Suffolk cousins, chapter by chapter, as she completed them. It is a tale of adultery, intrigue, and betrayal; of hidden identities, and sudden violent death, very much in keeping with the 'novels of sensation' then popular with the reading public. Edwards, evidently aware of contemporary popular taste, was canny enough to give her readers what they wanted.

In later years, she would dismiss *My Brother's Wife*, along with the two novels that followed it, as one of her 'juvenile efforts'.[45] Yet, when it came out in 1855, the book was favourably reviewed. One reviewer while noting a 'considerable dash of the melodramatic' in the novel's plot, described it as 'intelligently and artistically written'.[46] *My Brother's Wife* was reprinted in Edwards' lifetime, twice in American editions – for the last time in 1889.[47]

The novel's central story, with its bold treatment of what today would be called 'adult themes' – of a wealthy and attractive but feckless man's unfaithfulness to his wife – is told in the first person, from the perspective of Paul Latour, the husband's brother. It would not be the last time in Edwards' writing career, when a reviewer would remark that the confident male narrative voice suggested that – but for the author's name – the book might have been written by a man.[48]

My Brother's Wife was followed, in 1856, by *The Ladder of Life*, the tale of a young Swiss woman who finds herself adrift in London and survives by making a living on the operatic stage. One reviewer, while noting what he called the 'picturesque matter' of the subject, added that the novel was 'in many parts unusually well written'. Hardly an accolade, but not a rejection, either.[49]

Hand and Glove, which came out two years later, was praised for its 'good writing and liveliness of fancy'. The novel, with its ambiguous figure of a charismatic man who appears as if from nowhere, to act as Protestant clergyman to the congregation of an isolated French village, proved popular with the public. It went through six English-language editions after its first publication; and was translated into Italian by Croce, as *Il Guanto Fatale*.[50]

Even with her novels steadily gaining popular and critical success, Edwards was still doing a fair amount of hack work to earn money. Many years later, cousin Matilda – not always the most reliable of narrators – would assert that Amelia 'never wrote for money'. If she was going to earn enough to support herself and her elderly parents, at this precarious time in her life, Amelia had little choice.[51] Alongside the novels, she did a fair amount of hack work. *Etiquette for Gentlemen* (1857); a *History of France*; a translation from French of *A Lady's Captivity among Chinese Pirates*, by Fanny Loviot (1858); *Sights and Stories*, based on Edwards' travels in Belgium; and *The Story of Cervantes* (1862), were just some of the works she turned out during the late fifties and sixties, as she struggled to make her living.[52] Every year, she wrote half a dozen short stories for magazines, which kept her name in the public mind between the appearances of longer fictional works.

Then, in the summer of 1860, tragedy struck. On August 22, Edwards' father contracted a bronchial infection, and died. Just a few days after, Amelia's beloved mother died too. It was not only the suddenness of her parents' end, but Amelia's deep and abiding attachment to her mother, that made her loss almost unbearable. It left her feeling bereft of a dear friend, as well as of the woman who had sheltered her with her love since childhood, and later encouraged her to venture into the world. It was surely a source of regret that Alicia was not there to witness the success of her daughter's fourth novel, *Barbara's History* (1863). This was the novel that turned Edwards from a respected writer with a modest reputation and an appreciative following, into a literary celebrity.

Alone in the world, feeling herself adrift and lost in spite of her new fame, Amelia found a haven in the Kensington home of Ellen Drew Braysher, a friend she had known since her late twenties.

Ellen was twenty-seven years older than Amelia but shared her literary and social interests. Mrs Braysher wrote poetry and, like Amelia, loved the theatre. She knew William Macready personally, and other actors and impresarios of the London stage.[53] Her husband John, who had died in April 1863, three years after Amelia moved into the Braysher household, had corresponded with the poet Coleridge.[54]

Ellen took a keen interest in politics. She was supportive of women's rights, and of the cause of Italian independence. Her daughter Sarah received letters from the Italian republican leader Mazzini, in which he sent greetings and his thanks to Mrs Braysher (whether for her hospitality, or for more direct support for the republican cause, is not clear).[55]

A year after she was widowed, Ellen Braysher's beloved only child, Sarah, also died. She then decided to move to Westbury-on-Trym, at that time a quiet village on the outskirts of Bristol, where she arranged for her daughter's burial in the churchyard of nearby St Mary's, Henbury. Amelia joined Ellen there.

London, for both women, by now had associations of bereavement they must have been glad to leave behind. The Larches, the house they bought in Westbury-on-Trym, just over two miles from the western edge of Bristol, would be a shared home for both women till the end of their lives.

Reflecting with hindsight on the relationship between Amelia and Ellen, Amelia's cousin Matilda observes that the Edwards-Braysher relationship was, at least at first, far from being one of an emotionally needy older woman and financially dependent younger companion:

> Adoption in [Amelia's] case was a matter of affection, by no means of personal interest. Having lost both her parents within a week of each other, she accepted the shelter of a friendly roof, retaining as much independence as was possible under the circumstances.[56]

Amelia was largely able to keep financial independence through all the years she lived at The Larches. Retaining emotional independence in the relationship with Ellen Braysher might, it turned out, be more difficult.

It is sometimes assumed, in the face of evidence to the contrary, that the relationship between Ellen and Amelia was that of lovers. Whatever it meant to Mrs Braysher – possibly she adopted Amelia as a surrogate daughter – to Amelia, the older women seems to have been, at least in the early years of their relationship, a mother figure – a stand-in for the adored, deceased Alicia Edwards, who had been everything to Amelia until her untimely death.

At any rate, The Larches gave Amelia shelter. The house would be her safe retreat, a base from which to venture out to explore the world.

Edwards describes The Larches and its surroundings in an autobiographical article, 'My Home Life', written for the American magazine *Arena*.[57] The house stood along a main thoroughfare of the quiet, pretty village, on an acre of ground. High walls, thick shrubbery, and the tall larch trees that gave the place its name, kept the house and its occupants safe from intrusion. The secluded location suited Amelia well, enabling her to work undisturbed.

She came to dislike the summers, when she and Mrs Braysher went to stay in Weston-super-Mare. Saville Villa, Number 11, Park Place, which they rented from a friend of a friend, had many home comforts, with a spacious dining room and drawing room, and 'two large best bedrooms'. The outdoor surroundings were attractive, 'away from the noisy road, yet separated only by a pretty public (or rather private) garden, with a full view of the bay, and the carriages and the passers-by'.[58] They were waited on in the house by two servants employed by the owner, plus 'a very nice cook', and Mrs Braysher's personal maid. But Amelia had much less privacy there. Though she loved Ellen dearly, and had adopted her as a second mother, the older woman could be demanding – tyrannical even – in her claims upon Amelia's care and attention. While Amelia would have preferred to be back at The Larches – or off travelling, and somewhere else altogether – she considered Ellen's needs, and respected the older woman's belief that stays at Saville Villa were good for her health.

Although she now lived 120 miles away, Amelia did not cut herself off from London. In letters, and in occasional journeys out of Bristol by train, she still kept in touch for decades, with the many friends she had made there.

She was something of a celebrity hunter. Like many of her contemporaries, she collected famous people's autographs. She once made a list of the ninety or so famous people she had met in her life.[59] By the mid-1860s, however, she was becoming accepted as a celebrity herself, known as a fellow-writer by the London literati, even though she now lived tucked away in Westbury.

Some of the names on her list represented abiding friendships. She knew the poet Robert Browning, who was also acquainted with others in her social circle. He sent her a signed copy of his long poem, *The Ring and the Book*. In July 1869, Edwards invited Browning to stay at The Larches – an invitation he had regretfully to decline. He had postponed, he told her, another engagement, in order to come and see her; but an old friend had turned up unexpectedly. In July 1882, he was again unable to visit.[60] (It might have seemed quite a long way from London to Westbury-on-Trym in those days, in spite of Mr Brunel's Great Western Railway out of Paddington.) Browning did, however, ask to visit Miss Edwards some other time.

She became a good friend of John Addington Symonds, a well-known literary figure who lived in Bristol. She sent a copy of her *Ballads* to him and wrote him a verse tribute on the flyleaf. Neither the ballads – fairly banal song lyrics, intended to be sung to the melodies Edwards composed to go with them, nor the tribute to Symonds, are exactly Edwards' best work. Symonds, she hails as, 'thou whose gift of knowledge is so great . . ./ Whose mind is as a temple dedicate to Science . . .' As if aware of the shortcomings of her *Ballads*, Edwards ends her lines for Symonds by apologizing for 'So poor a tribute as these songs of mine'. She dedicated the book, however, not to Symonds, but to 'My Most Beloved Friend, Ellen Braysher'.[61]

She kept up a long-running correspondence with the artist and engraver Gustave Doré, who she sometimes met up with in London when he visited the city, and who in time would be a good friend.

Literary friendships were one thing. Where, though, would she find the intimate one-to-one love with another person, that seemed to elude her, after she broke off her engagement with Mr Bacon, back in the 1850s? After which, it seems, she knew that neither marriage, nor indeed any sexual relationships with men, were for her. Ellen Braysher became a dear and lifelong companion to Amelia – an older woman who mothered and cared for her, until Ellen herself became the one in need of care. Amelia, though, yearned for more than that.

While same-sex relations between women were not banned by law in Victorian England, they were not exactly celebrated, either. The state made no provision either for civil partnership, or for lesbian marriage. What, in North America, were sardonically referred to as 'Boston marriages', in England were lived out behind closed doors and tightly drawn lace curtains. Under such conditions, it was difficult for any woman who might find herself attracted to a member of her own sex, even to acknowledge her sexual orientation to herself, let alone to act upon her feelings.

Amelia Edwards was not afraid of her own sexuality in that way. She was brave enough, too, to defy the risk of social condemnation, by seeking out a like-minded woman to share her life. But the times in which she lived, the conventions of her day, were, even before she began her quest, setting her up for disappointment. Her search for the love of other women was all too likely to bring her sharply up against harsh realities.

2

Love lost – and found

'She does not love many people, for all her seeming geniality', said a dear friend of Amelia's, who knew her well. Though she had many acquaintances and correspondents, and was on friendly terms with her neighbours in Westbury, there were just a handful of people to whom she felt really close. It was a case, as the American poet Emily Dickinson put it, of 'The soul selects her own society'. But when Amelia Edwards did select, it was with a passionate intensity that could take the object of her love by storm.

In her novels, she writes about the dangerous power of love informed by sexual attraction (always, in her fiction, characterized as heterosexual) – the sheer overwhelming power of it, that overcomes all rationality, but also fills the lover with confidence and hope:

> Love is of all stimulants the most powerful. It sharpens the wits like danger, and the memory like hatred; it spurs the will like ambition; it exalts the imagination like hashish; it intoxicates like wine. A man of real power who, loving for the first time, loves with all the forces of his intellect and all the fire of his blood, feels himself capable of all things. He holds the world and its gifts in the hollow of his hand.[1]

Edwards had not been long in the Bristol area, when she made the acquaintance of Ellen Byrne and her husband, an ordained clergyman, the Reverend John Rice Byrne. They had a young son, Lionel, born in 1862, the year after their arrival in Bristol. They lived at 7 Cambridge Park in the west Bristol suburb of Redland, about two miles from Westbury-on-Trym, and quickly became friends with Amelia.

Although Byrne was employed full-time as an assistant inspector of schools, he still occasionally preached in a local church in nearby Horfield. Amelia went to hear him, inviting a neighbour to join her: 'Mr Byrne preaches tomorrow morning at Horfield', she wrote to Miss Cave; 'and if it is fine I mean to go.' She had a low opinion of the sermons given by their local clergyman, at the Westbury parish church of the Holy Trinity: 'Mr Elton is such an affliction that I thought you might be glad to exchange him for a really good preacher with a really good accent.'[2]

John Byrne was four years older than Amelia; his wife, six years her junior. Ellen was the youngest child of the Hon. Richard Webb, of Donnington Hall, a Georgian country seat in Herefordshire. Webb, a substantial landowner, a Justice of the Peace, and, for a time, High Sheriff of the county, had invested largely in local railway and canal excavation schemes, and was generally regarded as an important figure in his community. Although Edwards disliked snobbery, and satirized it in her novels, she was all the same romantic about old families with long ancestry and close ties to the land. True, the Webbs of Donnington could trace their origins back only a single century; but still, they had a coat of arms, and an imposing mansion. All this would no doubt have appealed to Amelia.

Ellen and Amelia had more substantive interests in common. Both women loved music; both did occasional work for charity; both had an interest in reforming the laws that discriminated against women. Ellen, Amelia, and Ellen Braysher all signed a petition of 1866, in support of giving women the vote.

Friendship between Ellen Byrne and Amelia soon deepened into love. Over a century before such arrangements became accepted as the law of the land, their relationship was consecrated by marriage. The poet and social critic John Addington Symonds, an advocate of free love and of same-sex relationships, told Havelock Ellis the story of Amelia and Ellen's marriage, a year after Edwards died:

> Another eminent female author among my friends, Miss Amelia B. Edwards, . . . made no secret to me of her lesbian tendencies. The *grande passion* of her life was for an English lady, married to a clergyman and inspector of schools. I knew them both quite well. The three made a ménage à trois together; and Miss Edwards told me that one day the husband married her to his wife at the altar of his church – having full knowledge of the state of affairs.[3]

Edwards herself called Symonds 'a dear friend of many years'. The closeness of their friendship has been questioned; it has been suggested that Amelia exaggerated.[4] But unless she had known him very well indeed, and trusted him, she would hardly have confided in him about something as sensitive as her same-sex marriage.

It is quite hard to imagine the three of them – the very proper clergyman and school inspector, ten years older than his wife and older than Amelia by four years; Ellen, fully six years' Amelia's junior, mother of a young son; and the ladylike, if highly-strung and passionate Amelia, engaging in a 'ménage à trois', in the fullest sense of the word. That the relationship was ever more than platonic, on the part of all of them, seems unlikely. But at an emotional level – to Edwards, at least – her love for Ellen Byrne mattered deeply.

Amelia and Ellen took part together in philanthropic fundraising in the Bristol area – an activity that both women would be involved in all their lives. In Westbury-on-Trym, in 1870, they organized a benefit concert, in aid of a convalescent fund for the nurses of King's Cross Hospital. The event was written up in the local press – the *Bristol Daily Post*, and the *Bristol Times and Mirror*.[5] Both women performed. Ellen sang a Schubert liede, 'On Every Tree', and the aria from Gluck's opera, *Orpheus and Eurydice*: 'Che farò senza Euridice' ('What shall I do without Eurydice?'), while Amelia accompanied her on the piano. Ellen, it was noted, was nervous at singing in front of an audience; but she was praised for her 'full and sweet' voice. 'In spite of nervousness', she 'rendered the cavatina very ably'. The concert, the press reported, resulted in 'very material assistance' (amount unspecified), to the convalescent fund.

In the following year, John Byrne accepted the post of Her Majesty's Inspector of Schools for Surrey. He and Ellen left Bristol and moved to Norwood, South London. Ellen went with him. Amelia was left behind.

To have expected Ellen to leave her husband for the love of another woman, let alone to live with her openly in defiance of the world and braving the consequent scandal, would have been asking a great deal of her. Same-sex relationships were regarded as depraved, if they were considered at all. Ellen had not only her child, but her husband's position as a clergyman and school inspector to think of. Her decision to follow John Byrne to London is fairly understandable. And Amelia had Ellen Braysher to consider.

For a woman like Amelia, however, who longed for love and abiding happiness with a member of her own sex, her situation was a lonely one indeed. The separation from Ellen hurt her to the core. 'It is like a death-blow to me', she told one of her neighbours. She had decided to go abroad, she told Mrs Cave. 'I suppose I shall start very soon after Mr and Mrs Byrne go away – for I must go somewhere to get over that great blow – the greatest that could befall me.'[6]

Amelia seems to have lost touch with the Byrnes after they went away. They made a new life in London, devoting themselves energetically to charity work there. Eight years after leaving Bristol, Ellen gave birth to a daughter, Evelyn. John helped found a church, St John the Evangelist in Norwood, becoming a trustee of the new foundation. It provided services for the community, supplying poor families with winter coal and blankets. Ellen, too, involved herself in good works. In 1896, she is on record as organizing a benefit concert for a local Seaman's Institute.[7] Husband and wife both became actively involved in the Primrose League, a movement established to promote support for the Conservative Party, with a strong jingoistic element that would have been distasteful to Edwards. If they had stayed in Bristol, she might, over time, have discovered that she and Ellen gradually had less and less in common. But, in 1871, how could she know that?

Ellen outlived her husband by seven years, dying in 1914, at the age of 77.

Left behind in Westbury, Amelia found comfort in her friendship with Marianne North, a clever and adventurous woman of about Amelia's age, whose sister was married to John Addington Symonds. North would make a career for herself as a distinguished botanist, famous for her exquisite paintings of plants, and of the exotic places where she collected them. She brought her specimens and stunning visual images back from travels in North America and the Middle and Far East, from Brazil, Jamaica, Australia and New Zealand – all over the world, in short.

Edwards addressed Marianne affectionately by her family nickname of 'Pop'. Like Amelia, she had once embarked on a career as a singer and been forced to give up when her singing voice failed her. She too, had lost her mother when in her twenties. Neither woman ever married. Both were intensely dedicated to their work. Both avid travellers. They were, in short, kindred spirits.

In her relationships, Marianne was assertive and self-confident. In a series of letters to Amelia, written in 1871, she challenges her friend about letting other people control her life. Ellen Braysher, it seems, is making Amelia's life unpleasant by emotional blackmail. She is being difficult about Amelia's wish to spend a few weeks with Marianne, who was shortly to set off on an expedition to North America. Marianne thinks Edwards is being 'rather weak' in failing to stand up to 'Mrs B', and to consult her own wishes. 'But do exactly what you like – only is it not something like cutting the dog's tail off by inches? This lingering and being bullied day after day?'[8]

Possibly Ellen Braysher is jealous of Amelia's intimate friendship with a younger woman? Marianne tries to encourage and reassure her. 'Do exactly what you think best for yourself', she again tells Amelia in another letter. 'Your friend . . . will not like doing without you for a few weeks', she concedes; but adds 'Your room [here] is all ready . . . You know how happy you will make me by coming.'[9]

In her next letters, Marianne pursues the theme. Amelia has tried to excuse Ellen Braysher's behaviour – Ellen, she says, is being possessive only out of love. To which Marianne sensibly retorts that while the quarrelling might for, all she knows, be an expression of love, 'it is not an agreeable way of showing it'.[10]

One sentence in this exchange of letters, has been the subject of some speculation: 'When the Byrne bullies you too much, come here.' Who is Marianne referring to here? It has been suggested that the 'Byrne' referred to might be Julia Clara Byrne, editor of the *Morning Post*.[11] This suggestion can be ruled out, however; the bully is clearly someone at close quarters, as Amelia is clearly able to escape from persecution by leaving the scene. It can hardly be Ellen Byrne, so much younger than both Amelia and Marianne, and so unlikely to be referred to as 'the Byrne'; or, indeed, to be in a position to bully Amelia. Ellen was in any case preparing to leave Bristol with her husband – or possibly had already left.[12] Could Marianne be referring to the Reverend Byrne – an Oxford graduate, a man with the social authority of a school inspector and clergyman? The most likely explanation though, surely, is that 'Byrne' is a slip of Marianne's pen. It is Ellen *Braysher* – not Ellen

Byrne, who by her jealous possessiveness is making Amelia miserable, trying to keep her from coming away from The Larches to stay with another woman.

Amelia finally manages to assert herself, telling her friend she will come to visit, after all. 'In spite of Mrs B', Marianne responds, with more than a touch of sarcasm; adding, 'I wonder? Seeing is believing . . .'[13]

Marianne North would go on writing to Edwards all through the next thirteen years of her travels abroad – long, detailed travelogue-like accounts of her work in exotic places.[14] If the tone of these later letters is impersonal, she may have had her reasons for keeping a certain distance. Before Marianne left for America, Amelia poured out expressions of her love for her departing friend; going so far as to offer her what seems to have been intended as an engagement ring. (Amelia's side of the correspondence has not survived; but North's responses to her letters give a sense of Amelia's passionate expressions of feeling.)

Marianne evidently thought it necessary to draw a line: 'Dear Amy – Bless you! what long letters you do write, what a pity to waste them on a woman! Don't waste your money on "massive gold glister rings". I never wear any out of England . . .'[15]

A few days later, she found it necessary to chide Amelia again: 'My dear Amy – What an unmitigated goose you are!' If Edwards intended her ring to be understood as a pledge of undying love, Marianne dismissed it as a toy – she had no need of 'playthings', she wrote, to remind her of absent friends. 'I have not the smallest intention', she added, 'of marrying you or anyone else . . . I shall have you bringing me up for a "breach of promise" case next'.

In case this rebuff was too cruel, North hastened to add that Amelia was still most welcome to come and visit her: 'I will not flatter you, when I say you will make me very happy by doing so.'[16]

Then North, like Ellen Byrne before her, went away. Edwards, too, left England, carrying her burden of rejection and loneliness.

She sought consolation in a journey she had always loved – over the Alps to Rome. On her way, she kept a journal – 'Reminiscences and Notes of a Tour in Germany, Bavaria, Tyrol and Italy'.[17] She would attend art classes in Rome, that winter of 1871–72 – visit art galleries and museums, and socialize with expatriate friends and acquaintances; all the while suffering under the weight of an intense depression. She felt inwardly quite dead. She wrote:

My heart no longer beats faster at the sight of a new or kindly and beautiful face. I hope nothing from it. I have come to the turn in the road of life when I expect no more love, when an act of genuine kindness, or an expression of genuine interest startles me and surprises me and fills me with gratitude, but ceases to give me hope.

She moved about in the world, unable to connect emotionally with her surroundings:

as one goes through the Hall of Busts at the Capitol, seeing only heads and looking for hearts no longer. To me my fellow creatures are busts only. I have come to ask nothing and expect nothing from them but a certain amount of intellectual stimulus . . . Men and women are not to me like my fellow creatures any longer, but as animate books, or pamphlets, or daily papers – talking shadows – things so far from and apart from me that, except as they amuse me, they do not seem to exist . . . Sometimes I feel as if I also were a mere bust – or, worse still, a terminal statue – head above and a marble column below. At other times I am scarcely conscious of even my head, and feel like a shadow moving among shadows – emotionless, passionless, unimpressed, almost without the consciousness of thought.

She struggled to engage with the world around her:

I have to look for things, in order to see them, and listen, in order to hear. My senses are no longer open and ready as of old. Moving to and fro among the sights and sounds of this wonderful city, I have to fix my attention upon objects – to compel myself to observe, or I should see nothing. This is real age – it is thus I know how the years have gone over my head.[18]

While still burdened with depression, she sought out the company of members of Rome's community of American expatriates. She made friends with an American fellow author, Anne Hampton Brewster. Like Edwards, Brewster was an independent single woman who had made a successful career for herself, and who earned a living as a journalist and novelist. Though Anne was thirteen years older than Amelia, the two women's shared interests no doubt made the age gap seem less important. They shared, too, a love of Italy, where the Philadelphia-born writer had made her second home.

Among the latter's personal papers, a few letters written by Amelia to Anne are the only record of their relationship. Most are undated. All the same, it is possible roughly to trace the course of their growing intimacy, from late in 1871 to Edwards' departure from Italy in the spring of 1872.[19]

The letters begin in formality. The first is polite, if enthusiastic, as Amelia thanks 'Miss Brewster' for an unexpected gift of flowers: 'I have had nothing so lovely to keep me company since I left my Gloucestershire roses to their long solitude.' Anne has invited Amelia to call on her, but Amelia has a prior commitment that day, and does not know what time she will be free. She signs her note as formally as she began, with 'Yours most truly', and 'Amelia B. Edwards'.

With the next message – again, a simple note – comes a dramatic change in tone: 'And shall I not see you till 8 tomorrow? It is a long time.' The letter now is signed, not 'Amelia B. Edwards', but, 'Yours everlovingly – ABE'.

A letter of January 13 shows Amelia as desperately, hopelessly in love with Anne. Also, in an intense state of depression, that Edwards attributes to other causes besides unrequited love:

I had a horrible fit of melancholy after leaving you yesterday – the first for many weeks. I had allowed myself to allude to things that I now never allow myself ever to think of, if I can help it. I ought either to have talked it all off my mind, or have kept silence. I told you the truth when I said there were only the dregs of me left. I shall perform the Hara-Kiri one of these days, when the black mood is on me – and exactly in the Japanese fashion, but in some more choice, European version of the same.

She longs for Brewster's company; and has made a point of arranging for lunch in her lodgings, to be sure of being there, in case Anne should call. Eating alone is, in any case, something she has come to dread:

My solitary dinner last evening was like a funeral feast. It seemed to me that I was solemnly burying my roast chicken, and pouring out libations to the manes of my forefathers. And tonight it is worse. I shall have to do something desperate – for another such evening is more than I can bear.

She must go to the theatre, she tells Anne, or invite friends in; or 'sling my guitar over my shoulder, & serenade you'. That probably will, she adds, with a touch of the bitter wit that asserts itself from time to time throughout this tormented, miserable letter, get her arrested by the Italian police.

Now she connects her desperate mood directly with her feelings for Anne:

Why have you brought this upon me? Why have you unsettled me – curdled my ink, paralysed my pen, & made even my own proofs unintelligible to me? It its very cruel. I think if you had known all the mischief you were going to do, you would not have betrayed me with that kiss … Do you often do this sort of thing? Where do you keep your collection of scalps …?

Then, as if embarrassed by this outpouring of feeling, she adds, 'I suppose this is the most incoherent letter you ever had in your life – but "tis not my fault"'. As if afraid of where the strength of her emotions might lead her, she will drop her letter at Anne's door on her way out of the hotel, without calling on her in person:

If I once came in, I should get no farther. I am afraid you are a mischievous fairy, and not a good one, after all – still, if you will only give me back my heart, I will immediately give it to you over again. With all my love (alas! for me that it is so).

In what seems to be the next letter in the sequence, the tone is calmer, but still passionate. The pretext – if it is that – is an apology. Amelia is returning two of Anne's letters that she picked up by mistake, thinking they were addressed to her. She begins tenderly – 'My dear little darling', and closes passionately: 'I kiss your lovely little hands half a million times . . . Very lovingly yours . . .'

In the next two letters, the tone has shifted again. Amelia complains that Anne – 'My dear little love' – has not been to see her. It is 'too bad' that she fills up her time with other engagements: 'I had understood that you had Friday and Saturday free . . .' Gone, however, is the emotional distress of the earlier letter, the desperate craving for companionship. Amelia now sounds busy and contented. She has been sketching; going to a studio to work on a portrait sculpture; going to the theatre; dining out with friends. And she mentions a further reason for being at once less obsessed with Anne, but at the same time keen to see her. Amelia wants to introduce Anne to a new woman in her life.

Thirty-nine-year-old Lucy Renshaw was the only child of a wealthy industrialist from the north of England. John Renshaw had died two years previously, leaving his unmarried daughter independent and with money at her disposal, free to roam the world. Now she was travelling with her maid for company, exploring Italy at her leisure. She and Edwards would form a bond that lasted to the end of Amelia's short life

'I do so much want you to know Miss Renshaw more', Amelia now writes to Anne Brewster; 'Two people I love so well ought to be better acquainted.' She regrets that the Rome Carnival disrupts the usual social round and makes meeting up more difficult.

The allusion to the Carnival indicates that Amelia was writing a few weeks before Easter.

Amelia's next letter mentions an engagement for an outdoor picnic. She apologizes for missing a reception given by Anne, and attending this 'suddenly improvised' event, instead. Is it coincidence that one member of the picnic party is Lucy Renshaw?

From now on, it seems, Amelia often finds herself too busy to call on Anne. 'I am so full of engagements', she writes. Her friend will not believe how difficult it is to find time for 'one thing more'. She has to go with someone to look at a shop. She has to attend a dinner party. She will have only half an hour free that day, and no doubt be 'horribly tired'. But she will *try* to find time to visit.

She has not, she assures Anne, stopped loving her. Anne should go on calling Amelia 'dear' and write 'mine' in her letters. 'I love you dearly', Amelia tells her; 'I insist on your loving me always. I never change when I love people – even if circumstances sweep me off into other paths'. Amelia will come and see Anne soon – 'if not today, then tomorrow'. She closes with, 'God bless you darling'.

A letter headed only 'Friday night', again mentions Lucy, who Edwards here nicknames 'Miranda'. Amelia could only stay with Lucy for half an hour, she tells Anne, because Lucy was not alone: 'Caliban was on guard'. (Is Caliban some kind of chaperone? Lucy's maid? Or another lover? A friend?) Whatever the case, when Amelia arrived, 'Miranda' and 'Caliban' were both going out for the evening. Amelia writes of walking home 'in the rain and slush', 'sad, weary, disappointed and utterly out of spirits . . . I have had a most wretched evening – hope and heart at zero, visions of sudden death . . . I wish tonight that I was dead too'. She confides in Anne about her feelings for 'Miranda', 'whose adorable name is Lucy'. She is, she tells Anne:

> in a bad way with regard to that young woman just at present. Her hands not so small as yours – & her nails won't bear any comparison – but it is a delicious hand for all that – soft, warm, yielding, like herself. Oh my!

> You know me well enough by this time to be quite sure that I am in the worst possible spirits when I write or speak in this restless, reckless way. I shall shoot myself one of these fine nights. When I feel as I do tonight I have a vast mind to take Miranda seriously, right away, for good & all – for better or for worse, to cleave to her in a semi-legitimate way, and settle down abroad. What do you say? Oh my! Again . . .

Whether Amelia ever made any sort of 'semi-legitimate' contract with Lucy, we shall never know. She certainly did not 'settle down' to live with her; although they went on journeys together, and remained in touch through the years, Edwards would continue to live at The Larches with Ellen Braysher, when not travelling abroad.

As if fearing she might have hurt Anne by this headlong declaration of love for Lucy, 'I am awfully fond of you', Amelia now adds; 'No one in the world could rob you of one bit of my affection'. But then she begs Anne, '. . . only spare me before her & the world, and don't shake her faith in me'. She ends with, 'Goodbye, my darling. Your everloving ABE'.

For all her assurances of continuing affection, the relationship with Anne was clearly on the wane. Amelia and Lucy were about to leave Rome, embarking together on new travels, new adventures.

In July of that year, Amelia wrote out a poem, 'To Lucy Renshaw', copying it by hand into the volume of her ballads published seven years before:

My love, in past and lonely years
When life was all too sad at times.
I wrote these melancholy rhymes,
And wrote them, not in ink, but tears.

None had I then, kinsman or friend
To love; & as I went my way

In darkness, sweet, I used to pray
That the long journey soon might end.

I never thought the sun would shine,
The roses bloom again for me.
How could I dream I should love thee,
And find my heaven in eyes of thine?

But so it is; & the dead Past
Is buried. Amen – let it go.
I love thee, and am loved – & lo!
The sun's up in God's heav'n at last![20]

3

Untrodden peaks

In April, 1872, Lucy and Amelia were in Salerno together, where they witnessed the eruption of Vesuvius. It was Lucy, as Amelia wrote up the event in her journal, who climbed up to the cone of Vesuvius and noted the shoots of black smoke jetting out from the crater. Both women, however, experienced 'the low thunderous rumble of the coming eruption', as Amelia described it – 'more like the dull ominous throbbing of a deep organ pipe than like any storm sound I ever heard'.[1]

Edwards' novel *Lord Brackenbury* contains a vivid account of the eruption. It began slowly:

Then the subterranean thunder rolled louder and longer; and the smoke poured out all black, rent with flashes of fire; and three small streams of lava, white and seething, began slowly crawling down the cone.

The thundering of the volcano became continuous – 'one solid implacable roar'.

The lava, now flooding down the volcano's sides, glowed 'crimson in the deepening dusk: creeping, twisting, writhing, lapping mass over mass, with something of a live horror in its motion, as of a reptile in agony.' The streets and railway station were filled with milling crowds of terrified people, lugging their possessions, struggling to get on the trains and escape to safety, leaving behind them their burning villages.

July found Amelia and Lucy on muleback, trekking among the peaks and precipices of the Dolomite mountains. They were venturing far off the beaten track, into a region of Italy where tourists normally didn't go – only a few naturalists and hardy mountaineers. Most English people had never even heard of the Dolomites. (Perhaps if they did hear the name, they imagined it to refer to some obscure religious sect, 'like the Mormons or the Druses'.) For Amelia, the trek into the mountains would mean an escape from the crowds of tourists and would-be artists, away from the hustle and bustle of the narrow Italian city streets, the baking summer heat of the lowlands.

It was a region that had long fascinated her. 'The Dolomites! It was full fifteen years since I had first seen sketches of them by a great artist not long since passed away, and their strange outlines and still stranger colouring, had haunted me ever since.'[2]

She would feel safer going there with Lucy Renshaw. She had found in Lucy a dependable companion, a seasoned traveller, sturdy and practical, who knew her maps, could cope with a rough, at times even dangerous, journey, was not fastidious about accommodation, and was well up to haggling with couriers and guides. Without Lucy's sturdy companionship, one feels, Amelia might never have embarked on the adventures she would later describe so graphically in her *Untrodden Peaks and Unfrequented Valleys*.

While Lucy shared Edwards' desire to travel into the mountains, she had concerns about their other companions. Lucy's maid Sophia, was 'delicate . . . less able for mountain work than ourselves'. And there was what looked like 'the supreme difficulty' of winning over a courier who had, until then, been conducting them through Italy. He was a 'gentleman of refined and expensive tastes', who 'abhorred what is generally understood by "roughing it"', despised primitive simplicity, and 'exacted that his employers should strictly limit their love of the picturesque to districts abundantly intersected by railways and well furnished with first-class hotels'.[3] Hardly a promising candidate, then, for a trek along rock-strewn mule tracks and among sheer mountain sides, to remote villages, where at day's end they might or might not find a comfortable bed and a decent meal.

Knowing the courier would object strongly to their proposed change of plan, the two women had to plot their new adventure behind his back, spreading out their maps in a summerhouse in the hotel garden, or holding 'stealthy indoor conferences', at times when they knew he would not be around.

Apart from the general direction of travel, Edwards and Lucy Renshaw were actually quite vague about their plans:

> We have Mayr's maps, Ball's Guide to the Eastern Alps, Gilbert and Churchill's book, and all sorts of means and appliances; but we have not the slightest idea where we are going, or what we shall do when we get there.[4]

One thing they did know, was that they could expect to travel for eight or ten hours daily, through rocky mountain passes, and on narrow unpaved tracks that often ran alongside an abyss.[5]

When he finally got to know about the planned expedition, the courier was, as the women had predicted, most upset. Edwards, disclaiming any pretence of 'moral courage', as she put it, left to Lucy the delicate task of talking him round. Their guide finally agreed to accompany them – but 'with such a nicely adjusted air of martyrdom and dignity as defies description'.[6]

Amelia and Lucy, on the other hand, were quite prepared to rough it on their journey through the Dolomites. Their route would take them on horseback and muleback, from Cortina to Caprile. They would explore the area around Caprile, with a two-day trip to Titian's birthplace of Pieve di Cadore, then travel on to Primiero, and back to Caprile. From there, they would go on to 'Corfara'(Corvara), to St Ulrich and Ratzes, before descending to the train station at Atzwang for the journey south. It was a rugged, unfrequented route along treacherous mountain passes, where strangers hardly ever ventured. But that, to Amelia and Lucy, was the whole point.

It was not long, though, before the reluctant courier decided the proposed adventure was not for him. Before they even left Cortina, he had made his mind up. They stayed at a somewhat primitive inn there, the Aquila Nera, run by an old man named Signor Ghedina. Old Ghedina was a leathery-complexioned man with 'a large, brown, flat face that looked as if it had been sat upon', who took the Englishwomen under his protection. Reassuring them with offers of help to prepare for their journey, he patted Amelia on the shoulder, as she says, 'with a paw like a Bengal tiger'.[7]

Lucy and Amelia came back from exploring the town and its surroundings, getting their bearings before the challenging trek that lay ahead, to learn of their courier's decision. He had already told his employers, he reminded them, that wilderness adventure was not for him. He was not impressed by the rough-and-ready, if generous, hospitality offered at the Aquila Nera. Now he had a clearer idea of exactly what lay ahead. 'The near prospect of being dragged over passes and up mountains, of having to ride on a mule for days in succession, and of living for many weeks to come in Tyrolean albergos, several degrees less comfortable than the Aquila Nera, was too much for the great man's philosophy.' He would be leaving them.

It was Lucy who had first employed this man to travel with her, months before she went with Amelia to Naples. So, it fell to her to settle accounts. Businesslike Northerner that she was, she 'transacted the whole affair with an amount of withering sang-froid which speedily reduced the offender to a condition of abject humility'. She rejected his offer to give two weeks' notice and paid him off forthwith.[8]

In spite of their relief at being free of the courier's gloomy presence – Lucy said she felt 'as if a necklace of millstones had been taken from round her neck' – his departure left them with a problem. Admittedly, the fastidious man would not have been much use to them on the rough road ahead. They needed a reliable local guide, who knew the way and could keep them safe in the trickier places.

A solution presented itself in the form of Old Ghedina's nephew, a dependable young man, well used to trekking through the mountains. They would pay him any transport costs, and wages, from which he would cover his own board and lodging. Amelia took an instant liking to Giuseppe – 'faithful, honest, courteous, untiring, intelligent'. She noted the way he constantly considered his new employers' needs before his own and was careful in managing their expenses. Although not a trained guide, he took trouble to find out as much as possible for his employers, about the places they journeyed through.[9]

As they rode on through the mountains, the travellers heard stories of natural disasters from the local people – of floods, and rock falls. Landslides were said to be a common occurrence. One particularly terrible one, though it had happened a hundred years before, was still vivid in collective memory. In 1771, at Alleghe, near Caprile, as the local people told it, 'the whole side of the mountain came down with a mighty rush and overwhelmed the sleepers, not one of whom escaped.' Two whole villages were buried under the rockfall. Others were drowned in the lake formed by the flooding of a nearby river. At times of the year when the water level dropped in the lake, remains of ruined walls and roofs became visible. Some people claimed the bells of the drowned church tolled at midnight to mourn the unburied dead.[10]

Another, more immediate, hazard, was that of extreme weather. In *Untrodden Peaks*, Edwards gives a dramatic account of a Dolomite thunderstorm, a description both painterly and precise:

> The lightning seemed to run slantwise along the clouds in jagged streams, and to end each time with a plunge straight down into the earth. These streams of electric fluid were in themselves blinding white, but the light they flashed over the landscape was a brilliant violet, as rich in colour as a burst of Bengal light. I never saw anything to equal the vividness of that violet light, or the way in which it not only stripped the darkness from the great mountains on the opposite side of the valley, but brought out with intense distinctness every separate leaf upon the trees, every tile upon the farthest house-tops, and every blade of grass in the piazza below. These flashes ... followed each other at intervals of not longer than fifteen seconds, and sometimes intervals of five; so that it almost seemed as if there were flashes of darkness as well as flashes of light.

The thunder was so loud, it often drowned out the ringing of the church bells; and the storm ended with 'a deafening final explosion, as if a mountain had blown up' – followed by a deluge of rain.[11]

During one of these frequent thunderstorms, while they were edging along a narrow, unfenced track, with tiny villages just visible a thousand feet beneath them, the horse Edwards was riding, startled by the lightning, pranced about wildly. She reined it back as it was on the brink of leaping over the cliff edge, taking her 'at a single bound' into the abyss.[12]

Although she had once listed riding as among her hobbies, and was fond of animals in general, Edwards was, it seems, a less confident rider than Lucy. Or perhaps just unlucky in her choices of a mount. She had particular difficulty after they left Caprile, when, since horses would be unable to negotiate the steep, rocky mountain paths, they exchanged the horses for mules. Amelia's new mount, a beast named Black Nessol, turned out to have a definite mind of his own. From their first meeting in the Caprile inn yard, he tested her patience to the limit. When she tried to climb on his back he dodged away from her – to the undisguised entertainment of the laughing villagers. After she made a dozen abortive attempts to get on board, a few of them took pity and came to her rescue. They hustled the rebellious mule into a corner of the yard, and 'pinned him against the wall by main force', while she climbed onto his back: 'I mounted ignominiously at last by the help of a chair.'[13]

Black Nessol soon showed other recalcitrant traits. In 'the matter of roads and turnings', Edwards observed, 'he invariably prefers his own opinion to that of his rider'. She was unable, either, to keep him from eating everything he came across, from farmers' crops to poison berries, to potato peelings and eggshells. 'He would eat the Encyclopaedia Britannica, if it came in his way.' Meanwhile, Lucy and her mule were turning out to be 'the best friends in the world'. She fed him with sugar, and he followed her about like a dog.[14] It is typical of Edwards that she finds humour in what must, as she struggled on day by day, have become a trying experience.

Back at Caprile, as Edwards and Lucy mounted their mules, they had left Lucy's maid Sophia at the village inn, in the care of the innkeeper's family, to look after their luggage, agreeing to return for her later. They had felt sure the onward journey would be too hard for her.

They had been wise to leave both Sophia, and the courier, behind. As they rode on into more challenging terrain, even Amelia and Lucy, both seasoned travellers, and used to physical exertion, found the journey hard going. In the Cereda pass between Agordo and Primiero, they found themselves making their difficult way along 'the bed of a small torrent . . . twice we have to dismount and make our way on foot from stone to stone across rushing streams some thirty feet in width'.

The going got ever more rugged. The mules had to be shoved and pulled up the steep ascents, or allowed to climb up without their riders, who could only scramble after them on foot.[15]

As always when she was abroad, Edwards carried her sketch book and water paints. She found plenty to record in this unknown territory. Fascinated as much by the people whose villages they rode through, as by the awe-inspiring landscape, she longed to record images of their colourful costumes, and scenes of their daily lives. In some districts in this remote part of Italy, they were reluctant to be sketched. Sometimes, though, the locals – young women especially – begged Edwards to draw them. Then she was able to make what she called a 'careful coloured study' of the various local costumes.

She was particularly impressed by one Tyrolean woman, a 'very handsome woman of Livinallungro', who allowed Edwards to paint her, 'tempted by the promise of a florin':

She was so tall, and so finely formed, that not even that hideous sacque and shapeless bodice could disguise the perfection of her figure . . . A more majestic face, I never saw, nor one so full of a sweet, impenetrable melancholy.

As Edwards worked on her study of the subject's face and clothing, they talked. The woman was a farm servant, aged twenty-three, and still unmarried.

'But that must be your own fault', I said.

She shook her head.

'Ah no', she replied, with a slightly heightened colour. 'Our young men do not marry without money. Who would think of me? I am too poor.'

I should have liked to know more of her history; but her natural dignity and reserve were such that I felt I must not question her further.

The woman reluctantly accepted the agreed payment for the modelling assignment – yielding to Edwards' insistence out of politeness, Amelia thought: 'more, as it seemed, through good-breeding than from inclination'.[16]

Between the visitors and the locals, fascination with and curiosity about, the Other, was mutual. In one place, where nobody visited from one year's end to the next, the whole village turned out to witness the unusual sight of foreigners. At Santa Croce, at the start of their journey, Amelia and Lucy had found themselves surrounded by 'the whole population of the place', come to inspect the strangers. Among the staring crowd, were three or four good-looking young women. They all had 'gay red and yellow handkerchiefs bound round their heads like turbans'. They were not shy at all:

> They crowd; they push; they chatter; they giggle. One invites me to take her portrait. Another wishes to know if I am married. A third discovers that I am like a certain Maria Rosa whom they all seem to know; whereupon every feature of my face is discussed separately, and for the most part to my disparagement.

Excited to be among the mountains she had dreamt about for so many years, Edwards settled down to try and paint – struggling all the while to keep off the flies, that 'settle upon me in clouds, walk over my sky, drown themselves in the water bottles, and leave their legs in the brown madder'.[17]

With her usual observant sensitivity to suffering – if compassion is at times mingled with a certain contempt for ignorance – Edwards noticed not only the picturesque aspects of the villages in the Dolomites, but their ubiquitous poverty. The horses, she remarked, were 'cruelly overworked'; but so were the villagers themselves. In Cortina, she came upon teams of people dragging sleds, with loads on them that looked 'as if they might be too much for an elephant'.[18] Often, the inns they stayed in were bare of furniture, and the food of the most basic. The inn in Cortina could provide its guests only with 'dry bread, eggs, butter, and a coarse, uneatable mountain cheese'. Amelia improved the menu by offering to cook eggs with butter – 'to the unbounded entertainment of the landlady and her servant' – who gave her the title of 'Signora Cuoca' (Mrs Cook). She was greeted by that title the next time she went there; and is 'remembered by it, doubtless, to this day'.[19]

Bad food seems to be a theme on this journey – and not always owing to poverty. After a day of sight-seeing in the town of Agordo and its surroundings, Amelia and Lucy came back to their inn, where an ambitious menu promised everything from ice cream and soup to trout and chicken – unexpected luxuries indeed, after days of the sparse mountain fare. They were in for a disappointment:

> Happily, we were not very hungry. I will not dwell upon the melancholy details. Enough if I observe that the boiled chicken not only came to table in its head-dress and feathers like an African chief 'en grande tenue', but also with the entrails still inside it – with its internal economy quite undisturbed . . . I believe to this day that the cook was a raving maniac.[20]

Sleeping accommodation could be primitive, too. In one village inn, Amelia and Lucy found the bedrooms so filthy, they preferred to camp out on the landing.[21]

In spite of their poverty, the local people did not take advantage of these travellers, so obviously much wealthier than themselves. Amelia found them kindly and courteous, with 'a friendliness that does not appear as an item in the bill'. The locals were always offering 'little friendly salutations', as Amelia called them – 'Sound sleep and happy dreams'; or 'Felicità', when somebody yawned. Even if conventional and spoken as a matter of habit, they all the same helped 'to keep warm the spirit of goodwill'.[22]

Manners were always important for Amelia. When a lapse occurred, she made a note of it. The one exception to the general politeness she describes, occurred at the inn in a place called Forno di Zoldo. As they were seated at table there, picking their way through a badly cooked meal, the young woman acting as their waitress walked, 'quite coolly', to a mirror at the far end of the room, and there took her time trying on Lucy's hat and Amelia's jewellery.[23]

This discourtesy was an exception to the rule, however. On the whole, Edwards came across people in the Dolomites for whose politeness and consideration she had nothing but praise.

As the women journeyed further into the unfamiliar region, it dawned on them how distinct the worlds of England and of this remote part of Italy were at that time. Many local people, for example, were genuinely puzzled that anyone would be trekking through their mountains for the fun of it. They failed to see any beauty in their surroundings. When the travellers announced their plan to climb up to the Sasso di Ronch – the tall spur rock, whose iconic image appears on the cover of *Untrodden Peaks* – the villagers thought them crazy.[24] Later on in the journey, as Edwards was sketching the Monte Serrata from the little village of Pieve, an elderly peasant woman came to find out what she was doing. This business of sketching seemed to her mysterious, and pointless. Edwards tried to explain that the sketch would help her to remember this place after she had left it and enable her to share the experience of her travels with friends at home who had never seen these mountains. Still the lady looked incredulous. She asked Edwards where she was from. 'And where is England?' she asked. 'Is it near Milan?' Being told that it was much further off than Milan, and in another direction, 'the woman could only shake her head in silence. "Gran' Dio!" she exclaimed at last, "Have you then no mountains and no trees in England?"' Another of the villagers told Edwards bluntly that he found the magnificent scenery he lived among, ugly ('brutto').[25]

Undeterred by the local sceptics, Amelia carried on sketching and painting. She also depicted the landscape in words. One description well conveys her intense feeling for the serene beauty of the mountains in the calm of a fine sunset:

> That wonderful rose-coloured vision ... broke upon us as we turned down again into the valley – that vision of the Civetta, looking more than ever like a mighty organ, with its million pipes all gilded in the light of the sunset. The sky above was all light; the wooded hills below were all shade. Monte Pezza, soaring out from a mist of purple haze, caught the rich glow upon its rocky summit. Caprile nestled snugly down in the hollow ... a couple of tender grey peaks, like hooded nuns, looked up to the Eastern sky, as if waiting for the evening star to rise.

The evening shadows lengthened across the valley:

> The sky turned a tender, greenish grey, flecked with golden films. The birds became silent in their nests. The grasshoppers burst into a shrill chorus. The torrent – steel-coloured now, with here and there a gleam of silver – rushed on, singing a wild song, and eager for the sea.[26]

She was less admiring of the religious practices of the local people. Always a little wary of the Roman Catholic faith, like many English people of her time – at her kindest, she regarded it as picturesque but delusive. (In an early novel, *The Ladder of Life*, she writes of 'that blind and touching piety which gilds the hollow shows of Romanism with a glory like that of the setting sun, and soothes with glittering hope the earthly trials of the confiding enthusiast'.)[27] She was sardonic about the religious decorations in one inn where they stayed, whose proprietor was even more pious than the norm. Scrupulously clean, but bare of carpets or curtains, the bedroom compensated for lack of physical comforts by its ample provision of what Edwards called 'spiritual adornments'. The walls were covered with prints 'of saints and martyrs in little black frames'; with, over the head of each bed, 'a coloured lithograph of the Madonna displaying a plump pink heart stuck full of daggers, and looking wonderfully like a Valentine'.[28]

Where their faith was concerned, 'The good people of Caprile', Amelia observed, were 'difficult to please in the matter of weather'. In case of a thunderstorm, the bellringers would get up at night and ring the church bells till dawn, in a bid to protect their homes against lightning. The following day, a procession would take place, again to pray for protection from the lightning. Afterwards, however, the people all went up to the church – to pray for rain. Edwards could not resist challenging one of the worshippers about this seeming contradiction. How would it be, she asked him, 'if, instead of praying against the thunder, and the lightning, and the drought, you just asked the Madonna to put the wind round to the South-west and send forty-eight hours of steady rain immediately?' The man half-saw her point. 'It may be so, Signora', he told her. But he would leave all such matters to the village priest, who understood them better than himself.

Amelia had no right to mock his faith, she reflected. She 'turned away, quite ashamed of my own levity'.[29]

On her way through the mountains, she visited a number of churches, but mainly to admire the frescoes there. Fascinated to see the house in Pieve di Cadore where Titian was born, she went to look at surviving examples of his early work, in the local church. There, she was greatly moved by a painting of the Angel of the Annunciation – 'bold, beautiful, buoyant as if just dropt down from heaven', who attended the Madonna 'on half-bended knee, with an exquisite air of mingled authority and reverence'. In contemplation of another image, also by Titian – an early work, of a Madonna and child, flanked by saints – the art critic in her asserted itself: 'The saints are not well-drawn', she noted; 'the whole design is poor, the treatment conventional'. And yet, gazing at the 'broad, calm face' of the Madonna, no student of Titian, she acknowledged 'could look at it for five minutes and doubt its authenticity'. She was moved, too, by the devotion to these works shown by the parish priest, Don Antonio, who proudly pointed to the cheap frames around the paintings, worth only a few pounds in English money, but which it had taken him years to save up for. Here, in spite of the cultural differences between the woman from Protestant England and the devoutly Catholic priest, their shared love of Titian led to mutual respect.[30]

Difference of another kind became apparent, between Amelia and Lucy's sense of themselves as women, and the more conservative and traditional views of the local people. For the village women, the principal goal in life was to find a good husband and raise a family. The spectacle of these two English ladies travelling alone, seemingly unprotected, and so far from their homes, aroused in them not only astonishment, but pity: 'Gran Dio! Alone, and not married! Poverine! poverine!' (Poor things, poor things), one group of local women exclaimed. Then they all cried together, 'poverine!' – with such 'genuine concern and compassion', that Amelia and Lucy felt 'almost ashamed' at being doubled up helpless with laughter.[31]

Not surprisingly, Edwards found most common ground with those local people who shared her interest in art, craftsmanship, or ideas. One such like-minded person, was the gentlemanly Signor Prospero, who she met in the little town of Primiero – 'gaitered, white-hatted, his garments buttoned all awry, and a striped silk umbrella under his arm'. She found him 'genial, fussy, courteous, enthusiastic, indefatigable, voluble'. Passionate about the life of the mind, Signor Prospero had progressive ideas, and was 'keen to promote culture in his native town'. Like Edwards herself, he was full of energy, endlessly at work on some new scheme. He had founded a theatre in his town, and had campaigned tirelessly, and successfully, for the building of a new road. He talked with Edwards for hours – about his admiration for British literary critics; about Darwin; about 'the Calculating Machine'; about prehistory, Universal Suffrage, the Suez Canal, and a host of other subjects. A 'kindly, benevolent, public-spirited old man' – a man after Edwards' own heart. Signor Prospero had hopes for the children of his town, who had started going to school; but he deplored the narrow-mindedness and ignorance of their parents, for whom even geography was 'an invention of – con rispetta – the Devil!'[32]

Another person with whom she sensed common ground, was a young Austrian, Franz Rottenara. Franz, a young man not yet in his mid-twenties, was the innkeeper's son. He was studying art in Vienna. From roof to basement drying room, the house in Corfara where Amelia and Lucy stayed the night, was filled with the young man's paintings. Communication was somewhat limited by the young man's shyness, and even more by the lack of a shared language. Franz knew no English, and only a little Italian, while Edwards had no more than basic German. But although they were unable to discuss the finer points of art, Edwards saw that Franz had 'all the steady industry, the patient ambition, and the deep inward enthusiasm of a German art-student'. He would, she believed, 'make his mark by-and-by'. She had fellow-feeling for this talented, creative young person from an obscure background. It must have reminded her of her own early struggles to make her way in the world.[33]

Sympathy with another Tyrolean artist, however, led to an embarrassing situation. In the Val di Zoppe, the travellers were introduced to Valentino Gamba, a self-taught wood carver. In his workroom, Edwards admired a carved bust, representing the spirit of Italy. The life-sized sculpture weighed, she estimated, as much as all her luggage put together. To carry it with them over the mountains would be far from easy. But she saw the light of hope in the sculptor's eyes as she admired the carving – clearly, he thought he might have a sale. The price, though, even if it was rather too high, was not the problem. She could not have travelled on muleback through the mountains weighed down with so heavy an object, any more than 'with the church steeple'. She took the sculptor's card, promising to tell all her friends about another piece, an elaborate carved frame, that he hoped to show at the Vienna Exhibition – and took her leave 'with the awkward consciousness of having said more than I intended'.

It all became more awkward still, when the artist turned up at Amelia and Lucy's lodgings in the village. Would Edwards make him an offer for the bust of Italia? He had lugged the heavy carving all the way from his home in Bragarezza. Edwards could picture the man 'toiling with it along the dusty road . . . pale, anxious-looking, out-at-elbows'. It now felt to her 'as if it were my fate to yield and buy'. Lucy and Giuseppe managed to talk her out of the idea – Giuseppe clinching the argument by pointing out that if she were to buy the sculpture, they would need an extra mule to carry the thing. Afraid of relenting if she saw him, Edwards hid away in her room, and sent down a message with a polite refusal. They would 'hear of the poor fellow no more'.[34]

After six weeks of strenuous trekking, Amelia and Lucy came back down from the mountains. Their journey ended at the foot of the Rittner plateau, where they would catch the train back to the south. Now, Amelia felt a sense of anti-climax: 'Here is Atzwang; here is the railway; Here is the hot, dusty, busy, dead-level World of Commonplace again!'[35]

Towards the end of her narrative, she made a prescient observation. If the Dolomites, she said, should ever become like much of the rest of Italy, a magnet for mass tourism, 'the simplicity, the poetry, the homely charm of the Dolomite district' would 'be gone for ever'.[36] Ironically, the popularity of her book – it went through five editions during her lifetime – may have played a small part in hastening the day when that fate would arrive. But the opening up of remote valleys by modern technology probably has more to do with it. On smooth metalled roads, journeys that once took a whole day can now be done in an hour by car. Amelia and Lucy would hardly recognize the secluded villages they knew – not only for their enhanced communications, but for the greater prosperity of their well-educated residents, their lives now connected to the world beyond the Dolomites. Only the enduring mountains are hardly changed.

In November 1873, Anne Brewster received a letter from Amelia. Enclosed with it, a copy of *Untrodden Peaks and Unfrequented Valleys*. Amelia drew attention to the dedication, 'to my American friends in Rome' – pointing out that it implicitly included Anne.[37] Tellingly, though, her novel *In the Days of My Youth* that also appeared that year, carried a handwritten inscription to Lucy on an advance copy, a Christmas gift in December 1872, before the novel appeared in the bookshops the following year. The wording – 'The Doggie to his owner' – playfully depicts Amelia as Lucy's faithful hound – ready to follow and obey.

The bond between Lucy Renshaw and Amelia Edwards was one that lasted well beyond the days of their travels together – indeed, for the rest of their lives.

'My dear charming friend', is how Amelia now addresses Anne. (No longer 'my darling'.) In her letter, she mainly recalls externals – 'your pretty rooms, & all your pretty dainty wraps'. Edwards had been in England, working on an anthology of contemporary English poetry, and seeing to the publication of *Untrodden Peaks*. Now she and Lucy were on the road again. They had been in central France, where Edwards had been sketching and making notes on her impressions. They might go home via Italy, Amelia told Anne; in which case it would be 'a great pleasure to see Rome and you again'. But it was more likely that, after having gone further afield to 'see a little of the East', they would travel back to England via Athens.

Whatever the assurances, the promises to keep in touch, Amelia was leaving Anne behind.

Amelia and Lucy were on their way to Brindisi, to take ship for Egypt. A new chapter in Amelia's life was about to start.

4

The Nile

On Sunday, December 14, 1873, Edwards, with Lucy Renshaw, went down to the brink of the Nile in Cairo and boarded the sailing barge *Philae*, for a journey upriver. They would go as far as Abu Simbel, and the fringes of Nubia, on a voyage that would become the subject of Edwards next travel book, *A Thousand Miles Up the Nile*.[1]

Lucy, (as always, referred to only as 'L'), appears in Edwards' narrative of the Nile journey almost entirely in her role as shipboard medical officer – treating the *Philae*'s crew, and other local people, for minor ailments and injuries. She was accompanied by a different maid, this time – Jenny Lane, an intelligent, observant, thoughtful young woman, who kept her own log of the voyage.[2]

Following behind, in a second boat, were friends made in Alexandria – a Marianne Brocklehurst, with her companion, 'Miss Booth' (called 'the M. Bs', in *A Thousand Miles*), with Marianne's nephew Alfred, and a resourceful, imperturbable manservant, George.

Edwards – who refers to herself throughout *A Thousand Miles* simply as The Writer – tells us little about most of these passengers – though she does offer a lively account of the many-talented George. Hailing from 'the wilds of Lancashire', George was a man 'gifted with a comic gravity of countenance that no surprises and no disasters' could upset for a moment. George could skin a game bird 'like a practiced taxidermist'. He could wash and iron. He was 'groom, footman, housemaid, laundry-maid, stroke oar, game-keeper and general factotum'. And he picked up Arabic 'as if it were his mother tongue'. In his English groom's coat with gaiters, and a tall hat, he rode his donkey over the sands near the Pyramids, 'with his long legs dangling within an inch of the ground', as to the manner born. 'One would have sworn that he had been brought up on pyramids from his earliest childhood.'[3] The reader might hope to hear more of this appealing, eccentric character; but after this attractive sketch, he disappears from the story.

As Edwards tells it to her readers, the decision to go to Egypt and journey up the Nile was taken on the spur of the moment, when, during a sketching holiday in Northern Europe, Amelia and Lucy encountered 'the wettest of wet weather'. They 'drifted' to Egypt, she claims, 'by accident, with no excuse of health, or business, or any serious object whatever; and had just taken refuge in Egypt as one might turn aside into the Burlington Arcade or the Passage des Panoramas – to get out of the rain'.

Their choice of destination was not quite as spontaneous however, as this account makes it seem. In fact, Longman the publisher, who had already published her book on the Dolomites, had written to Edwards, with a specific request: 'Mr Longman wrote off at once to me saying, 'pray go up the Nile . . . write us a book about Egypt.'[4]

The *Philae*'s intrepid passengers were sailing up the Nile in comfort. On board the traditional flat-bottomed Egyptian sailing barge, or dahabeeyah, they had individual cabins, with a bathroom for the passengers; and a well-furnished, carpeted saloon, with a piano, a cushioned divan, and shelves of books. Amelia and Lucy brought in vases of flowers. An awning on the cabin roof made it pleasant for the passengers to dine in the open air. Their meals were cooked in a shed located between the mast and the boat's prow. Amelia wondered at the skill of the cook, who could turn out delicious meals – the 'elaborate dinners that are the pride of a Nile cook's heart' – from such a primitive kitchen. How they managed 'when wind-storms and sand-storms are blowing, and every breath is laden with the fine grit of the desert, is little short of miraculous'.[5]

It was a large boat – a hundred feet in length, from prow to stern. It had a large crew. Along with the boat's captain – Reis Hassan, 'short, stern-looking, authoritative', a steersman and twelve sailors, the crew in addition comprised a cook, an assistant cook, two waiters, and 'the boy who cooked for the crew'. There was also a dragoman, or guide. The last-mentioned, a man named Elias Talhamy, became a close companion of Edwards and her friends.

Less comfortably accommodated than their passengers, the crew slept wrapped in blankets on the boards of the lower deck, and subsisted on a monotonous diet of bread, beans and lentils, 'with a little coffee twice a day, and now and then a handful of dates'. Coffee and tobacco were the only luxuries the crew ever bought for themselves, 'and our poor fellows were never more grateful than when we distributed among them a few pounds of cheap native tobacco'. Reis Hassan, better off than the others, was said to have a small house in Cairo, returning there to his wife after each voyage.[6]

Edwards quickly got to know the crew members' names. Like Talhamy, and the 'wizened old cordon bleu' cook, Hassan Bedawee, the waiters Habeeb and Michael were Syrians from Beirut. The latters' names indicate that they were Christians. Other crew members – the 'gentle' Mehemet Ali; Salame, Khaleefah, Riskali, Moosa – were from Upper Egypt. Salame, a native of Aswan, was, Amelia writes, 'young, active, intelligent, full of fun, hot-tempered'; and 'as thorough a gentleman as I have ever had the pleasure of knowing'.[7]

In the course of their journey, the passengers came to like and trust all the sailors. None of them 'ever went on shore without one or two of them to act as guards and attendants'.[8]

They took the journey upriver at a steady pace, visiting the pharaonic sites in order, beginning where known ancient Egyptian history began, with Saqqara and the Pyramids of Lower Egypt, and progressing from there to sites of later construction, at al-Minia, Assiut, Denderah, Luxor and Aswan, and on to Philae and Abu Simbel. Edwards was critical of those who rushed the journey upstream, viewing all the antiquities in the wrong chronological order. The local guides, she complained, seldom grasped the necessity of working upstream in systematic fashion. She and her party, though, 'began the Great Book' as 'it always should be begun – at its first page; thereby acquiring just that necessary insight without which many an after-chapter must have lost more than half its interest'.[9]

After ten days on the river, at the town of Minia just before Christmas, they were joined on board the *Philae* by a painter friend, Andrew McCallum – 'short, slight, with dark skin and hair, small, dark, deep set eyes, and an energetic and dramatic personality'. He is always referred to in *A Thousand Miles* as The Painter. McCallum enjoyed a reputation in England as a fashionable painter of landscapes. He hoped, Edwards said, to produce a great work of art, as a result of his travels. The artist spoke some Arabic, was friendly with governors and consuls all along the Nile, and 'great on the subject of what to eat, drink and avoid'.[10] Mr and Mrs Eyre, a young newly-wed couple, with their maid, came on board at the same time as McCallum. For some reason, Amelia always calls this 'Happy Couple', 'the Idle Man' and 'the Little Lady'. (Edwards' use of initials or nicknames for all the passengers, may have been partly a device to protect their anonymity. Her nicknames for the Eyres do, however, sound a little disparaging. It seems she regarded them very lightly.)[11]

She had greater respect for the Painter, McCallum – as a fellow-artist, no doubt, but also for his practical qualities. Having sailed up the Nile three times before, he 'knew the ropes'– quite literally, being well acquainted with the river's currents, winds and sandbanks.

The leisurely pace at which the *Philae* travelled, offered Edwards ample time for note-making, sketching and painting – with a particular focus on temples. Between Philae and Abu Simbel, there were fourteen of them – 'to say nothing of grottoes, tombs, and other ruins'. While the Happy Couple soon went on strike where antiquities were concerned, and started skipping temple visits, Edwards' own enthusiasm was 'insatiable, and grew with what it fed upon'. She went over them all: 'I took notes of them all. I sketched them every one.'[12]

Besides evocative watercolours and pen-and-ink sketches, the journey as a whole yielded vivid descriptions of the Nile and its surroundings. With her painterly eye, and feeling for the spirit of place, Edwards gives us a number of scenes that, as she says, were done not only for her readers' benefit, but to fix them lastingly in her mind's eye. As she writes of the Great Hall of Karnak, 'swathed in coiled shadows and broad bands of light', she has the sense of being back there: 'I stand once more among those mighty columns, which radiate into avenues from whatever point one takes them.' The Great Hall and its columns are 'photographed in some dark corner of my brain for as long as I have memory'. 'I see them painted and sculptured with shapes of Gods and Kings.'[13]

They lingered at Luxor, both on the upstream journey, and on their way back, when they rode on donkeys on the western bank of the Nile, passing the Colossi of Memnon:

> How well I remember that morning ride across the Western plain of Thebes – the young barley rippling for miles in the sun; the little water-channel running beside the path; the white butterflies circling in couples; the wayside grave with its tiny dome and prayer-mat, its well . . . inviting the passer-by to drink and pray . . . How the great statues glistened in the morning light! How they towered up against the soft blue of the sky! Battered and featureless, they sat in the old patient attitude, looking as if they mourned the vanished springs.[14]

With careful accuracy, she recorded the dramatic spectacle of a dust storm over the desert:

> A fitful breeze springs up, blowing in little gusts and swirling the dust in circles round our feet. At the same moment, like a beautiful spectre, there rises from the desert close by an undulating semi-transparent stalk of yellow sand, which grows higher every moment, and begins moving northward across the plain. Almost at the same instant, another appears a long way off towards the south, and a third comes gliding mysteriously along the opposite bank . . . the first begins throwing off a . . . kind of plume, which follows it, waving and melting in air. And now the stranger from the south comes up at a smooth, tremendous pace, towering at least 500 feet above the desert; till, meeting some cross-current, it is snapped suddenly in twain.[15]

As elsewhere in her work, Edwards' impressions are full of wit and humour. As she sat one day with her easel, 'a pair of self-important hoopoes', the colourful insect-eating birds that fly everywhere in Egypt, perched overhead and watched her as she sketched, 'nodding their crested polls and chattering disparagingly, like a couple of critics'. Another day, going ashore from the *Philae*, she and her friends passed five of their sailors, who were having their hair shampooed. The barber was 'complacently surveying the effect of his work' as 'an artistic cook' might admire 'a dish of particularly successful meringues à la crème'. The meringues, she said, 'looked very sheepish' when the English people laughed at them as they went by.[16]

In similarly humorous terms, she described her first – and presumably last – encounter with a camel, when, between Aswan and the island of Philae, the travellers left their boat and decided to trek on overland. The ensuing ride was not a comfortable one. The camel, while 'irreproachable as a beast of burden' is, we are told, 'open to many objections as a steed':

> You know that he hates you, from the moment you first walk round him, wondering where and how to begin the ascent of his hump. He swears freely while you are taking your seat, snarls if you but move in your saddle; and stares you angrily in the face, if you attempt to turn his head in any direction save that which he himself prefers. Should you persevere, he tries to bite your feet. If biting your feet does not answer, he lies down.

Being stuck on a camel for hours was, Edwards said, a punishment no human being should be subjected to – 'not even a reviewer'. Only tourists, she claimed, ever submitted themselves to the ordeal of camel riding. The local people always got about on donkeys.[17]

While Amelia was having these mundane adventures, something else was happening to her. The Nile, the desert – above all the mysterious temples and tombs – were awakening her imagination. More and more, there grew upon her, as she wandered among the shadowy halls, or pondered the images on some vivid fresco, a sense of being in communication with the past.

Finding herself standing against the huge stones of the Great Pyramid; measuring her height against one; actually touching it as the giant shape towered slanting out of view, she had a sudden revelation of what before had been merely an abstraction: the pyramid was now in its 'seventh millenary':

> These remote dates had never presented themselves . . . until this moment as anything but abstract numerals. Now, for the first time, they resolved themselves into something concrete, definite . . . The consciousness of that moment will never, perhaps, quite wear away. It was as if one had been snatched up for an instant to some vast height overlooking the plains of Time, and had seen the centuries mapped out beneath one's feet.[18]

Wherever she went in Egypt, Edwards was struck by cultural links between the present and the ancient past. The 'zaghareet' or 'joy cry' of the modern Egyptian peasant woman, like the death-wail she uttered in mourning, and the work songs of farmers as they drove their oxen or drew up water for their land, had been 'handed down from generation to generation through an untold succession of ages'.[19] Nubian small boys still wore the single sidelock of hair, as depicted in paintings in Egyptian tombs. At Wady Sabooah near Dakka, she met with a portly middle-aged man, 'dressed in a kilt and carrying a palm staff', in whom she recognized a startling likeness to a well-known wooden statue in the museum at Boulaq.[20]

The 'essentially processional' ceremonies of ancient Egypt had, she believed, influenced the later rituals of Christian churches. She attended a

Coptic (Egyptian Christian) church service in Luxor, where she heard the liturgy chanted in the Coptic language. She recognized that, even though the language must have changed drastically since pharaonic times, she was all the same hearing 'the last lingering echoes of that ancient speech', recited by those most closely descended from the ancient Egyptians.[21]

As they were sailing upriver, the *Philae* was boarded by a mendicant Coptic monk, who swam across the river and clambered on board. He was 'a fine shapely man, aged about forty, with splendid eyes and teeth, a well-formed head', and skin 'the colour of a copper beech leaf'. But it made 'one's heart ache', the Writer said, to note the expression on the man's face, of 'such ignorance, timidity, and half-savage watchfulness'. Hardly the face of a dignified descendant of the Pharaohs, such as she might wish to see. Even so, Edwards thought she detected in him some resemblance to the images of his ancestors she had recently seen depicted in the tomb of Ti at Saqqara. As the poor man's teeth were chattering with cold, the travellers gave the monk a generous baksheesh, 'for all he represents in the history of the world' and sent him on his way.[22]

Coming to Egypt brought for Edwards, as she says, reunions with 'old half-forgotten friends' – the images in the illustrated *Manners and Customs of the Ancient Egyptians*, a book she loved as a child. 'I had read every line of the old six-volume edition over and over again. I knew every one of the six hundred illustrations by heart'. Here, in the tombs in Thebes, were the originals of the scenes in those pages: 'Every subject on these wonderful walls was already familiar to me. Only the framework, only the colouring, only the sand under-foot, only the mountain slope outside, were new and strange.' Here were the well-loved images – the soul of the dead being weighed in the presence of Osiris – the musicians at the feast – the fowler hidden crouching in the rushes, with a basket of decoys: 'One withered hand is lifted to his mouth; his lips form the call; his thin hair blows in the breeze. I see now that he has placed himself to the leeward of the game; but that subtlety escaped me in the reading days of my youth.'

All the human figures in the tomb paintings were as familiar to her as living people: 'It seemed to me that I had met all these kindly brown people years ago – perhaps in some previous stage of existence; that I had walked with them in their gardens; listened to the music of their lutes and tambourines; pledged them at their feasts.'[23]

The long period she spent inside the shadowy sacred spaces of the ancient religion, began to have strange effects on her mind. In the dark halls of the Temple of Denderah, 'Hurrying along by the light of a few flaring candles', Edwards wrote, 'one cannot but feel oppressed by the strangeness and awfulness of the place. We speak with bated breath . . .' The sculptured frieze on the staircase to the temple roof represented a magnificent ritual procession, of pharaoh and priests, with an uncanny air of reality:

> Their attitudes are so natural, their forms so roundly cut, that one could almost fancy them in motion as the lights flicker by. Surely there must be

some one weird night in the year when they step out from their places, and take up the next verse of their chanted hymn, and, to the sound of instruments long mute and songs long silent, pace the moonlit roof in ghostly order!'[24]

She recalls how, when the great Serapeum at Memphis was first opened, the French Egyptologist Auguste Mariette went in there alone; 'and there, on the thin layer of sand that covered the floor, he found the footprints of the workmen who, 3,700 years before, had laid that shapeless mummy in its tomb and closed the doors upon it.'[25]

Approaching the temple of Philae, Edwards was struck by the preservation of its outer walls, 'solid, stately, perfect'. The interior, too, with its bas-reliefs and elaborate ceiling paintings looked pristine. 'Here is a place in which time seems to have stood as still as in that immortal palace where everything went to sleep for a hundred years': If 'a sound of antique chanting was to be borne along the quiet air – if a procession of white-robed priests bearing aloft the veiled ark of the God, was to come sweeping round between the palms and pylons – we should not think it strange'. Nor would it surprise her 'to find masons here tomorrow morning, or the sculptor with mallet and chisel, at work on a carved frieze of lotus buds'. It was hard to believe that twenty-two centuries had passed, since 'they all struck work for ever'.[26]

After they reached Abu Simbel, she spent days wandering through the temple's inner chambers, in the late afternoon. It was 'a wonderful place to be alone in – a place in which the very darkness and silence are old, and in which Time himself seems to have fallen asleep':

Wandering to and fro among these sculptured halls, like a shade among shadows, one seems to have left the world behind, to have done with the teachings of the present; to belong, oneself, to the past. The very Gods assert their ancient influence over those who question them in solitude. Seen in the fast-deepening gloom of evening, they look instinct with supernatural life. There were times when I should scarcely have been surprised to hear them speak . . . There were times when I felt I believed in them.

Wonderful, as she says – but never wholly comfortable. There was something 'weird and awful' about Abu Simbel. If Salame, the crew member from the *Philae* who usually came with her on her expeditions, was nearby, she felt able to walk about freely in the inmost recesses of the temple. When completely alone there, though, she seldom went further in than the entrance hall. On the one occasion when she did venture alone all the way to the inner sanctuary and sat down 'at the feet of the Gods' there, she grew paralysed with terror. A conviction overcame her that the whole weight of the mountain above the rock-cut temple was about to fall down and crush her. She found herself unable to move, or even make a sound: 'I felt I could not have called for help, though it had been to save my life.'[27]

Gazing at the giant sculptures of Rameses II, to whom the temple at Abu Simbel is dedicated, Edwards could write of the 'terms of respectful intimacy' on which she found herself with this particular Pharaoh: 'We seem to know the man – to feel his presence – to hear his name in the air.' His features 'are as familiar to us as those of Henry the Eighth or Louis the Fourteenth'. His signature cartouches were everywhere in Egypt, with the gigantic structures that extolled his conquests and his power.[28]

She was far from idealizing Rameses, however, or any of the other Pharaohs who ordered the building of magnificent monuments. She estimated the human cost. Each gigantic stone block laid in place in a palace or temple, represented the sacrifice of a life: 'Every breath that wanders down the painted aisles of Karnak seems to echo back the sighs of those who perished in the quarry, at the oar, and under the chariot-wheels of the conqueror.'[29]

Other encounters with the past proved disturbing for different reasons – those with the physical remains of the ancient Egyptian dead. Edwards recounts her shock at Saqqara, as she and her companions wandered in the desert near the Pyramids, at discovering the land around them was pitted with violated graves; and strewn with fragments of bone and desiccated flesh. But after the first shudder, 'We soon became quite hardened to such sights, and learned to rummage among dusty sepulchres with no more compunction than would have befitted a gang of professional body snatchers'. 'So overmastering is the passion for relic-hunting', she added, 'that I do not doubt we should again do the same things under the same circumstances.'[30]

In an encounter with a newly discovered mummy at Luxor, however. she experienced the shock of empathy. It was one thing to look at mummies 'lodged and catalogued' in a museum, she pointed out, where one might regard them as 'specimens', and forget 'that they were once living beings like ourselves'. Quite another, to see a wrapped body freshly unearthed from a tomb. This 'poor mummy' seemed to her 'startlingly human and pathetic, lying at the bottom of its grave in the morning sunlight'. As with her attitudes to living Egyptians, Edwards' feelings about the ancient Egyptian dead were complex, constantly shifting.[31] Her encounters with contemporary Egyptians blended criticism and revulsion; compassion, liberal guilt; occasional admiration and respect, and an anthropological curiosity about people's manners, beliefs, and customs.

As well-to-do foreigners, the passengers enjoyed hospitality only with upper-class Egyptians – mainly with the Turkish officials who largely made up the governing class. In *A Thousand Miles*, some members of this class come in for a good deal of satire. Edwards was amused by a Nubian Sheykh who thought himself too grand to put food in his own mouth, and had to be fed. When he came visiting on the *Philae*, the guide Talhamy was appointed to perform the role of feeder, putting 'every morsel into our guest's august mouth, as if the said guest were a baby'. Amelia, Lucy, and Mrs Eyre, then plied him with fruit and jam for dessert, until 'the poor man . . . laid his hand pathetically over the region next his heart, and cried for mercy'.[32]

She was impressed by the beautiful manners of one Turkish official. At Erment, near Luxor, the town's Bey or governor, came on board the *Philae* to pay a formal visit. He gave the travellers presents – samples from his sugar factory, and a Scarab ring, that he gave to the Little Lady, who politely hesitated to accept it. Insisting the ring was nothing, 'a toy', the Bey persuaded her to take it. What impressed Edwards, was the graceful way he did it: 'The readiness, the courtesy, the lofty indifference of it, were alike admirable.' Edwards always appreciated good manners; and here encountered perfect tact and politeness, in this Turkish member of the upper classes.[33]

She had real, if condescending, affection for the Egyptian and Levantine crew who kept the *Philae* travelling smoothly on her way up the Nile:

> More docile, active, good-tempered, friendly fellows never pulled an oar. Simple and trustful as children, frugal as anchorites, they worked cheerfully from sunrise to sunset, sometimes towing the dahabeeyah on a rope all day long, like barge-horses; sometimes punting for hours, which is the hardest work of all; yet always singing at their task, always smiling when spoken to, and made as happy as princes with a handful of coarse Egyptian tobacco.

Amelia and Lucy took trouble to get to know the sailors, tended their minor injuries; and 'a feeling of genuine friendliness was speedily established between us'.[34]

Much as she liked the men, she all the same found it hard to consider most of the Egyptians she met, as equals. 'Child-like' is her commonest adjective in *A Thousand Miles*, for the crew of the *Philae*. She writes, for instance, of the 'child-like enjoyment' with which the sailors gather, 'cross-legged and happy', round the pot where they have cooked a sheep given them by the passengers. Set to clean up a giant head of Rameses at Abu Simbel, they are described as all 'delighted as children at play'. They are 'simple and trustful as children'. At other times, the men are 'poor fellows' – helpless even in going about their own work; always 'bruising their feet, wounding their hands, getting sunstrokes and whitlows, and sprains, and disabling themselves in some way'; coming to Lucy, as acting ship's doctor, for first aid. These tough, hard-working men – although clearly grateful to Lucy for her care, and eager to thank her with small gestures of courtesy and kindness – giving her wild flowers, singing her Arabic songs – would surely have been surprised – quite likely, offended – to learn to what extent they were regarded by the passengers as not quite fully adult.[35]

The Egyptian peasant, Edwards believed, was:

> half a savage ... a singularly transparent piece of humanity; easily amused, easily deceived, easily angered, easily pacified. He steals a little, cheats a little, lies a great deal; but on the other hand he is patient, hospitable, affectionate, trustful ... He commits no great crimes. He is incapable of revenge.[36]

This last statement seems particularly odd, in the context of the murderous revenge feuds between families – the 'Tar' of Upper Egypt – that, like the Sicilian vendetta, might carry on down whole generations.

When, sailing upriver past Aswan, the travellers came into Nubia, they had partly left the Arab world; they were on the borders of black Africa. Here, Edwards' perceptions were unfortunately even more influenced by the racist assumptions of her culture. The Nubians, she claimed, belonged 'to a lower ethnological type', than the Egyptians of Arab descent. These 'primitive' people paddled about the river using palm logs as boats; they had (to the European eye), barbaric-looking jewellery; they threw 'boomerangs', and carried spears. Their children went about almost naked. In short, the Nubians were 'savages au fond', their 'old war-paint' only 'half-disguised under a thin veneer' of Islam.[37]

To many European travellers, the Nubians were most definitely the Other in threatening form. The Europeans went in actual fear of them. What Edwards and her companions seemed to find most alarming, was the way the local people tended to turn up in crowds. The *Philae*'s passengers would set out to interact with an individual, only to find they were dealing with a whole village.

One day, going along the riverbank, Edwards came upon the Eyres and Lucy Renshaw backed up against a tree, surrounded by 'an immense crowd' of villagers. The people were not hostile – just desperate to sell things to these wealthy tourists. But sailors had to be fetched from the *Philae* to help the travellers escape. Edwards believed that everywhere in Nubia, 'where the traveller's life was scarcely safe fifty years ago', English people going about unescorted, were still 'pretty certain to be disagreeably mobbed'.[38]

The Idle Man, Mr Eyre – who seemed to have a gift for getting out of his depth in his dealings with the local people – bought a necklace from a Nubian villager. This local man turned up later, with 'half the village at his heels'. He had been cheated, he claimed – he demanded a fairer price. After acting out his rage – tearing off his turban, brandishing a spear, the seller and his supporters sat down on the riverbank, while a steadily growing crowd gathered behind them. The *Philae*'s captain looked troubled at this turn of events but the situation was hardly one of life and death. After all, the crew had only to cast off, and sail the boat away to some other place, up or down the river.

As it happened, the angry villagers turned up just as the *Philae*'s passengers were at Sunday worship. The Idle Man was below decks in the saloon, reading the lesson. Edwards volunteered to go on deck and ask everyone to calm down. She explained that the English people were at prayer, and that the racket outside the boat meant no one could hear the service. The effect on the shouting villagers was instantaneous. A reverent hush fell over the crowd. They calmed down and waited quietly till the service was over. In the newly-restored calm, Mr Eyre was able to renegotiate his deal with the angry seller, to the satisfaction of both parties.

The conclusion Edwards draws from this incident is interesting. The reverent hush that fell on the Nubians, she takes as evidence of 'the sincerity of the religious sentiment in the minds of a semi-savage people'.[39] That her comment betrays a degree of surprise, however, suggests she regards the Nubians' respect for faith as little more than a civilized veneer, laid over their alleged 'savagery'. Like her companions, Edwards was hampered in her efforts to relate to the ethnic Other, by false Darwinian-derived notions about racial hierarchy, which assigned Africans to the near-animal level. In the eyes of the *Philae*'s passengers, the Nubians, being of African descent, were never entirely to be trusted.

Fear of the Nubian crowd led to an unpleasant incident, as the *Philae* sailed back from Nubia. As Edwards tells the story in *A Thousand Miles*, Mr Eyre, while onshore to shoot quail, accidentally injured a four-year-old child, who was crouching down unseen in a field of barley. The enraged villagers seized hold of Eyre and grabbed the gun away from him. Someone hit him from behind with a large stone. Mehemet Ali, one of the *Philae* sailors, went to Eyre's rescue. After being knocked about and getting his clothing torn, he managed to bring Eyre with him back to the boat. The gangplank was drawn up. With a whole village, a furious crowd 'all raving, shouting, gesticulating' on the riverbank, the English people felt besieged on the boat.

Talhamy the dragoman went onshore to negotiate. He succeeded in pacifying the crowd, by offering to have the injured child treated on board the *Philae*. Reassured that the foreigners meant to make amends for what they had done, the villagers sat on the bank to await developments. 'When a Nubian sits down', Edwards comments, 'you may be sure that he is no longer dangerous.'

After a while, an elderly man appeared with a few companions, carrying the injured child, wrapped in a blanket. Here in her story, Edwards is just to the Nubians – noting that they not only trusted these foreigners to treat the child the Englishman had injured, but also returned Eyre's gun, undamaged.

The ever-practical Lucy got out the medical kit. The little boy's shoulder, 'slightly grazed' in several places by the shotgun cartridges, was washed, and sticking plasters applied. His father was given money in compensation for the child's injuries.[40]

The matter now seemed to have been resolved. All the same, it was thought safer to move the boat away from the village. It was decided to sail down to Philae, where Edwards could do some sketching.

There the whole affair might have ended; if Eyre and McCallum had not opted to make a formal complaint to McCallum's friend the governor, in

Aswan. They thought it necessary to do this 'for the protection of future travellers' – mainly, it seems, because Eyre, who had offered no resistance when the villagers surrounded him and seized his gun, had been 'treacherously' (Edwards' word) hit from behind with a stone.

There is no way of telling what Eyre and McCallum expected the governor to do about their complaint. Perhaps they thought the villagers would get a reprimand, and a warning. In fact, the governor had fifteen villagers arrested. Eyre had to go and appeal for their freedom.

Edwards, having gone with the boat to Philae, could, presumably, tell what happened next, only from hearsay. The men were brought in before the governor – 'I am ashamed to write it!', she tells us – in single file, chained, neck to neck. Appalled at this drastic outcome of his complaint, Eyre persuaded the governor to free fourteen of the men on the spot, and to reduce the proposed punishment of the man who had struck him on the back. Instead of 150 strokes of the cane, the culprit would receive six. Eyre had to stand and see the punishment carried out. As each blow fell on the soles of his bare feet, the man cried out, 'God save the Governor! God save the Moodeer! God save the Howadji! (the foreigners).' All the men were then released – overjoyed, we are told, to be let off so lightly. Eyre went away too – not before the governor had assured him that 'his only wish was to be agreeable to the English, and that the whole village should have been bastinadoed, had his Excellency desired it'.[41]

Critics have focused on Edwards' attitude in telling the story of the injuring of the child, and the men's arrest, finding her treatment of it somewhat cold-hearted; especially where she writes about the small boy. Possibly she found the whole incident upsetting, and resorted to ironic distancing to deal with it? She does not, however, seem to question Eyre's sense of entitlement to go hunting in a densely populated area, on farmland near a village, where the chances of hitting a human being must have been fairly high. All the same, her imagined account of the treatment of the unfortunate villagers, shows keen awareness of the arbitrary brutality of Egyptian 'justice'; of the governor's contemptuous attitude towards the villagers; and his servility, towards the Englishman.

When attention focuses on individuals, racist generalities tend to break down. While Edwards may write the received opinion of Nubians – that they are ethnically inferior semi-savages – when confronted with the pain of a single human being, the negative view that distances a whole race as the threatening Other, is nowhere in sight. Generalization is replaced by empathy. Bereavement and separation in particular seem to evoke compassion – as in Amelia's meeting with an elderly Nubian woman, who came to the *Philae* to ask the sailors if they had news of her son. The young man had gone to Cairo to earn a living. The mother no longer heard from him – had not heard for months – and she was afraid he might be dead. Since he had been gone, she had become destitute, and was forced to beg for a living. Any scrap of information would be welcome; but the crew were unable to tell her anything. 'It made one's heart ache', Edwards writes, 'to see the tremulous eagerness with which the poor soul put her questions, and the crushed look in her face when she turned away'.[42]

Another time, the travellers witnessed a Nubian funeral. Again, there was a mother in the case. A bereaved woman was burying the body of her son. At his grave, she broke down: 'The tears began to make channels down her cheeks – her voice became choked with sobs – and falling down in a sort of helpless heap, like a broken-hearted dog, she lay there with her face to the ground . . .'[43]

Was Edwards so touched at this sight, perhaps, remembering the loss of her own dearly-loved mother?

She had compassion for the hardships that ordinary Egyptians endured. Seeing 'our poor fellows', the sailors of the *Philae*, struggling to tow the boat upstream when the wind dropped, 'harnessed to a rope like barge-horses', made Edwards deeply uncomfortable. Although, she says, they got used to it in time, still, 'It looked like slaves' work, and shocked our English notions disagreeably.'[44]

Edwards was keenly aware, too, of the sufferings of the fellaheen, the peasant farmers, in the towns and villages along the Nile bank – of the 'poverty, sickness and squalor' of their villages – the wholly preventable eye diseases of the children there, owing to the mothers' ignorance about the need to fend off flies; the appalling infant mortality rates. She learned to avoid these places, feeling helpless to do anything about such conditions. They might not be worse, she thought, than in 'many an Irish village'; but the misery in these Nile-side communities was so upsetting to her, 'that one would willingly go any number of miles out of the way', rather than witness such suffering, 'without the power to alleviate it'.[45]

She knew about the corvée, the forcible conscription of villagers, taken from their homes to do public works for the government. During their time of servitude, these conscripts were 'little better off, for the time being, than the captives of the ancient Empire'. Meagrely paid, once the work was done, they often were not provided with transport home, but left, far from their villages, to make their own way back as best they could. While they were away, the whole family suffered. Often, the man's land back home, left untended, became the property of others.[46]

She tried to see another side of the question. If no one were brought to repair the canals and irrigation ditches, she pointed out, Egypt's entire agricultural system would collapse. Curiously, it did not seem to occur to her, that the exploited fellaheen might still do the work, but do it better if offered decent working conditions, and proper wages.

Middle-class Egyptian women, she empathized with for a different reason. While in Luxor, she visited a family where the women of the house, confined to the harem, never got out. It was a situation that an active woman of the world like Edwards, would have found intolerable. These women, although they expected nothing different out of life, were clearly unhappy.

Though they were 'all good-nature and gentleness', their faces wore 'the expression of people who are habitually bored . . . One could see that time hung heavy on their hands'. The harem life was particularly oppressive for middle-class women, Edwards noted. Women of the upper classes rode out in their carriages from time to time. Even if veiled and chaperoned, they might attend the opera and other public entertainments. A few, active behind the scenes, took an interest in politics. (In a later generation, such involvement would inspire the powerful Egyptian feminist movement.) Peasant women, meanwhile, even if 'bitterly poor' seemed to Edwards the happiest. At least they had 'the fresh air, the sunshine, and the open fields'.[47]

In spite of her powerful evocations of others' grief and suffering, in her observations of contemporary Egyptian life the social historian in Edwards often asserted itself. As she witnessed a village funeral, she noted the similarities between contemporary rites, with the wailing and shrieking of the female mourners, throwing dust over their heads, and those depicted in pharaonic wall paintings. Like an eager photojournalist of our own modern world, she wanted, too to portray visually, or in word-painting, everything she saw. The result was some wonderful word-portraits – of two young men from Khartoum, for example, with their 'small proud heads and delicate aristocratic features . . . intensely, lustrously, magnificently black . . . like young and beautiful Dantes'.[48] She admired many of the women, both Arab and Nubian, for their dignity and grace. Near Dakkeh, 100 miles to the north-east of Abu Simbel, she saw a Nubian bride being ferried across the river to her wedding – 'a chocolate beauty with magnificent eyes', with her hair elaborately braided, her face and neck decked in gold jewellery. She stood in the moving boat, surrounded by her female attendants, 'proud of her finery, and pleased to be stared at by the Ingleezeh'.[49]

Elsewhere, she reminded herself of the danger of loss of empathy, in her quest for vivid material. But the scenes she passed through were all so 'picturesque . . . so biblical, so poetical', that:

one is almost in danger of forgetting that places are something more than beautiful backgrounds, and that people are not merely appropriate figures placed there for the delight of sketchers, but are made of living flesh and blood, and moved by hopes, and fears, and sorrows, like our own.[50]

Her depictions of the countryside in A Thousand Miles are undeniably both accurate and beautiful – as when, late in the voyage, she described fields at harvest time:

steering their way by unseen paths, go strings of camels; their gawky necks and humped backs undulating above the surface of the corn, like galleys with fantastic prows upon a sea of rippling green. The pigeons fly in great clouds from village to village. The larks are singing and circling madly in the clear depths overhead. The bee-eaters flash like emeralds across our path . . . the brown reapers, barelegged and naked to the waist, are at work with their sickles . . .[51]

Sometimes, in her eagerness to portray the picturesque scene, she forgot her own warnings against treating her surroundings as subjects for art and literature, and overstepped the mark into voyeurism. In the town of Aswan, where they stopped off on the journey upriver, the *Philae*'s passengers received a visit on board from the governor, and other dignitaries. Edwards was tactless enough to express a wish to visit the slave market in Aswan, in order to sketch it. They had no political objective, she assured the governor; her only object was to depict something she imagined would be 'most curious and pathetic'. Her request triggered a minor diplomatic incident:

The smile vanished from the Governor's face. The Mudeer set down a glass of fizzing lemonade untasted. The Kadee all but dropped his cigar. If a shell had burst in the saloon, their consternation could scarcely have been greater.

The distinguished guests hastened to insist that no such market existed: 'It is forbidden.' Undeterred, the English people continued to insist that it did – they had heard about it from other European travellers. 'An awkward silence followed. We felt we had committed an enormous blunder, and were disconcerted accordingly.'

The Governor had the presence of mind to defuse the situation, by changing the subject: 'He rose, opened the piano, and asked for some music; whereupon the Little Lady played the liveliest thing she could remember, which happened to be a waltz by Verdi'.[52]

The Egyptian people Edwards got closest to, were the sailors and other crew members of the *Philae*. Each of them told her his story, in which 'the local oppressor', and the 'dreaded' military conscription, were invariably central themes. They confided to her 'their hopes, their wrongs, their sorrows . . . Through sympathy with these one comes to know the men; and through the men, the nation'.[53]

When the English group, on their way back from exploring a temple, were alarmed to find themselves lost in the dark, they were grateful to the *Philae*'s crew, for coming out to find them:

A whole bevy of dancing lanterns and friendly brown faces comes gleaming out from among a plantation of sugar-canes, to welcome and guide us home. Dear, sturdy, faithful little Reis Hassan, honest Khaleefeh, laughing Salame, gentle Mehemet Ali, and Moosa – 'black but comely' – they were all there. What a shaking of hands there was – what a gleaming of white teeth – what a shower of mutually unintelligible congratulations! I was never much more rejoiced at a meeting in my life.[54]

Late in their voyage, as the *Philae* was sailing back down the Nile, the sailors' food supplies ran out. The hunger among the crew distressed the passengers; although Talhamy the dragoman was unmoved by their plight:

> 'Hungry? Well yes – no doubt they are hungry. But what of that? They are Arabs; and Arabs bear hunger as camels bear thirst. They have often been hungry before – they will often be hungry again. Enough! It is not for the ladies to trouble themselves about such fellows as these!'[55]

Ignoring Talhamy's objections, Edwards and the other women raided his supplies, to feed the 'poor lads' with eggs and biscuits, until they could buy food at the next town. The dragoman thought them quite crazy.

If she made rash generalizations about Egyptians in general, Edwards conceived great liking and respect for particular people. Talhamy was one of them. At first, she was irked by the dragoman's 'air of melancholy resignation which he always assumed when not allowed to have his own way'. 'You will come to learn the value of a wind, when you have been longer on the Nile', he told her once, when she and her fellow passengers insisted on staying longer in one place and risked missing a favourable breeze. (In fact, he could have been right, because the fair wind dropped, just as they were making ready to leave.) Talhamy was 'an indolent, good-tempered man', Edwards remarked; but 'that air of resignation came to be aggravating in time.' All the same, she learned to respect his good sense, and genuinely to like Talhamy. He would travel with her and her friends all the way to Beirut, when their Egyptian tour was done, and they left Cairo at the beginning of May; and they parted from him with sadness.[56]

She had respect for the cool nerves and unflappable calm of the Nubian Sheykh of the Cataract, who took over as temporary commander of the *Philae* to manoeuvre the boat through the threatening Aswan rapids. At first sight, not an impressive-looking character – 'flat-faced, fishy-eyed', wearing an old yellow bandanna, and endlessly smoking his long-stemmed Turkish pipe – the Sheykh had inspired the travellers' mistrust on their way upriver, by refusing to mobilize his men to tow the boat up through the rapids. Fate, he said, was against them. McCallum had sworn volubly at the Sheykh in Arabic. Whether the swearing had the desired effect; or whether Fate had changed its mind, is unclear; but the following day the Sheykh, who had decamped in a rage, saying the *Philae* 'might stay where she was till doomsday', returned with all his men, who, with Herculean effort, towed the boat up to the head of the rapids and into calm water.[57]

On the way down the Cataract on the return voyage, the Sheykh once again took command, directing his own experienced rowers, while the *Philae* captain and sailors looked on. The moments before the descent were full of nervous tension: 'Everybody looks grave . . . even the Arabs are silent.' Everyone gazed down at the narrow channel 'through which, at a steep incline', there rushed a roaring torrent. 'The whole Nile, in fact, seems to be thundering in wild waves down that terrible channel.' As the boat drifted towards the channel, everyone on the boat felt it tilting sharply towards the chasm. 'We feel the leap – the dead fall – the staggering rush forward. Instantly the waves are foaming and boiling up on all sides . . .'

The men stopped rowing and let the boat plunge forward of its own accord. Now the Sheykh really came into his own – looking 'quite majestic', as he stood absolutely still, armed raised to give a signal. At the end of the channel was a sharp turn to the right – 'as sharp as a street corner in a London thoroughfare' – with a hundred feet of wooden boat to get around it. Suddenly, the uplifted arm was waved – the Sheykh thundered, 'Daffet!' (helm) – an order to swing the boat and turn the corner. The men, 'steady and prompt, put the helm about'. The boat, 'answering splendidly to the word of command', began to turn. Shooting round the bend with only inches to spare, the *Philae* came out safe and sound, 'with only an oar broken'.

Everyone burst into shouts of joy and sheer relief. There were thanks to God, and handshakes all round. And horseplay – the Sheykh's men snatched off Talhamy's headcloth and danced away with it as a trophy. Amid all the excitement, only the Sheykh of the Cataract was unmoved. His brief burst of energy over, 'He slouches back with the old stolid face; slips on his shoes; drops on his heels, lights his pipe; looks more like an owl than ever'.

Amelia was awed by the whole performance. She doubted whether any English boatmen 'would venture to take such a boat down such a rapid, and between such rocks'.[58]

She had great liking for the intelligent, fun-loving young sailor Salame, who often went with her on sketching expeditions, and acted as a guardian. One day, she had him accompany her while she sketched the temple at Esna. It must have been 'dull work', she reflected, to sit with her while she painted. But he sat watching her every move – adjusting her parasol, handing her water, or paints, as required. He might have gone into town, and enjoyed himself, she thought; but he 'betrayed no discontent'.

She gave Salame money to buy himself food and bring it back to where she sat painting. Time went by, and Edwards, absorbed in her work, had forgotten all about her own (quite elaborate) lunch. Only when she finally started to eat, did she notice that Salame had not touched his own meal, although it was four hours after his usual lunchtime. When she finally remembered to eat, he wolfed down his own lunch, ravenously. Edwards reproached him for starving himself; at which Salame exclaimed, 'Am I a pig or a dog, that I should eat when the Sitt (Lady) was fasting?'

Edwards recorded this incident as indicating Salame's personal devotion to her needs. For the young native of Aswan, however, his behaviour was no more than normal good manners, and a way of showing respect for the English lady, his employer.[59]

Wherever she went in the world, Edwards took an interest – if at times tinged with sarcasm – in people's religious customs. She was moved by the unselfconscious piety of ordinary Muslims at prayer – remarking how believers prayed at the appointed hour, wherever they might be. 'So the camel driver would dismount and pray in the dust at the roadside, or a merchant unselfconsciously spread his prayer mat and bow down in prayer on the steps of his shop amid the bustle of the marketplace.' 'We could not but be impressed by their profound and unaffected devotion.'[60]

Raised in the decorous formality of the Church of England, Edwards was much less taken with the frenzied ecstasies of a band of dervishes, who worshipped publicly before a crowd of curious tourists in Cairo. Disturbed by the violent, rhythmic spontaneity of the zikr, she could only describe the ceremony in terms of 'writhing and shrieking'. It was, she thought, 'a horrible sight', needing 'only darkness and torchlight to be quite diabolical'. The zikr violated all the norms of what a well-brought-up English Protestant lady might regard as reverent worship.[61]

At least where the Cairo dervishes were concerned, Edwards could hardly doubt their sincerity. About various 'holy men' encountered as she journeyed on the Nile, she was more sceptical. A case in point was the Holy Sheykh Cotton, who on one occasion visited the *Philae*. The Sheykh was 'a well-fed, healthy-looking young man' of about thirty. Plied with money by the adoring sailors, the holy man accepted their little offerings 'with the air of a Pope receiving St Peter's Pence'. Then, dripping wet, and smiling 'like an affable Triton', he blessed the boat. The crew were convinced that with the blessings of the holy man upon it, their voyage could only go well. They would have favourable winds and get back to Cairo safely. But what, Edwards wondered, had the Sheykh done to earn his title, or his revered reputation? He didn't fast more than anyone else. He was financially supported by the faithful. He had two wives. He never did 'a stroke of work'; and he looked 'the picture of sleek prosperity'. All the same, he would be honoured after he died, said to have worked miracles; and his eldest son would succeed him in the business.[62]

Edwards formed an equally low opinion of one Sheykh Seleem at Farshut: 'Holiest of the holy, dirtiest of the dirty, white-pated, white-bearded, withered bent and knotted up', Sheykh Seleem had sat, naked and unwashed, on the same dust-heap, winter and summer, allegedly for fifty years, 'never even lifting his hand to his mouth; depending on charity not only for his food but for his feeding'. He was 'not nice to look at', in Edwards' own view; but the sailors thought him 'quite beautiful', and called out for him to bless them, as they sailed by.[63]

As she travelled, Edwards was growing increasingly aware of the shocking neglect everywhere, of Egypt's precious cultural heritage. She came upon a temple at Esna 'buried to the chin', as she put it, in rubble that had accumulated over centuries. The temple at Amada was actually threatened with total inundation in the sand, so that within a few generations, the entire building seemed likely to disappear completely. Until Auguste Mariette, as Egypt's Director of Conservation of National Antiquities, had them demolished, Edfu temple had sixty-four houses built on its roof, where families lived with their chickens, dogs and donkeys.[64]

For one particular instance of neglect, Edwards could only hold her own people to blame. A gigantic statue of the pharaoh Rameses the Great had been given to the British Museum – whose people were, as she remarked dryly, 'too economical', to remove it. So, the colossus lay face-down in the mud, drowned every year by the Nile, 'visible only when the pools left by the inundation have evaporated, and all the muddy hollows are dried up'.[65]

Damage to monuments took many forms. Tourists scribbled on them; local people carted off masonry for their own building needs; even professional scholars, taking prints of precious wall paintings, used a method that over time destroyed all the original colour. Unscrupulous excavators carried off temple statuary for foreign museums, or for their own private collections – at one tomb in Assiut, even hacking off entire inscriptions from the walls. Most of the time, there was no one around to prevent the destruction.

Some of the damage done in the past had been motivated by religious fanaticism – as with the beautiful Greco-Egyptian bas-reliefs at Denderah, vandalized by early Christians, who chopped away the faces from all the images, and carried off pharaonic stones for new church buildings. Then an edict from Byzantium of AD 379 outlawed the old religion completely, with the destruction of scores of temples.[66] 'The gods are avenged now,' Edwards claimed; for in Nubia, Christianity had died out, to be replaced by Islam.[67]

There had been systematic looting. On the West Bank of the Nile at Luxor, whole families made their living by looting the tombs and selling what they found to whoever would buy. In interviews she would give later to newspapers in America, Edwards made potentially racist statements shocking in their brutal directness, blaming 'the Arabs' for 'breaking up and selling piecemeal priceless specimens', and naming them as the chief enemies of conservation. In *A Thousand Miles*, however, she offers a more nuanced view, blaming the untutored Egyptian villagers for this practice, less than the European buyers who made the trade in antiquities so profitable: 'The museums of Berlin, of Turin, of Florence are rich in spoils which tell their own lamentable tale. When science leads the way, is it wonderful that ignorance should follow?'[68] She did not include the British Museum in her list of institutions, though it was equally complicit in the plunder.

Egyptian rulers, too, had played their part in looting the treasures of Egypt. It had been the practice for the reigning Khedive, when he wished to honour some important foreign visitor, to grant him permission to excavate a historic site; where the excavator was allowed to keep anything he found. It was not unheard of, under this 'pick-your-own' system, Edwards claims, for recently found grave goods or other treasures to be put back in a tomb, so that the distinguished guest might have the thrill of 'discovering' them.[69]

The painter, McCallum, while out exploring on his own at Abu Simbel, did make a genuinely original discovery of a new ancient site. He sent a message back to the *Philae*: 'I have found the entrance to a tomb. Please send some sandwiches.'

Excited by this news, everyone, passengers and crew alike, left the boat and went to investigate. And to excavate. They all got down on their knees, and, with no more sophisticated equipment than a broom, a shovel, wicker baskets and their bare hands, worked madly to clear away the sand blocking the entrance. 'Everyone helped; even the dragoman and the two maids.' The local Sheykh turned up, followed by a hundred of his men, to join the digging. He claimed, and received, payment for his efforts, though not as much as he demanded.

The discovery, as it turned out, was not a tomb, but a beautifully decorated side-chamber to a temple – the temple's library, perhaps. The *Philae* travellers wrote their names on the chamber wall, with the date – February 16, 1874. It was, Amelia said, 'the only occasion on which any of us left our names upon an Egyptian monument'.[70]

She does confess, however, that, while in Luxor with Lucy Renshaw, she engaged in some illegal antiquity-buying of her own; even though she knew it was breaking the law. 'We enjoyed it none the less because it was illegal. Perhaps we enjoyed it the more.'[71]

Despite indulging in the guilty pleasures of illegal antiquity hunting, Edwards thought a new ban on exporting antiquities, introduced by the Khedive Ismail, was a positive step. Precious artefacts, that formerly were shipped out of Egypt wholesale and without official scrutiny, were now to be bought, sold, or shipped abroad, only under license. (This, at least, was the ideal.) The new system of regulation was, it seems, working up to a point: Egypt's treasures were increasingly being collected and conserved in Egypt. The Boulaq Museum, founded in 1861 – the embryonic Egyptian Museum that exists in central Cairo to this day – is largely the product of digs organized and overseen by Mariette. His workers had strict instructions to send him any mummy case found during excavations, unopened and intact.[72]

Edwards and her friends also made a minor contribution to restoration work. While at Abu Simbel, Andrew McCallum had the *Philae*'s crew climb on improvised scaffolding to clean and restore the huge face of Rameses II on the temple, which had bits of plaster sticking all over it, where a plaster cast had been taken of the head: 'A scaffolding of spars and oars was at once improvised, and the men, delighted as children at play, were soon swarming all over the huge head, just as carvers may have swarmed over it in the days when Rameses was king.' After scraping off every scrap of plaster, the sailors covered up the white marks left behind, by dabbing the white patches with coffee-soaked sponges held on sticks. Hassan the cook was appalled at the gallons of coffee consumed daily in the restoration work: 'Never before had he been called upon to provide for a guest whose mouth measured three feet and a half in width.'[73] The amateur restorers could now claim to have made amends, however small, for the Europeans' many acts of theft and vandalism in Egypt.

In the three years that went by, between Edwards' return to England, and the appearance in print of *A Thousand Miles Up the Nile*, she had thoroughly researched many aspects of the history of ancient Egypt. She read up on all that was known about the dynastic history of its rulers, and the social history of the ordinary people. She relentlessly badgered eminent scholars and archaeologists, to learn from them all she could. She taught herself to read hieroglyphics. By the time she came to write her account of the Nile journey, she was able not merely to describe the scenes and adventures of her travels, but to give a substantive scholarly account of Egypt's magnificent, if neglected, temples and other antiquities. She could offer her readers imaginative glimpses into the life of that remote past.

For all we know, the idea of a society to promote excavation and conservation in Egypt may have been forming in her mind, even as she and her companions journeyed back down the Nile. Or it took root, perhaps, when she was home at The Larches, settling down to write about her Egyptian journey.

Whenever it was she finally resolved to set up the Egypt Exploration Fund, she can hardly have realized what a daunting task it would be. Or how the new commitment would consume her life.

5

Inventing Egypt

As Edwards completed *A Thousand Miles Up the Nile*, Longman rushed the book out in time for the Christmas season. She was still writing the preface even as the first pages were being sewn up for binding. The book was in the shops in December 1876 (though it appeared in print with the date 1877, suggesting that the publisher had given up hope of having it ready by Christmas).

Word quickly got around, that she was working on a new project. In the year before *A Thousand Miles* was published, a gossip columnist was already telling readers of the *Belfast News-Letter* that 'Miss Amelia B. Edwards has hidden herself away in a cottage in Somersetshire, close to the sea and some interesting ecclesiastical ruins ... in a garden the trees of which are one mass of delicious blossom.' (Presumably this colourful account refers to the house, Saville Villa in Weston-super-Mare, where Amelia would go once or twice a year, for the sake of Ellen Braysher's health.) She was, the Belfast journalist went on, hard at work in her seaside idyll, on 'another charming book', to be called 'A Thousand Miles Up the Nile'. Irrelevantly, and with more than a touch of sexism, 'That's where I would like to be at this very moment,' the writer added; 'and I shouldn't object to the society of Miss Amelia B. Edwards!'[1]

'A delightful gossiping book', one reviewer called *A Thousand Miles*, when it first appeared. It would 'impart a new dignity and grace to the drawing-room tables on which it reposes'. The *Saturday Review* praised the book for giving what it called 'a woman's view' of its subject. Amelia Edwards, 'unlike some other literary ladies', was 'the last person in the world to think of renouncing her sex, and assuming a masculine swagger'.[2]

Others took the new work more seriously. Its blend of travellers' tales with scholarly erudition appealed to a wide readership. *The Globe* praised it for 'Cultured writing, beautiful typography, and graphic illustrations'. (Something for everyone here, then.) 'What more', the writer demanded 'could the most exacting ask for in a book of travels?' It had to be admitted, however, that there wasn't much in the way of dramatic incident – no 'hairbreadth escapes', or 'fortuitous slaughter of great game and natives'. (Readers of 'anything pertaining to Africa' apparently expected an element of 'sensation'.) And there was perhaps a little too much history and scholarship in places, for this reviewer's taste – although, it was conceded, this would not necessarily be viewed as a flaw by everyone. A book for 'more refined tastes', the reviewer concluded. 'A labour of love and enthusiasm', the *Pall Mall Gazette* called *A Thousand Miles;* admiring the thoroughness of the research, if sometimes finding the accounts of pharaonic monuments went on a bit. (Edwards' readers, it was thought, might be 'less ardent after antiquities' than the author herself.) Parts of the book, though, were found to be 'fresh and lively'. Edwards' beautiful illustrations, according to the reviewer, left 'nothing to desire'.[3]

More personal responses came from acquaintances and friends. The artist and humorous writer Edward Lear (best known today for 'The Owl and the Pussy Cat' and other verses), wrote to praise what he called, 'Your Egyptian Book'.[4] Lear was elderly by now, frail and ill, but he appreciated Edwards' gift of the copy of *A Thousand Miles*. 'I value it much', he wrote, 'and shall continue to do so for what I suppose is the very short span of time I have yet to live'. His Italian manservant was also 'a fervent admirer' of *A Thousand Miles*; having lived for several years in Cairo. For both of them, Amelia was now 'La Signora del Nilo'.[5] Her book, Lear told her, had inspired him to consider publishing his own 'Egyptian diaries'.[6]

She received a letter from a friend in America, the painter Frederick Church. In congratulating Edwards on her new book, he expressed the surprise, that others might also feel, at the unexpected turn her career had taken. He had read her novel, *In the Days of My Youth,* and enjoyed her book about travel in the Dolomites – although he still had not 'gotten over the astonishment I experienced at the diversity of the subjects'. And now here she was, 'with the lantern of science casting its rays into the gloom of the tombs of the Pharaohs'.[7]

Anyone who had known Amelia Edwards as a young girl would have been less surprised at her only seemingly novel passion for Egyptian archaeology, if they recalled how ancient Egypt had been part of her imaginative world since she first turned the pages of the books in her parents' library. As she herself wrote, her fascination with the land and history of ancient Egypt 'began with my childhood, and will only die with me'.[8]

Another artist who admired her writing, was the engraver and painter Gustave Doré. They first got to know one another in London in 1869, after Edwards wrote a favourable review of his work for the *Morning Post*.[9] Doré gave her a copy of his illustrated *Don Quichotte*, with a handwritten dedication from 'an ami affectueux'. They became firm friends; and although the artist lived in Paris and visited Britain only occasionally, they corresponded for years.

Doré often expressed appreciation of Edwards' work. He particularly liked her non-fiction – the Dolomites book, and *A Thousand Miles Up the Nile*. He called her 'encyclopaedic', admiring her versatility in various arts, and her unusual capacity for absorbing information – 'une faculté d'assimilation bien rare'. A letter of August 1877 contains lengthy praise of

A Thousand Miles Up the Nile. He appreciated the sheer amount of research that had gone into the book. That he greatly admired its illustrations, she would have taken as a high compliment from so famous and accomplished an artist. He wanted to know why she hadn't put her name to them. In any case, 'Mille Bravos sincères'.[10]

The Egyptologist and linguist Gaston Maspero was still in his early thirties, a professor at the Collège de France in Paris, when he wrote to express his appreciation of *A Thousand Miles*.[11] His distinguished career as Director General of Excavations and Antiquities for the Egyptian government, and co-founder of the Egyptian national museum, still lay some years in the future.

The young professor already knew and admired Edwards' novels, having first come across her short stories in Charles Dickens' *Household Words*. He wrote to her respectfully, as an older woman with an established literary reputation. Maspero made an interesting suggestion about common ground between the work of the novelist, and that of the Egyptologist. 'Archaeology', he wrote:

is, in its way, a kind of fiction . . . We too aim to make characters come alive, think, speak, act, die. Where others see only grinning mummies, we see real men and women. Novels are, after all, the history of people and things that might have existed.

The narratives of history, then, can be viewed as 'fiction about things and people that did actually exist'. It was a gracious, tactful letter, and a perceptive one, paving the way for friendly relations between the novelist and the Egyptologist. It would lead to fruitful collaboration between them in years to come.

A Thousand Miles went through seven different reprints in Edwards' lifetime, including a translation into Polish. Its lavish use of coloured illustrations made the book expensive for circulating libraries to buy, and in 1888 a new, cheaper edition was produced, bringing it within the reach of less affluent readers.[12] It has been reprinted several times in recent years. To this day, it remains among the best known of Edwards' works.

All through the 1870s, from the first days of her return from the Nile, Edwards was teaching herself hieroglyphics, and reading everything she could get hold of, to learn about almost thirty centuries of Egyptian history. At first, these studies were, she claimed, an exercise undertaken as a break from other activities – as 'one might take up the dumb-bells' for exercise, 'after three or four hours at the desk'.[13] If indeed they were begun merely as a diversion from more central concerns, they came to claim more and more of her attention, and her time. As well as reading, she consulted scholars at the British Museum. Between June 1874 and January 1875, as she worked on *A Thousand Miles up the Nile*, she wrote to Joseph Bonomi, a museum curator and draftsman, who pointed her in the direction of source material on Abu Simbel to be found in the British Museum;[14] and to Dr Samuel Birch, Keeper of the museum's Department of Oriental Antiquities. She contacted Birch at least five times, with queries about the meanings of inscriptions on temple walls; about potsherds, about ancient vases, about the fragments of a mummy case.

By the time she wrote to him again, in 1876, she must have been aware of trying Birch's patience. Her tone, as she asks for his help in deciphering two pharaonic cartouches, is both playful and apologetic: 'I should think you must have been hoping I was dead or mummified, as I have been quiet for some little time. Now, however, I rise again to torment you.' Though clearly aware the eminent Egyptologist is by now thoroughly sick of her importunate queries, she cannot resist seeking his advice. Her compulsion to know everything there is to be known, overrides all considerations of tact.[15]

As in other fields where she applied herself with untiring diligence and attention to detail, Edwards' capacity for self-education bore fruit. After six months of study, she knew enough about the field, to read a paper at the 1874 Oriental Congress in Vienna, on 'Recent Excavations in the Necropolis of Abydos'.[16] In 1891, her *Pharaohs, Fellahs and Explorers*, was published. The book is a compilation based on public lectures she gave while on tour in America and all over Britain. It gives a good measure of her erudition on the subject of ancient Egypt by this time; of knowledge gathered over the seventeen years since she had begun systematic study in the field.[17] The reviewers were impressed. Gone was the patronizing tone of some responses to *A Thousand Miles*. The new work was properly recognized as one that, while written in an engaging style and directed to the general reader, was based on careful scholarship, that had to be taken seriously. The *Morning Post* called it 'one of the best books on Egyptian antiquities ever published'.[18] For the *North London News*, the book deserved 'to rank among the very best of its kind'.[19] And a review for *The Graphic* – although the reviewer complained the book was 'disfigured' by American spelling (!) – acknowledged that it had the capacity both to educate and to entertain: 'The story of the discovery of buried cities beneath the mounds of the Delta is capitally told in such a fashion as to interest those who have never paid any particular heed to the subject.'[20] The prestigious *Athenaeum* took the opportunity to comment on Edwards' achievement as a popularizer, in making complex information understandable and interesting to a wide reading public: 'No English Egyptologist possesses in greater perfection the art of lucid exposition and the analogical grasp which are essential to the popular treatment of a complicated subject.'

In a time of growing public interest in the world of ancient Egypt, she sought to share her own passion. Audiences would pack halls across Britain and America, to hear her impart not just her knowledge, but her love, of her subject. Like Maspero, she aimed to kindle people's imaginations; to remind them of our shared humanity with the long-dead Egyptians.

She brought to her writings and talks the imaginative vision of a novelist. 'It rarely happens', an editor of the *Century* magazine, writing in 1890, observed, 'that the pen of ... a gifted and favourite author' is 'inspired by archaeological facts'. Yet Amelia Edwards 'has found the Valley of the Nile more enchanting and its soil full of tales more strange than fiction'.[21] It is precisely Edwards' imaginative vision, that brings a long-dead world to life. She can evoke a sense of awe, at the idea of a vast unknown world beneath the desert sands, as yet undiscovered, but only awaiting the tread of the explorer:

If you but stamp your foot upon the sands, you know that it probably awakens an echo in some dark vault or corridor, untrodden of man for three or four thousand years.'[22]

When, in 1871, Arab workmen employed at Meydûm first opened the tomb where they found the statues of Prince Rahotep and his wife Nofret, 'they first drew back in terror; and then, believing them to be inhabited by demons, were with difficulty restrained from smashing them'. Their fright, Edwards comments, 'was natural enough':

Looking into the eyes of this wonderful pair, and seeing how the light shifts in their liquid depths, it is difficult not to believe that they look at us, even as we look at them, and that their gaze is not following us as we move from group to group in the hall of the museum where they sit enthroned. But how strangely and luridly those eyes of quartz and crystal must have gleamed from the depths of that dark sepulchre of Meydûm![23]

These people of ancient times are alive in our imaginations, Edwards suggests. To their contemporary descendants in the early 1880s, even more so. By unbroken continuity with the past, they are members of the modern community.

She tells of the extraordinary discovery in 1881, at Deir el-Bahari near Luxor, of dozens of royal mummies, all found together in a single underground chamber. What followed, as the mummies were loaded onto steamboats to be carried downriver for safe storage in Cairo, was perhaps more remarkable still. The villagers turned out *en masse*, not merely to stare at the piled decks as the steamers went by, but to show respect for the illustrious dead. Women with dishevelled hair running along the banks and shrieking the death wail, men ranged in solemn silence and firing their guns in the air, greeted the Pharaohs as they passed. Never, assuredly, did history repeat itself more strangely than when Rameses and his peers, after more than three thousand years of sepulture, were borne along the Nile with funeral honours.[24]

'We had, I suppose, been so accustomed to think of the ancient Egyptians as mummies', Edwards said, echoing Maspero, 'that we scarcely remembered they were men'.[25] An observation that may recur to us, as we read her description of the mother and child also discovered entombed at Deir el-Bahari:

> Queen Maut-em-Hat, for all her high-sounding dignities, is only sixteen inches long. Makar [her mother] died in child-birth, and this tiny infant – superscribed with every title which was already hers by right of birth . . . was, after all, no more than a little dead letter addressed to the Land of Shadows.'[26]

Edwards reminds us of the variety of touchingly human objects found in the graves of long-dead Egyptians, all speaking of their human needs, affections, attachments: a pet gazelle; a musician buried with his cymbals; dolls and balls in the tombs of children; bows and arrows; work tools; rouge pots, a mirror. From a much later period, that of Greek colonization, in *Pharaohs, Fellahs, Explorers*, she tells us about 'the great Homer Papyrus', found in an Egyptian grave in 1889:

> The owner's head was pillowed upon it. She had been apparently a beautiful woman, with little ivory teeth, and long, silky black hair. The inscription on her coffin was illegible, and we are alike ignorant of her name, her nationality, and her history. She may have been an Egyptian, but she was more probably a Greek. We only know that she was young and fair, and she so loved her Homer that those who laid her in her last resting place buried her precious papyrus in her grave.[27]

To bring the remote Pharaonic past to life for her readers, she asks them to picture themselves stepping into the frame, and imagining themselves as ancient Egyptians; becoming, for instance, a traveller in the time of Rameses II, approaching the town of Tanis. The place, in the north-east of the Egyptian Delta, close to Sinai, was in Rameses' day an important centre of royal power. The whole region at that time was criss-crossed by waterways, long since vanished into sand.

In Edwards' imagined scenario, the visitor approaches Tanis by boat, along a river, travelling through a plain dotted with villages, with glimpses of other boats sailing along a nearby canal; while 'far away to the northward, whence a mass of storm-cloud is driving up from the coast, a pallid far-distant gleam tells the story of the sea'. Nearing the town, he is confronted by a gigantic statue of Rameses II, 'fourteen times the height of a man', so colossal he at first mistakes it for a tower.

The visitor goes on into Tanis, where he witnesses the victory parade of Rameses, returning in triumph to Tanis from making war in Syria:

> Clad in a loose robe of fine muslin, girdled by a jewelled belt, on his head a helmet covered with leopard-skin, on his neck and arms rich collars and

bracelets set with gems, in his left hand a bow, in his right a curved scimitar, the Son of Ra stands in his gorgeous chariot, upright, haughty, immovable as one of his own statues.

Edwards piles on the pictorial detail, until the imagined picture rises vividly before our eyes:

Upon his horses' heads are nodding plumes; his young sons, carrying aloft great fans of ostrich feathers, walk beside his chariot wheels; his tame lion follows after. And now the maidens fling their flowers, and the children clap their hands, and the men prostrate themselves, and, amid a great roar of acclamation, Pharaoh passes.[28]

As an artist herself, Edwards was, naturally, interested in the art of Egypt, in all its varied historical manifestations. And she brings expert knowledge to explaining how it was done. She can, for example, tell her readers about the materials and methods used to create the celebrated so-called Fayûm portraits – the arresting Greco-Roman images that were found at the Fayûm site, painted on mummy cases of the period. Powdered colours, mixed with soft wax, she explains, were 'laid on with a stiff reed-brush fuzzed out at the end, such as had been used by the old Egyptian painters from time immemorial'. After laying on a coat of distemper, the artist painted on the ground colour for the portrait – generally 'of a leaden tint for the background, and of a flesh tint for the face and neck'. Then the painter would trace out the outline of the features, using the brush – 'this being generally done in a purple hue'. Finally, the artist was ready to work in the surface colour, or 'painting proper', the hot sun of Egypt 'sufficing to keep the wax in a creamy and manageable condition ... No artificial heat was needed ... and the colours were undoubtedly applied with the reed-brush, the fibres of which are clearly traceable in these Fayûm portraits'.[29]

As for the subjects of the Fayûm portraits, they become another means of bringing us – quite literally – face to face with the common humanity we share with these long-dead Egyptians: 'There is not a face in the whole series which we might not meet any day in the streets of London or New York.' While we should not be surprised at this fact, Edwards points out, we are so used to thinking of 'men and women of the far past' as the 'dramatis personae of ancient history, and as belonging to another age', that it is 'with a shock of something like incredulous astonishment that we find them so precisely like ourselves':

The truth probably is that as regards features, stature, and complexion, the ancient Egyptians differed very little, if at all, from the Copts of the present day ... Past or present, we are in truth but members of one great family ... and as we look through this ancient and interesting portrait-gallery, we cannot but recognize our kinship with these men and women, these youths and maidens, who lived and loved and died nearly two thousand years ago. Yet even these are but things of yesterday compared with the Ethiopian subjects in the tomb of Hui at El Kab, or with the paintings of the four races of men in the tombs of the kings at Thebes. And in these we see depicted racial types which survive unchanged to the present day in Nubia and Palestine.[30]

She writes learnedly of the successive styles of Egyptian art down the centuries: 'the Memphite school, which was the earliest; the Twelfth Dynasty school, the Theban, the Saïte'. The changing styles 'mark a succession of decadences and renaissances of art, each renaissance being distinguished by its own special characteristics'.[31] Probably of greater interest to the general reader, however, is what Edwards has to say about the art's purpose and function in its relationship to Egyptian religious beliefs:

All these schools, all these renaissances, had . . . one essential principle in common: they were primarily exponents of the religious idea. In the hands of the sculptor and the painter, the gods were made manifest to the eyes of their worshippers; the terrors of Hades and the delights of Elysium were depicted with curious minuteness of detail; and the art of portraiture continued to be, from first to last, the concrete expression of one of the most singular, obscure, and fantastic religious beliefs which was ever inculcated by a priesthood, or by which the mind of a people was influenced.

How, she invites us to wonder, did the Egyptian artist arrive at such a level of skill in the art of portraiture? The explanation lies, according to *Pharaohs, Fellahs and Explorers*, in the religious imperative that drove those who carved the statues and painted the mummy cases, to offer the most faithfully lifelike image of the deceased of which they were capable. The statue or the portrait provided a physical home for the life, the Ka, of the deceased to inhabit after death: 'The life needed a body in which to abide, just as it needed bread, meats, fruit, wine, and milk for its sustenance. The Ka informed the statue, dwelt within it, felt through it, just as the life informs, dwells in, and feels through the living body':

When we speak of an Egyptian statue of the time of the Ancient Empire – that is to say, of the most archaic period known – we refer to a figure modelled direct from the life, and treated on ultranaturalistic lines. We now know why the art of the Memphite school was so essentially realistic. We now know that these statues are, one and all, Ka-statues, and that the sculptors who produced them were governed by the necessity of providing a faithful likeness for the benefit of the Ka. But the marvel of their execution remains the same.[32]

In her discussion of ancient Egyptian art, as in other areas of her work, Edwards is, unfortunately, captured by mistaken nineteenth-century conceptions about the 'evolution' of the human race, from a state of inferiority, ignorance and savagery, to a more civilized level. Accomplishment in art was said to be no exception to the alleged evolutionary rule. 'It is impossible', she writes:

> even to conjecture the length of time during which the Egyptians must have been gradually working their way upward through higher and higher levels of civilization, in order to arrive at these results. When we first become acquainted with them as sculptors and builders, they are already adults; and as yet we have found no relics of their infancy.[33]

(Before we judge Edwards too hastily for her views on the evolutionary model of the development of art, it is worth bearing in mind that the marvellous cave paintings of Altamira in Spain had been discovered only thirteen years before the publication of *Pharaohs, Fellahs and Explorers*; and that their 36,000 years of existence remained a matter of fierce controversy, until early in the twentieth century.)[34] Moreover, she is quick to recognize how mistaken is the public image of pharaonic art as uniformly stiff and un-lifelike.[35]

In her writing, as in her public talks – using 'magic lantern' slides to illustrate the latter – she sets out to persuade her audiences to look at ancient Egyptian art with new eyes. With a view to convincing us, in *Pharaohs, Fellahs* she 'reads' a series of portrait images, suggesting how the personality of the subject might be perceived and understood, even thousands of years after the portrait was completed, helping out her verbal interpretations with accompanying pen-and-ink sketches. We are introduced to Ra-em-Ka, the 'Wooden Man of Bulaq', 'a stout, commonplace, elderly Egyptian . . . who was an overseer of public works in the time of the Fourth Dynasty'. She notes the 'good-natured, contented face' of the carved wooden figure, which is most probably 'carefully studied from the life'.[36] She invents a hypothetical biography for a statue of a kneeling scribe, found in the tomb of a prosperous man of the fifth century, presumably the scribe's employer:

> This humble dependent kneels with crossed hands, as though awaiting his lord's instructions. His vacant and deprecating smile expresses the patient resignation of a life of servitude. He has no will, and no opinions of his own. His back is well acquainted with the time-honoured 'stick', and he is so well trained in the virtues of obedience and submission that he not only takes his punishment without a murmur, but is ready to kiss the hand by which it is administered.[37]

(Was Edwards thinking here of the incidents she had witnessed in modern Egypt, during her travels on the Nile? In particular, perhaps, of the man who shouted 'God save the governor' after taking a flogging on the soles of his feet?)

Pharaohs, Fellahs, Explorers must be among the first popular texts to draw readers' attention to pharaonic influences upon the art of Greece. From finds at the Greek settlement of Naukratis in the Egyptian Delta, 45 miles to the southeast of Alexandria – a site where Edwards directly helped to sponsor excavations by Flinders Petrie – it became clear how much early Greek sculpture and decoration owed to ancient Egypt. From the images of the lotus and the Sphinx (originally an avatar of the Egyptian god Horus), to some of the first Greek statuary, to an image of a dancing girl that, in the sideways positioning of the body and the angular thrust of the arms, could almost have come from a decorative painting in an Egyptian tomb, Naukratis and other Greek settlements in Egypt gave the key to artistic influences on the cultural world of mainland Greece. (By the way, Edwards did not necessarily find much merit in some of these. The dancing girl painting, in particular, she found grotesque. Her artistic ideals were firmly rooted, for better or worse, in photographic realism; she tended to reject anything stylized. While she described the face as quite 'naturally' drawn, the body, she said, had 'all the Egyptian conventionalities grossly exaggerated ... being shown frontwise to the waist, while the legs and feet are placed sidewise, the breadth of the shoulders and the length of the arms being ludicrously out of proportion'.)[38]

Over time, the cultural debts between Greece and Egypt were paid in both directions; with Egyptians of the second century AD painting realistic portraits on a flat panel in the Greek manner, 'the semblance of relief being given by light, shadow, and foreshortening'. This 'bold, last step', Edwards considers, was truly liberating for Egyptian art: 'Fettered as the Egyptians had been by the traditions of their schools, they would scarcely have recognized the properties of light and shadow, or the value of colour in transition, unless their eyes had been opened by teachers from without.' The Greek influence, however, was only the payment of 'one instalment' of the 'enormous debt' of Greece to Egypt.[39]

Though Edwards shared the mistaken belief of her contemporaries in the 'primitive' nature of black Africans, her love of portraiture – her studies and sketches of the faces in tomb sculptures, on mummy cases, or depicted on temple walls – inevitably made her conscious of the diversity of ethnic groups in ancient Egypt, in some ways more akin to the thinking of the early twenty-first century, than to that of the nineteenth. She would never make the error of regarding 'pharaonic' peoples as a single homogeneous whole. There were, she knew – from having carefully studied their portraits – Canaanites, Libyans, Black African Nubians, at different times within the borders of Egypt – the last-mentioned having been for a period, rulers of a kingdom. The Hyksos people, too – 'a race of hard-featured warriors, with wide and high cheek-bones, open nostrils, and mouths curved sternly downward at the corners' – had also once ruled in Egypt.[40] Hebrews had been settled within Egypt's borders for centuries before their enslavement and the ensuing Exodus, and risen to power and prosperity there. There had been colonies of Greek traders. The Greek settlement of Daphnae (Tahpanhes), had given shelter to the daughters of King Zedekiah and their followers, who fled into Egypt, after Nebuchadnezzar attacked Jerusalem: 'we read of it in the forty-third chapter of the Book of the Prophet Jeremiah as "Pharaoh's house at Tahpanhes".'[41]

In the time of Rameses II, a contingent of Sardinians served in the Pharaoh's army, and they too found artists to document their presence:

> In the heads of the Sardinian body-guard . . . as we see them depicted in the famous battle-subject on the north wall of the Great Temple of Abû-Simbel, we find these fair-skinned, blue-eyed, and small-featured islanders represented with a freshness and vivacity which seem to point to the delight of the draughtsman in a new subject.

Syrians and other 'Asiatics' captured in war were brought into the country as slaves. Each of these ethnic groups is recognizable from the stereotypical manner in which the artists depicted them. Libyans, for example, conventionally 'allowed their hair to grow in a long lock on the right side of the head, but shaved it on the left'.[42]

In her writings on Egyptian 'literature' (in the broadest sense of the word), and the talks on which she based them, Edwards aimed at raising awareness of the sheer abundance and diversity of written texts, that circulated in Egypt over millennia. For ancient Egyptian literary culture, she makes large claims. In the sense that they had libraries and privately owned collections of papyruses, the Egyptians, she says, are 'the first people of the ancient world who had a literature of this kind: who wrote books, and read books; who possessed books, and loved them'.

She indicates the sheer variety of fields in which ancient Egyptian writings exist: not only 'moral and educational treatises; state-papers; works on geometry, medicine, astronomy, and magic'; but 'travels, tales, fables, heroic poems, love-songs, and essays in the form of letters'. There are religious and magical texts: 'hymns, dirges, rituals'; and 'last, not least, that extraordinary collection of prayers, invocations, and religious formulae known as The Book of the Dead'.[43]

We learn of an 'Egyptian *Iliad*', 'full of incident and dialogue', that relates in detail the bitter, but ultimately victorious, campaign of Rameses II against the armies of Syria and Asia Minor. And of a collection of maxims, supposedly delivered by the sage Ptah-hotep, and written down almost four thousand years before Edwards' time. 'Be not proud because of thy learning. Converse with the ignorant as freely as with the scholar, for the gates of knowledge should never be closed', is a saying that no doubt appealed to Edwards herself, who loved to share what she knew with a broad public. Another saying would have had, for Bible-reading Victorians, a strong religious resonance: 'If thou art exalted after having been low, if thou art rich after having been needy, harden not thy heart because of thy elevation. Thou hast but become a steward of the good things belonging to the gods.' A later collection, attributed to 'the Scribe Ani', focuses on relations with others: 'Beware of giving pain by the words of thy mouth, and make not thyself to be feared'; 'He who speaks evil, reaps evil'; 'Do not eat bread in the presence of one who stands and waits, without putting forth thine hand towards the loaf for him'.[44]

Edwards calls the ancient Egyptians – 'at their best', as she says – 'a gentle, kindly, law-abiding race, anxious to cultivate peace and goodwill, and to inculcate those rules of good conduct whereby their own lives had been guided'. Her idealized Egyptians are not given to abstruse intellectual speculation or profound metaphysics: 'To live happily, to live long, to deserve the favour of their superiors, to train their children in sane thinking and right-doing, to be respected in life and honourably remembered by posterity, represented the sum of their desires.' Theirs was a simple philosophy 'of utility and good-will, in which the ideal has no part'.[45] This view seems inconsistent with what is known of the elaborate Egyptian cosmology, in which sophisticated mathematical calculations and astronomical knowledge were employed in the service of powerfully poetic religious ideas. No doubt, as in many other cultures, the beliefs and values of the farmer in a village differed from those of, say, the pharaonic priesthood. All the same, it has to be admitted that Edwards simplifies the Egyptians here, and possibly sentimentalizes them too.

She is back on stronger ground, as she once again wittily dismisses the notion that the ancient Egyptians must have been, like their mummies, dry, shrivelled and generally unappealing – 'a people who were destined to be spiced, bandaged, and ultimately consigned to glass-cases in modern museums'. We might be surprised to learn that they told fantastical stories of magical adventures and wrote love songs. Edwards goes on to tell of striking parallels between stories from Pharaonic Egypt, and tales and fables found in Aesop, and the Arabian nights. The well-known fable of 'The Lion and the Mouse', for instance, 'was discovered by Dr. Brugsch in an Egyptian papyrus a few years ago'. There are romantic stories – of a Pharaoh who finds a beautiful young woman's lost sandal, or a lock of her hair, and orders a search for her, that ends in marriage – themes that find later echoes in the story of Cinderella. A besieging general takes a city by hiding five hundred soldiers in huge jars, that are carried inside the city gates – a story that Edwards suggests as an early forerunner of 'Ali Baba and the Forty Thieves'. (Possibly, one might add, of the tale of the Trojan Horse?) A story called 'The Shipwrecked Mariner' contains elements that turn up again in 'Sindbad the Sailor'.[46]

Versions of the work songs of ancient Egypt could still be heard in the fields by the Nile, when Edwards travelled there in the nineteenth century. She cites one example – the threshing song the driver chants to his oxen, as they tread the corn with their hooves. The chant, dating from around 1650 BC, was found on the walls of a tomb in Upper Egypt. Although the tune that went with it is lost, 'no one who has listened to the monotonous songs of the Egyptian labourers as they ply the shadûf or the waterwheel, can fail to be struck by their evident antiquity'. It seems probable the same chant somewhere still survives 'among those so often heard by the modern traveller, as his boat glides along the broad waters of the sacred river':

> Thresh the corn, oh ye oxen!
> Thresh for yourselves, oh oxen!
> The fodder for eating,
> The grain for your master!

In the wall-painting illustrating these words, 'we see the oxen at work, just as in the Egypt of today, treading in a measured circle, with the driver seated on his revolving stool in the middle'.[47]

Pharaohs, Fellahs and Explorers cites one example of a love-poem, one sung by a young woman to her lover:

> Oh, flower of henna! My heart stands still in thy presence. I have made mine eyes brilliant for thee with kohl. When I behold thee, I fly to thee, oh my Beloved! Oh, Lord of my heart, sweet is this hour. An hour passed with thee is worth an hour of eternity! Oh, flower of marjoram! Fain would I be to thee as the garden in which I have planted flowers and sweet-smelling shrubs! the garden watered by pleasant runlets, and refreshed by the north breeze! Here let us walk, oh my Beloved, hand in hand, our hearts filled with joy!

Each verse compares the lover to a different flower, a poetic structure in which Edwards sees a similarity to Tuscan folk songs. As for the subject matter, it is, as she remarks, 'the old, old story'; and the story itself is 'yet older than the song'.[48]

Other surviving examples of Egyptian poetry are powerfully erotic. In one, 'When we kiss, and her warm lips half open, / I fly cloud-high without beer!' In another, a woman tells her lover boldly, 'Would you leave because you want something to drink? / Here, take my breasts! They are full to overflowing, and all for you!'[49]

Edwards was certainly no prude and surely must have enjoyed such poems. But she also knew her middle- and upper-class Victorian audiences and would have been careful to refrain from citing anything that might disturb or shock them.

She did give talks with distinctly feminist undertones – a lecture on 'Queen Hatasu and the Women of Egypt', for instance, reproduced in *Pharaohs, Fellahs and Explorers*, that she delivered in both America and England.[50] As a fervent supporter of the right of women to participate in political life, she could hardly fail to be interested in the history of Queen Hatasu, or Hatshepsut, 'one of the most magnificent builder-sovereigns of Egypt'. Hatshepsut ordered hundreds of construction projects in her lifetime; among them, her magnificent mortuary temple at Deir el-Bahari. Her reign, according to Edwards, unlike those of other, more warlike, male pharaohs, was marked by 'profound peace'.[51] The Queen sent a trading expedition to Punt, on the eastern coast of Africa, to bring back exotic animals, trees and plants, ivory, gold, and the costly spices used in temple ceremonies. Edwards believed that Hatshepsut also ordered the digging of a canal linking the Red Sea to the Nile. (It was known that such a canal had once existed, but there was controversy as to the identity of the ruler who had commissioned it.) 'It would seem, indeed', Edwards asserted boldly, 'as if the great woman-Pharaoh who first conceived the daring project of launching her ships upon an unknown sea, was by far the most likely person to canalize that channel by which alone, so far as we can see, it would have been possible for them to go forth.' Hatshepsut was, in fact, 'the scientific ancestress' of De Lesseps, the architect of the modern Suez Canal.[52]

That Edwards calls Hatshepsut 'the Queen Elizabeth of Egyptian history', can hardly be accidental. By implication – in a hint that her audiences could not fail to take note of – England too had known a powerful woman, who played a leading role in the political life of her country – and a woman might do so again.[53]

In her public talks in the 1880s, Edwards returned often to feminist themes. One of her lectures was titled, 'The Social and Political Position of Women in Ancient Egypt'. In the 1880s and 90s, access of women to political and economic life, and their status within marriage, were still highly contentious topics on both sides of the Atlantic. By the late 1880s, the public was growing ever more involved in debates about voting rights for women – and not all were in favour. Edwards, herself a vocal supporter of legal reforms, knew the need for sensitivity in discussing even so arcane a topic, as women's status in ancient Egypt. But in everything she said publicly on the subject, there lurked a quietly stated feminist sub-text.[54]

In pharaonic Egypt, she told her audience, royal descent was, for centuries, inherited through the maternal line. This was certainly true of Rameses the Great, 'and all the mighty Pharaohs of the Theban dynasties'.[55] Children were known by their mother's name – as, for instance, 'Horus, whose mother is Senerius'.[56] A husband took the name of his wife. A woman, moreover, could be highly respected for her learning – like the lady Tanii who was, her funerary inscription tells, 'a marvel among those gifted with knowledge – a woman blest by the praises which issued from the august mouth of her sovereign'. At her death, it was said, 'many were the proofs of regard' for her wisdom.[57]

Women in ancient Egypt commonly engaged in trade, bought and sold real estate, lent money at interest, took out loans or imposed conditions on their debtors, 'without the smallest reference to their husbands'.[58] In marriage, a woman became the controller of her husband's property and of the family budget; undertaking in return to feed and clothe him, and to provide for his funeral. Marriage, Edwards pointed out, was – unlike the traditional institution in Victorian England – purely a secular contract, a business arrangement, without religious implications. Couples were free to divorce – something far from easy to do in Victorian England – and a woman could remarry afterwards.

In case all this startling information might be found unsettling for her hearers and readers, Edwards is careful to distance herself from its most radical implications. In case her audience might think she, herself, endorses ancient Egyptian customs, she is careful to say that women's rights in ancient Egypt were curtailed under the rule of the Hellenic Ptolemies, as if to correct the excesses of matriarchal power. With tongue firmly in cheek, she then apologizes for speaking at length on what she calls, 'a very dry subject'. To claim that the topic is boring, is to disclaim any strong personal interest in it – to say, in effect, 'We / I don't really care about all that tedious social history, that does not concern us today'.

She ends with another ironic distancing gesture: 'I only hope that the picture I have drawn of the Social and Political Position of Women in ancient Egypt may not have excited a sentiment of retrospective envy in the hearts of the ladies here present.' That was then, this is now, she implies. She concludes with an awkward joke: 'I should indeed be grieved if they went home lamenting that they had not lived in the days of the Pharaohs, and that they are not at this moment occupying the proud position of mummies in the British Museum.'[59] As if to say – again with irony – 'those legal and economic rights of women belong to those who are dead and gone. I hope you don't imagine I could be advocating anything like that for women nowadays'.

To her evocations of ancient Egypt, Edwards brought her talents and experience as novelist, artist, traveller and self-trained Egyptologist, with the wit, poise and charm that made her a compelling public speaker. All of this uniquely equipped her to awaken the interest and inspire the curiosity of the public. Above all, she was able to communicate her own infectious enthusiasm for a subject that, in other hands, could have remained abstract and remote:

> I have sometimes been asked, for instance, how it happens that I – erewhile a novelist, and therefore a professed student of men and manners as they are – can take so lively an interest in the men and manners of five or six thousand years ago. But it is precisely because these men of five or six thousand years ago had manners, a written language, a literature, a school of art, and a settled government that we find them so interesting. Ourselves the creatures of a day, we delight in studies which help us to realize that we stand between the eternity of the past and the eternity of the future. Hence the charm of those sciences which unfold to us, page by page, the unwritten records of the world we live in.[60]

Egyptology was, in fact, a source of fascination to Edwards' contemporaries – perhaps more than she herself realized. The ongoing excitement of ever-new finds under the sands of the Delta and in Upper Egypt, generated a public interest that can only be likened to that with which twenty-first century people follow discoveries about the world of outer space. In both cases, the lure of the unknown is what compels, and the quest for fresh understanding.

Edwards had, as she quickly discovered, a coveted gift to share.

6

Founding the Fund

While Amelia Edwards had come to love the study of ancient Egypt with passion, and for its own sake, she wanted not only to share that passion, to inform and entertain, but also to raise awareness that Egypt's antiquities were both precious and vulnerable. She wanted people to know about the deplorable state of the temples of Upper Egypt, their columns broken, their courtyards choked with rubble; about the fallen statues, like the fallen Colossus of Rameses, that no one seemed to have the money, or the will, to raise and restore;[1] about the giant mounds of debris all across the Delta, their treasures buried deep under the rubbish of centuries, only waiting for the archaeologist who would come to reveal them, as the last resting-places of once-thriving ancient cities.

It was with the rescue of Egypt's neglected antiquities in mind, that she formed the idea of the Egypt Exploration Fund. The money raised by such a fund could be used to restore and house precious antiquities, whether in the Egyptian Museum even then being organized in Cairo under the direction of Auguste Mariette (and then of Gaston Maspero, after 1881), or in collections in Britain. It could pay for the work of archaeologists – for travel money, accommodation, provisions, tools, and the hire of workmen to use them – to enable new discoveries that might throw further revealing light upon the ancient past.

She began by sounding out distinguished Egyptologist at the British Museum, starting with Dr Samuel Birch. Birch was dismissive – 'sentimental', he called the Exploration Fund idea (a conveniently stereotypical epithet, one might think, when the proposal came from a woman). More to the point than the alleged sentimentality, was his concern that any objects found during excavations in Egypt should be given to the British Museum, not to the embryonic Egyptian museum at Boulaq, or to the Louvre.[2] Edwards herself expressed a more generous attitude. 'I should like to see an international scheme free of all jealousies', she told Poole in a letter of September that year.[3]

Early in 1880, she wrote to a number of well-known figures in Britain, either soliciting funds, or asking them to write articles in the *Morning Post*, which had recently opened its pages to pieces on the subject of ancient Egypt, and inviting all of them to support her project for an Exploration Fund.

The first responses were not encouraging. She tried Henry Villiers Stuart, the MP for Waterford, who told her flatly that, 'at present Rich Landlords have very little leisure for literary pursuits'.[4] The Assyriologist Ernest Wallis Budge told Edwards he would gladly support anything to do with Assyrians, but that he had little expertise – or, it would seem, much interest, where ancient Egypt was concerned.[5] She tried the speculative religious thinker Ernst de Bunsen. He told Edwards that matters of 'chronology' and ethnic origins had to be better understood before excavations could proceed – an egregious example, one would have thought, of putting the cart before the horse.[6]

Anyone less determined than Edwards might have given up.

At last, she found an ally in Stuart Poole, the British Museum's Keeper of Coins and Medals, and an enthusiast student of Egyptology. He encouraged her to select articles to stimulate greater interest in Egyptology, for the *Morning Post*. They should, Poole wrote, be chosen by 'someone who is at once acquainted with the scientific literature of the subject and knows at the same time how much the public can understand'. He could think of no one 'so well qualified as you are'.[7] Poole would become Edwards' chief supporter in launching and promoting the Egyptian Exploration Fund.

Support for Edwards' project now began to trickle in. Learning that the *Morning Post* was publishing articles on Egyptology for a general readership, the German scholar, Heinrich Brugsch, agreed to contribute an article weekly. Encouraged by the growing interest, Edwards and her allies felt confident enough to start making the Fund a reality. On June 11, 1880, a small group of scholars and archaeologists met to discuss the proposal. Stuart Poole, of the British Museum, was there, and Ernst de Bunsen – both of whom acknowledged Edwards as founder of the infant Fund; also the Swiss Egyptologist Henri Edouard Naville, an expert on hieroglyphic inscriptions, who would be asked to undertake the Fund's first archaeological dig.[8] A report of the meeting appeared in *The Academy*: 'Last Wednesday several ladies and gentlemen interested in Egyptology held a private meeting in the Council Room of University College London, to consider the desirability of promoting research in Egyptology.'[9]

In August that year, Edwards had a letter from Henry Howarth MP. 'Although I am a member of the House of Commons', Howarth wrote, 'my heart is not there but in archaeology . . . how very much you have taught me and how great a delight it is to me at all times to read what you write'. If he could be of service 'to the cause of Egyptian exploration', Howarth continued, 'or to the preservation of Egyptian monuments in any way I shall be very pleased to be so'. The British government, he thought, should pay for the importation of Egyptian antiquities, like the Rameses statue, that it had received as gifts from the Egyptians. Could Miss Edwards perhaps write a letter to *The Times* about it?[10]

It was another small, hopeful, sign that new support would be forthcoming. Two more years would go by, before Edwards' dream at last became reality; but the first steps had been taken.

On March 27, 1882, the Egypt Exploration Fund met to convene its first committee meeting; and the new organization formally came into existence. Amelia Edwards was appointed joint Honorary Secretary, with Stuart Poole. Sir Erasmus Wilson, a wealthy surgeon and amateur Egyptologist (who in 1877 would sponsor and help fund the transportation of the obelisk known as 'Cleopatra's Needle', from Alexandria to the Embankment in London), was later appointed President.[11] Poole's assistant Barclay Head, and Charles Newton, Head of the Department of Greek and Roman Antiquities, would play an informal, but influential role in decisions of the Fund – as will shortly be seen, not always with Edwards' consent or approval.

One important fact, Edwards wrote, 'must never be overlooked', when discussing the ancient Egyptians and their beliefs: 'They were the first in the history of the world who recognized, and held fast by, the doctrine of the immortality of the soul.' They lived their lives 'looking forward to an eternal future'. She believed that much of the exotic iconography of ancient Egyptian religion had, in its early years, contained symbolic meanings that were forgotten over the centuries, until the religion became ever more literal in its interpretations, and the symbolic significance was forgotten.[12]

To Victorians, this belief of the Egyptians in immortality mattered greatly and in some surprising ways. For instance, in the *Preston Herald* for December 13, 1890, we find an anonymous feature writer regarding the god Osiris as a type and forerunner of Christ. Like Christ, the Egyptian god receives and blesses the souls of the sanctified dead. We have this insight, the author comments, thanks to the 'glorious lustre, archaeological and otherwise', that scholarly investigations in Egypt have 'shed on the fuller story of the Cross'. Amelia Edwards, the writer thought, seemed to know more about these matters. She ought to be invited to give a lecture in Preston.[13]

People in the nineteenth century therefore had particular, pressing, reasons for wanting to investigate and explore the ancient past of the Near East – of Syria, Palestine, Mesopotamia and Egypt. These were the 'Bible lands' where events believed to be central to orthodox Christian faith were said to have unfolded. The ideas of Darwin, and contemporary findings in geology that indicated the immense age of the earth, well beyond the simple imaginings of the faithful, had induced a profound crisis of religious doubt. The quest for the real existence of biblical figures like Joseph and Moses; for the route taken by the Hebrews in their Exodus from Egypt; or for tangible evidence of the structures the Hebrews had built during their enslavement in Egypt, seemed to offer touchstones for faith to hold onto, amid the swirling currents of scepticism. As historian David Gange has observed, for many Victorians the quest for evidence to bolster faltering religious faith, was a far more important motive for promoting Egyptology, than any interest in boosting national pride.[14]

Egypt is mentioned over six hundred times in the Hebrew Bible. Whether or not religious seekers had done the arithmetic, they certainly were aware of the importance of the land of the Pharaohs in the Old Testament story. They hoped the ancient land might hold clues to validate Bible stories and Bible teachings. They sought, for instance (as did Amelia Edwards), to identify particular pharaonic rulers referred to in the Bible. Thus, Rameses II was claimed as the cruel pharaoh of the Hebrews' Egyptian captivity. The Pharaoh Apepi, who reigned at Tanis in the sixteenth century BC, would come to be identified by early Christian writers as the ruler in the story of Joseph, who stored up grain in time of famine.[15]

Given such enthusiasm for tracing Biblical roots, it is hardly surprising that among the first supporters of Edwards' new Fund were, as Edwards stated, in a notice she placed in *The Times* of March 1882, 'the Archbishop of Canterbury, the Bishops of Bath and Wells, Durham and Lincoln, the chief Rabbi, Archdeacon Arason ... Canon Cook ... the Dean of Manchester'.[16] (Robert Browning and the Earl of Caervarvon are also named; but religious figures predominate.)

In an article in *The Academy*, Edwards sought to convince the wider public that Egyptology was 'a cause of such supreme interest, biblically, historically, archaeologically, that one marvels how it should need advocating at all' – one that promised to reward the seeker with 'momentous discoveries'. There was a need to awaken the 'Bible-loving', church-going English people 'from their long sloth', and 'to make them see that now, if ever', it was 'a serious duty, and not a mere archaeological pastime', to contribute money for excavations in Egypt.[17]

Edwards was herself an early member of the Society of Biblical Archaeology, and one of its first female members. She wrote a series of articles for a popular magazine, with the challenging title, 'Was Rameses II the pharaoh of the Exodus?'[18] She, too, was keenly interested in the issue of whatever biblical traces might be found in ancient Egypt. Stuart Poole shared her interest. In a scholarly article for *The Academy*, he confidently omitted the question mark, asserting categorically that excavations had turned up 'final proof' that Rameses II was indeed the pharaoh of the Captivity, and that Tel-el-Maskhuta, in the north-east of Egypt, was the place from which the Exodus had begun.[19]

Although the question of biblical connections with Egypt fascinated Edwards, it seems to have been for her more a matter of academic interest, than of passionate religious devotion. Which is not to call her a hypocrite. Like most of her Victorian contemporaries, she was a member of the Church of England, if hardly a very zealous one. But enlisting the backing of prominent religious figures was for her as much about building support and credibility for her new Fund, as any personal religious enthusiasm. She would also reach out to the artistic community, to art historians and scholarly experts on ancient Greece, seeking financial support from them on the grounds of interest in the influence of ancient Egypt on Greek culture.[20] (In the late nineteenth century, that influence, today taken as proven, was far from accepted as a given.)

The new organization promised to combine public education with protection of existing Egyptian antiquities; and most importantly, to fund archaeological missions in quest of new discoveries. These goals were mutually supportive: the more the public knew and understood about Egyptology, the more they would take an interest in the preservation of Egypt's treasures; and the keener they would be to pay for new excavations.

Edwards took on the work of recruiting new members to the Fund, and collecting their subscriptions, which were set at the attractively low rate of one guinea. The new organization quickly attracted hundreds of members, 150 of whom Edwards recruited herself.[21] In a letter to the young scholar Flinders Petrie, (who would become a leading figure in archaeology, largely thanks to Edwards), she explained her strategy for enlisting support:

> I first of all select a *likely* person . . . then I write him a beautiful letter, pointing out to him how the aims of our society are precisely *his* aims; and how valuable our publications will be to him; and how, being who and what he is – his name and support will be peculiarly precious to us.

To Lord Shaftesbury, she wrote about the ancient city of Pithom, and its possible connection to the story of the Exodus. To the Bishop of Durham, she mentioned discoveries of Greek papyruses (which, she said, induced him to increase and make permanent the subscription he had been thinking of cancelling). Jewish people did not care to hear too much about the Captivity in Egypt, or the Exodus, but were interested in the story of Joseph in Egypt, and the centuries of Hebrew power and prosperity. Aesthetes liked to be wooed with the hope of discovering more Greek art in Egypt; clergymen, 'with the chances of a 1st or 2nd century New Testament'. Quakers, apparently, preferred to hear about findings related to the Old Testament. 'These special letters rarely fail', Edwards wrote, 'and I have got most of my good subscribers that way. 'But', she added, 'it takes a terrible amount of valuable time.'[22]

Fundraising was one thing – sponsoring excavations in Egypt, quite another matter. Local politics, to begin with, had to be taken into account. Who ruled Egypt at a given time, could have drastic implications for Egyptology.

By the 1880s, thanks to new legislation by the Egyptian government, and the careful conservation work of the Director of Antiquities, Auguste Mariette, wholesale freelance plundering and sale of antiquities had been to some extent brought under control. Newly discovered artefacts were sent, either to the new museum at Boulaq or, under government licence, to museums abroad. In 1882, however, British and French forces invaded Egypt to support their client, the Khedive Tewfik, against the challenge to his power from a popular army officer, Ahmad Orabi. Fighting broke out across the Delta, as Egyptian forces, led by Orabi, battled unsuccessfully to repel 40,000 British troops.

The chaos thus unleashed meant a crisis for Egyptian archaeology, and for the French citizens then in charge of it. Gaston Maspero had succeeded his compatriot Auguste Mariette, as Director General of Excavations and Antiquities, only a year before the British invasion. He had gone to Egypt in 1880, as head of the archaeological project that would become the French Institute of Archaeology. He succeeded Mariette as Director General of Excavations, the following year. (It was Maspero who that year dispatched a team to Deir el-Bahari, where the forty royal mummies were found.) [23]

That Maspero was not in the least interested in politics, only in Egyptology, did not save him, or his projects, from being overtaken by the revolution. Excavations ground to a halt, as workmen were conscripted to fight the British invaders. Food and other provisions ran out. Maspero had to close the school of archaeology he had recently founded. When his wife fell ill, the couple left together for Paris.

Although it was hardly the most propitious time to start a new project for Egyptian Exploration, Edwards bided her time. She wrote round privately, for donations to help Maspero in his troubles. And, being Amelia Edwards, she could not resist a letter to the press, on the dramatic events in Egypt. No doubt partly – but not entirely – with an eye to attracting more support to the Egypt Exploration Fund, she offered a historical and biblical 'take' – on the invasion. The British forces fighting their way from Ismailia to Zagazig, she pointed out, were following the course of a valley that 'anciently formed part of the Land of Goshen'.[24]

By late November of 1882, Maspero felt able to return to Egypt, and was re-established at Boulaq, where he took on the duties of chief curator of the expanding Boulaq museum. (Apart from a three years' absence, from 1886 to 1889, he stayed in post as Egypt's Director of Antiquities, until his retirement in 1914.)

Edwards had been friendly with Auguste Mariette, Maspero's predecessor. Eight months before Mariette's death in 1881, she wrote a letter paying tribute to him, to the *Morning Post*. Thanks to Mariette's work, a museum 'that had no existence twenty years ago', she wrote, had built a collection, 'one of the richest in the world'. With her letter she attached a translation of his final report on the rebuilding of the museum to protect its treasures from the Nile floods.[25] She had been keen to involve Mariette with plans for the Fund's work in Egypt; but Poole had been reluctant, perhaps fearing loss of control to the French.[26] However, she soon established friendly relations with Mariette's successor, with whom she corresponded regularly throughout the first half of the 1880s. Like Maspero himself, Amelia had little interest in national glory; she merely wanted to see the treasures of Egypt preserved and protected. She wrote to Samuel Birch at the British Museum, expressing the hope that 'something may at last be done in the way of co-operation with the French on Egyptian soil'. 'If we do not cooperate', she added, understanding how to touch Birch on a sensitive point, 'there will be a German invasion of the Delta, and English scholars and lovers of Egyptology will be nowhere'. French and British archaeologists and Egyptologists needed to work together, 'in the interests of science'.[27]

In a letter to Poole of November 15, 1882, Maspero came to an agreement with the Exploration Fund, in which he laid down rules for the EEF's activities. All objects found in excavations were by law the property of the Egyptian government. Oversight of excavations was, and would remain, under the remit of Egypt's Department of Antiquities. The EEF would meet all the expenses of any excavation, including the wages and other expenses for diggers and overseers. Any dig would be limited to a specific site, and last only for a specific, limited, period of time. Maspero made clear that he would visit from time to time, or send an assistant, to ensure that these conditions were met. In choosing an archaeologist for the work, 'Envoyez-moi un savant' ('Send me a scientist'), he stressed to Poole. He wanted no mercenaries or looters directing archaeological work – only dedicated scholars. In return for meeting these conditions, he would do all in his power to facilitate the work of the EEF, including interceding with the Egyptian government on the Fund's behalf. After the EEF committee agreed to these conditions, Maspero persuaded the Khedive to send Erasmus Wilson two choice pieces of sculpture – a granite falcon and a kneeling human figure, which were deposited in the British Museum.[28]

An amicable arrangement with Maspero and the Egyptian government was worked out, whereby antiquities found would be shared between the Boulaq museum and the Fund, with the Egypt Exploration Fund covering all the costs of excavation. Large objects found would go to Boulaq, unless a 'duplicate' existed; in which case, the Exploration Fund might seek permission to acquire it, paying for the object's transport to Britain. The Fund – and indeed an individual archaeologist – would be permitted to buy half of any smaller finds, after submitting the proposed purchases for Maspero's approval. Work at excavation sites would also be shared, with French archaeologists investigating sites in Upper Egypt, and the British undertaking digs in the Delta.

The French, wrote the Swiss archaeologist Edouard Naville, were happy for the British to excavate in the Delta, provided the work was done in a spirit of genuine scientific inquiry. 'What Maspero does not want', he emphasized, 'is for people to dig with the commercial aim of finding objects and selling them. If at any time he suspects any such motive, he will refuse authorization.'[29] But the system of 'partage' whereby an excavator might buy smaller items found on site, subject to licensing by the Egyptian government, meant that 'the realities of dispersion' did, as one historian observes, mean that the antiquities approved for export 'oscillated' between classification as gifts to foreign institutions, and commodities for sale to individuals.[30] So long as individual excavators were allowed to take a proportion of their finds as personal property, it was inevitable that not everything would end up in a museum collection, whether in Egypt or abroad. Amelia herself acquired a substantial collection of small artefacts, most of which she bought from Flinders Petrie after his work in the Delta.

All the same, Edwards demurred regarding the idea of taking large objects out of Egypt. They belonged to the land, she thought, and ought to stay there. Poole replied that statues and other monuments exposed to the elements, were 'perishing in the damp air' of the Delta – adding that it was 'of utmost consequence that we should obtain some large objects'. Whether or not she was fully convinced by Poole's arguments, Edwards gave in.[31]

There was, whether she acknowledged it or not, a darker side to the work of the EEF. Even though the stated aim of the new organization was conservation of Egypt's endangered treasures – a goal in which Amelia believed wholeheartedly – the outcome of some of the Fund's activities was stripping ancient sites of everything that evoked the ancient past. By 1890, when one traveller reached the site of Bubastis, formerly sacred to the cat goddess Bast, he exclaimed in dismay that there was nothing left to see. Approximately 125 tonnes of material had been lifted from Bubastis, 'around two-thirds of which were shipped abroad by the EEF'. In the space of decades, artefacts from other Egyptian sites found their way to museums in, among other countries, Canada, Switzerland, Australia, Mexico, Japan and the United States. As a twenty-first century museum curator remarks in relation to the despoliation of Bubastis, 'the line between preservation and destruction is a fine one'.[32]

Whatever the EEF did with the monuments, it could not be as bad as the random snatching of Egyptian antiquities that had gone on in the past. In the unscrupulous ransacking of ancient sites, all sense of context and historical significance had been lost, in the race to acquire Egyptian objects as examples of 'art'. Museums in Turin and elsewhere – the British Museum not excepted – acquired such objects piecemeal. Edwards rightly condemned the indiscriminate plunder – if only because of the resulting loss of historical context:

> It never occurred to these so-called 'patrons of the arts' that such monuments are concrete history, and that it is of special importance to identify every object with the place of the discovery. Schools, periods, dynasties, were nothing to [the collectors]. They paid, and asked no questions, and it was in the dealers' interest to keep silence.[33]

Soon, the Fund's committee had raised enough from wealthy benefactors and subscriptions, not only to acquire already found objects, but to consider funding new excavations of their own. Edwards contacted Heinrich Schliemann, who was interested in ancient Egypt as a possible new field for his own archaeological researches. She had been on friendly terms with the famous archaeologist since, on her way back from the Middle East in 1874, she had visited him at his home in Athens. They had discussed his work, and he gave her a portrait of his wife wearing the gold headdress he had unearthed at Troy.[34]

Schliemann, who had signed a statement of support for the new Exploration Fund, now offered to contribute his practical skills, for a dig at Naukratis, on the western side of the Nile Delta, or, alternatively in the area of Tel-el-Maskhuta, and the biblical Land of Goshen. However, his proposals were firmly vetoed by Gaston Maspero. 'M. Schliemann's intervention', Maspero wrote, 'seems to me unfortunate in every respect . . . M. Schliemann does not include discretion among his virtues. He likes a fuss, articles in sensational papers.' Maspero was afraid Schliemann's lack of diplomacy might offend Egypt's ruler, the Khedive Tewfik or other members of the Egyptian government.[35]

In the New Year of 1883, the Fund appointed Edouard Naville, to undertake the first EEF-funded excavation. Well-known all over Europe as a distinguished scholar of ancient Egyptian texts, Naville was friendly with the senior staff of the British Museum. With EEF sponsorship, he spent three months in Egypt, excavating at Tel-el-Maskhuta, once an important town in the Eastern Delta, ten miles to the west of Ismailia. Naville identified the site with the 'store city' of Pithom mentioned in the Book of Exodus. Though this finding was later challenged by twentieth-century scholars, Naville's work at the site was a source of great excitement at the time; and he found imposing temple sculptures, and ceramics from the Hyksos period.

In 1885–6, Naville would work for the EEF again, this time at Wadi Tumilat in 'the land of Goshen' – in the dried-up bed of the ancient canal, that once had linked the Nile with the Red Sea. From Bubastis (Tel Basta), where he worked for three years (with intervening excavation work at Tel-el-Yahudiya in 1887), Naville would bring back the giant sculptured head of Amenemhat III, now in the British Museum. The EEF had truly launched the career of this erstwhile scholar of manuscripts, as a practical archaeologist in the field.

Naville would go on working at sites in Egypt until well into the 1890s – at Herakleiopolis, Mendes and Tel Mukdam, Deir el-Bahari.

In the year Naville began work at Tel-el-Maskhuta, the EEF recruited a new worker in the field – a certain Flinders Petrie. A surveyor by training, Petrie and his work had come to the attention of Fund committee members, through his recent impressively comprehensive survey of the Great Pyramid at Giza, published when he was just thirty. Petrie himself, meanwhile, had written to his friend Archibald Sayce for information about this new organization that was raising money to support archaeologists. When Naville left off excavation work to return to his first interest, the study of ancient Egyptian texts, the Fund committee offered employment to Petrie. Edwards was sceptical at first – she knew little about the newcomer. After reading Petrie's recently published *The Pyramids and Temples of Giza*, however, she was impressed and agreed to the Fund engaging him.[36]

In January 1884, Petrie signed a contract directly with Maspero, acting on behalf of the Egyptian government, allowing him to buy objects directly from workers at the excavation site. He was required to submit these purchases to the authorities for inspection, who would allow him to keep them, or reimburse him for any that would be taken for the museum at Boulaq. After June 1884, he took out of Egypt sixteen crates of pottery and other small artefacts. Naville disapproved, fearing that Petrie's wholesale purchase of such items might 'easily some day wreck the entente cordiale' that had long existed with Maspero and the Boulaq museum.[37] Edwards, however, did not object. (Indeed, she herself bought artefacts Petrie brought back to England from his excavations.)

Sponsored by the EEF, Petrie began to dig at that former important seat of pharaonic royal power, the buried city of Tanis, near the modern town of San al Hagar, and forty miles to the west of the Suez Canal. He stayed on there until well into the summer of 1884, finding pottery, papyri, a splendid gold necklace, and the remains of a colossus of Rameses II. The finds were shared between Boulaq, and museums in Britain, where he exhibited them at the Royal Archaeological Institute.

Petrie would do several more excavations for the Fund – at Tel Nebesheh in the northeast of the Delta (1886–88); at the fortress of Defennah, and at Naukratis, forty-five miles to the south of Alexandria. At the last-mentioned site, he found pottery that showed beyond all doubt that Naukratis had been a Greek settlement and trading town. Even more importantly for the future development of the science of archaeology, he evolved a method of identifying stages of historical development on any given site, by comparing the changes over time in pottery styles, an approach still used by archaeologists today.

At Naukratis, there was division of labour. While Petrie dug, Naville collaborated with him on translation and publication of whatever inscriptions were found.

Edwards liked and greatly respected Petrie. She admired, she wrote in a letter to Anne, Petrie's mother, 'not merely his unselfishness, but his self-denial – his generosity, his largeness of soul'. Indeed, she named him as one of the few people for whom she felt real affection. 'I am fond of Petrie', she once said; adding, however, that for all the affection she got from him in return,[38] 'one might as well be fond of a young obelisk'.[39] More than twenty years her junior, he very much became her protégé; and her choice to occupy the Chair of Egyptology she would fund, at University College, London.

She could hardly have been unaware of his irascible temperament, or of the personal tensions that quickly developed between himself and Stuart Poole; or of Petrie's growing hostility towards Edouard Naville. With Edwards herself, however, there were no such tensions. She and Petrie were, in some respects, alike – both conscientious, dedicated workers, who in their work paid an almost obsessive attention to detail. Edwards liked, too, the frugality – he was careful with money to the point of stinginess – with which he managed the limited financial resources of the EEF while out on field work.

It was Petrie who pioneered the practice of salvaging every small item, however seemingly unimportant, found at an excavation. Formerly, it had been the practice to discard all small finds, retaining only larger items, in a manner that would appal the modern archaeologist. Edwards shared Petrie's understanding that, in some cases, a scrap of pottery or a half-rotted strip of leather, might have greater scientific significance, than a giant monument. With good reason, therefore, she came to trust his work more than that of Naville. Petrie would work over a site more slowly, but with greater thoroughness.

By 1892, Edwards could proudly report that for a decade, 'the Egypt Exploration Fund has sent out explorers every season, having sometimes two, and even three, simultaneously at work in different parts of the Delta'. Every year had been 'fruitful in discoveries':

Ancient geographical boundaries have been traced; the sites of famous cities have been identified; sculptures, inscriptions, arms, papyri, jewellery, painted pottery, beautiful objects in glass, porcelain, bronze, gold, silver, and even textile fabrics, have been found; a flood of unexpected light has been cast upon the Biblical history of the Hebrews; the early stages of the route of the Exodus have been defined; an important chapter in the history of Greek art and Greek epigraphy has been recovered from oblivion; and an archæological survey of the Delta has been made, nearly all the larger mounds having been measured and mapped.[40]

To the armchair Egyptologist, reading these reports back in Britain, it must all have sounded wonderful. In 'The Explorer in Egypt', however, one of the public talks she reproduced in *Pharaohs, Fellahs and Explorers*, Edwards sets out to dispel whatever romantic ideas her audience might entertain about the working life of an archaeologist:

Few . . . of those who 'sit at home at ease' have any clear notion of the qualifications which go to make an explorer of the right sort – still less of the kind of life he is wont to lead when engaged in the work of exploration. They know that he goes to Egypt just as our November fogs are coming on, and that he thereby escapes our miserable English winter. They also know that he lives in a tent, and that he spends his time in 'discovering things'. Now what can be more romantic than life in a tent? And what can possibly be more charming than discovering things'? They may not be very clear as to the nature of the 'things' in question; but they, at all events, conceive of his life as a series of delightful surprises, and of himself as the favorite of fortune, having but to dip his hand into a sort of archæological lottery-box, and take out nothing but prizes.

Most people, Edwards says, have no idea of 'the judgment, the patience, the skill which are needed when choosing a site for excavation', of 'the vigilance which has to be exercised while the excavations are in progress', or of 'the firm but good-humoured authority' required to manage a workforce of diggers – not to mention 'the range of knowledge indispensable for the interpretation and classification of the objects which may be discovered'. Of all this, the general public had no more conception, she said, than Edwards herself had of the skills and experience required to command a battleship. In addition to the above qualities, the archaeologist 'must have a fair knowledge of colloquial Arabic, no small share of diplomatic tact, a strong will, an equable temper, and a good constitution'. He also needs to be well-versed in 'Egyptian, Biblical, Babylonian, Assyrian, Greek, and Roman history'. His working day will be one of 'unrelenting routine toil, beginning at sunrise, when the diggers turn up for work, and he spends an hour and a half allocating tasks to each worker'. After breakfast in his tent, the archaeologist is back on site:

> He now helps, perhaps, to move a huge block or two, stirs up the lazy digger, catches a pilferer in the act and dismisses him, separates gossips, copies inscriptions, or takes photographs, with the sun blazing overhead and the thermometer standing at 99 degrees in the shade.

In the evening, his work begins again: 'He writes reports, journals, and letters; classifies and catalogues the objects discovered during the day; draws plans, makes up his accounts, and so forth.' Even in bed, he gets little rest, as the field mice and rats get active and keep him awake. At the excavation at Tanis, the field mice 'would not walk into traps like civilized mice', so 'the explorer's only resource was to burn a night-light and shoot them'. 'Flies, of course, are legion, and the white ant is a perpetual plague of the first water.'[41]

Even so, in the spring of 1883 Edwards might well have begun to envy the archaeologist, as the enormity of the task she had taken on in launching the EEF became clear to her. Already, after only a year, she had become a victim of her own success. 'It is like the old story of Frankenstein', she wrote. 'I have created a monster and it is hunting me to death.' She scarcely had time to snatch half a solid meal at home; accepting others' invitations to dinner, was out of the question. She was 'driven to the last verge of overwork'.[42] Her labours for the Fund were entirely voluntary: the work that kept her up until two a.m. every night, 'does not bring me a penny'. In fact, it was costing her money, as she was obliged to turn down novel-writing contracts that would have brought in new income. She had made a commitment, however, to develop the Exploration Fund; and she would not shirk her duty.

When not writing fundraising letters, she worked for the EEF on public relations. In August 1886, she struggled to complete media publicity for an exhibition in London, of Petrie's latest finds.[43] Then there were book reviews; arrangements for shipping of antiquities; responses to supporters' queries. She wrote hundreds of letters for the Fund every year – four thousand of them in 1886 alone.[44] With work piling up all around her, in 1887 she seriously considered giving up the position of Honorary Secretary.[45] Still, she struggled on.

Some pressure was taken off her, by the delegation of fundraising and recruiting responsibilities to a growing network of local Honorary Secretaries. It was built up gradually, beginning early in 1887. Like the EEF executive, these dedicated people – one-third of them women – were all volunteers. Their expenses were paid; and they got the glory of receiving donations of artefacts from the Exploration Fund, to be placed in their local museums.

Amelia was always glad to undertake initiatives that empowered women. When a branch of the EEF was started in America, she found plenty of willing female volunteers. 'The majority are, I am happy to say, ladies', she wrote of these American Hon. Secretaries, in her EEF Report of 1887; adding, in a somewhat cynical joke, that when it came to fundraising, women made 'the best beggars', as men found it harder to refuse their appeals.

Joking aside, the system established by Edwards did, as one historian has noted, give a 'key role' to women, in securing Egyptian artefacts for local museums.[46]

Edwards went on writing articles, and letters to the press, to promote the Fund. Between 1877 and 1891, there were seventy-four articles for *The Times*, and over a hundred for *The Academy*, for which Poole gave advice on the scholarly notes. Erasmus Wilson gave moral support, encouraging Amelia to contribute to the popular press as much as possible. 'Academising and journalism are excellent', he advised; 'they give you a status among experts; but you must show yourself as a writer for the Public as well . . . no more ponderous books!'[47] (To Edwards' grief, Wilson died in August 1884, having been the EEF's President for just over eighteen months.)

Clearly, she hardly needed the advice to do more popular work. She wrote not only the pieces on Rameses II for *Knowledge,* previously mentioned; but an entry on 'Mummy', for the Encyclopaedia Britannica; and her name appears as the editor of *Baedeker's Handbook to Egypt* (1878). In July 1886, she produced an article for *The Graphic* on Rameses II as the Pharaoh of the Book of Exodus.[48] In a letter to the *Morning Post* of February 15, 1877, she weighed into the controversy over the biblical story that Mary and Joseph with the baby Jesus fled from Judea into Egypt, to escape the wicked king Herod. Though she stated cautiously that she felt unqualified 'to pass judgment on so difficult a point of Biblical criticism', all the same, she doubted the story of the Holy Family's journey to Bethlehem to be counted in a census; she pointed out that the only known Roman census in Palestine had taken place long after Herod's death.[49]

Edwards' public lectures were, if anything, even more popular than her articles, if the reaction in the press is anything to go by. In September 1886, she was said to have 'interested a large audience', with a lecture on papyri found at Thebes and Fayûm.[50] In November 1887, she was in Manchester, talking about 'The Buried Cities of Ancient Egypt'. A report in the *Manchester Courier* conveys the excitement of this event, where, as usual, she illustrated her lecture with sketches, and on this occasion with examples of finds from the EEF's excavations. As she spoke about uncovering famous cities of antiquity, discovering marvellous artefacts, bringing fresh information to our understanding of the past, 'a flood of unexpected light' was 'cast upon the Biblical history of the Hebrews.' She held her audience spellbound, it was said – 'and of course she appealed for funds'.[51] When she made another lecturing visit to Manchester, a few months later, the town hall was filled with an expectant audience. Latecomers had to be turned away.[52] She spoke to enthusiastic audiences all over the Midlands, the North of England and Scotland – about women in ancient Egypt; about Egyptian influences on Greek art; on Egyptian portraits; on the excavation of Egypt's buried ancient cities. She gave the lectures all she had, seemingly tireless – until at last exhaustion took its toll, and illness slowed her down.

If Edwards struggled with the burden of overwork, the Egypt Exploration Fund as an organization faced difficulties of its own. For one thing, there were growing challenges to the EEF's academic credibility. In one way, this might be viewed as a measure of the Fund's success. Its archaeologists and scholars were now at the forefront of discovery and academic influence, and attracting greater public attention. Some scholars not directly involved with the new project clearly felt threatened by the organization's growing authority.

Some of the challenges were maliciously expressed. An American academic, Frederic Cope Whitehouse, questioned Naville's claim that Tel-el-Maskhuta was the Biblical 'treasure city' of Pithom. Whitehouse may, in fact, have been correct; but the manner in which he phrased his critique seems to have been offensively personal. It was, Edwards wrote to Poole contemptuously, 'low, vulgar, disgusting'.[53] She was deeply upset: not only was this attack on his reputation unpleasant for Naville; but the reputation of the EEF itself was at stake. In the end, however, she thought it best to ignore the Whitehouse challenge.

Four years after this incident, Edwards was again upset – this time, by letters from a Canon Taylor, who doubted her identification of a particular sculptured head as being of Hyksos origin.[54] Edwards, who had taught herself as an Egyptologist, no doubt sometimes felt vulnerable to criticism from scholars with more formal training.

She was irritated for different reasons, by a complaint to the EEF from Peter le Page Renouf, of the British Museum's Oriental Department. The Fund had sent him a collection of artefacts – for which he was not grateful. He wrote to Amelia, to tell her that he could not accept what he described as 'valueless objects'. Where were the 'missing antiquities'? Edwards was understandably annoyed by Renouf's tone of what she termed 'autocratic impertinence'. The EEF, she said, was 'not the servant' of the Oriental Department – which did not even help to support the Fund financially. 'It is too much to be endured, that Mr Renouf should take this tone', she wrote crossly to a colleague, Francis Llewellyn Griffith, a co-worker for the Fund.

One would think that he had 'bought and paid for' the objects he complained about, rather than receiving them as gifts.[55]

Sometimes she had to fend off well-meaning conservationists. Edward Poynter, an Orientalist pre-Raphaelite painter, and a leading figure in the Society for the Preservation of the Monuments of Ancient Egypt, wanted Edwards to join him in a public criticism of the way monuments left at their original sites in Egypt, were still exposed to neglect. Poynter thought a loud protest in the British press might be effective. Edwards, who was herself a member of the Society, and supported its work for the securing of Egyptian monuments with gates, lockable doors and the employment of security guards, wrote back that she judged it better, where possible to provide the monuments with 'a haven of safety' – whether within Egypt, or overseas – either 'at Gizeh or Bloomsburg', as she put it. She was wary of making any public censure either of the Egyptian government, or of the British occupation administration, that by now held the real power in Egypt. The very existence of the EEF, she pointed out, was 'dependent on the goodwill of both'.[56]

The growing popularity of the EEF, and its expanding membership, on both sides of the Atlantic, brought other challenges. Much financial support for the Fund now came from subscribers and donors in America, giving Edwards the idea of starting an EEF branch there. Stuart Poole was less enthusiastic, owing both to the complexities of collecting and recording subscriptions long-distance, and the possibility of what he called 'Dual Control' – by which, presumably, he meant the rise of an autonomous American EEF to rival the founding organization in Britain. And Americans would want to receive some of the finds from excavations. But, as Edwards pointed out, the Americans were, by 1888, giving more to the EEF than their British counterparts. So, the Fund as a whole would benefit in the long run.[57]

Edwards succeeded in persuading Poole and the other EEF committee members, that one of the Fund's key supporters in America, the Reverend William Copley Winslow, would make a reliable treasurer for an American branch. Poole then agreed to set priorities for entitlements to receive donations of artefacts: London and the British Museum would come first – then in descending order of entitlement, America, Bristol, Sydney, and Lancashire, where Edwards' contacts, and her speaking engagements, had drummed up support.

All through the mid-1880s, Amelia struggled, with insufficient time and personnel, to manage the Fund, a project that had grown beyond her expectations, and her resources. It did not help that, as Ellen Braysher became older and more frail, she felt committed to spending much time with her at Westbury-on-Trym, while other key members of the EEF committee were based in London. Though she corresponded regularly with Poole – in February 1885 writing him four letters over four days, on subjects ranging from book production costs to ancient Egyptian burial customs – and made occasional visits to join the committee members in London – many of the EEF's decisions were, perhaps of necessity, taken by others. It angered her, though, when it became apparent that Poole, and Barclay Head, his assistant in the British Museum's Coin Room, along with Charles Newton of the Department of Classical Antiquities, were making decisions without her knowledge or consent. 'I do not', she wrote, 'see the use of my giving up everything, earnings, time, health and home duties – if I do not have the least confidence reposed in me by the Committee, and am only told things after they are done'.[58]

In 1885, she grew concerned about the Fund's finances, and how they were being used – warning Poole in February that year, of the 'danger of running through our little capital.' If they overstretched themselves financially, she warned again, six months later, 'The Society must collapse and end in nothing'.[59]

Waste of money continued to be a concern. In July, she tried to insist on handling contracts with printers and publishers; confident that, as a self-described 'real woman of business', she could deal with the commercial side of book production most efficiently.[60]

In August the following year, she complained to Barclay Head, that because letters and reports she sent to London were not dealt with in a timely manner, the work kept having to be repeated – a great waste of her energy, and valuable time.[61]

Whatever she might think privately, in public Edwards was always at pains to protect the Fund against allegations of financial or administrative incompetence. In 1888, she wrote to a Fund supporter, Professor Hayter Lewis, to defend the EEF against such charges.[62] Behind the scenes, though, she remained concerned.

That year, publication costs were still an issue for her. 'I protest strongly', she wrote to Poole, at the prices the publisher Trubner was charging the Fund for producing its scholarly publications. She was sure the work could be done far more cheaply if the contract were offered to a firm in the West Country.[63] In July 1889, she also charged Poole with poor administration. How could her stock records be kept, she demanded to know, 'if one so high in authority as yourself acts irregularly'.[64] The irritable tone, from one who was usually so courteous and correct, gives some indication of the intense strain she was under that year.

Edwards herself could be impractical, when carried away with what she thought was a clever 'marketing' notion. Believing that the bricks without straw found at Pithom must be the very bricks produced at the site by the enslaved Hebrews, she hit on the idea of asking for a thousand of these bricks to be imported, for distribution to EES supporters – physical evidence, supposedly, of the Captivity. Fortunately, Poole and Petrie firmly quashed the idea. Petrie was not about to waste a week of excavation time, he told her, in packing bricks. And, he added, most Egyptian bricks had been made without straw, in any case, from time immemorial. Pithom bricks were nothing special. Edwards' idea was quietly let drop.

She had offered, subject to Committee approval, to serve as acting administrative secretary for the Fund, on her return from reading a paper at the 1886 Oriental Congress at Vienna.[65] In practice, she seems to have been performing these duties already; and this in spite of being already burdened and drained of energy. The previous year had ended with her ill, exhausted, and bedridden with flu. 'My eyes have suffered very much this year from overwork', she wrote in October 1886.[66]

All through 1885 and 1886, the stress was intensified by the tensions that built up between Flinders Petrie and his older, more established male colleagues. In January 1885, Edouard Naville felt driven to protest that Petrie had done nothing but complain about him – 'one string of complaints', he alleged – about his commentaries on, and translations of, materials brought by Petrie from Naukratis. For Naville – an established Egyptologist and linguist, with an international reputation, the negative criticism from a man ten years his junior, and far from an expert in the reading of hieroglyphics, must have been hard to take.[67]

In the last half of 1886, Petrie had a serious falling out with Stuart Poole. Poole was annoyed that Petrie had failed to submit his accounts from the last excavation. He was offended by what he perceived as Petrie's vanity – which exceeded, Poole said, 'that of Rameses'.[68] Petrie, for his part, charged that the EEF slighted his suggestions, and mismanaged the arrangements for his excavation projects. Famous for his obsessive frugality, he complained that they had overspent, when arranging the printing of his illustrations for the report on Tanis.[69] In addition, since he had been so much more responsible in handling his own expenses, he did not see why he should not use the remainder of his excavation allowance in Britain, on his return from Egypt. (In the end, he would donate it to University College, London. The dispute was, perhaps, less about sums of money, than about getting his own way.)

As we have seen, Petrie's charges against the Fund officers, of inefficient administration, may have been quite well-founded – he was understandably furious when Poole refused to print both parts of his report of his excavations at Naukratis in the same year. 'Naucratis Part II, then, would be "two years stale" and subsequent volumes even more out of date.'[70] But the rows arose partly from a clash of temperament. Petrie was young, decisive and ultra-self-confident, apt to be sure of the rightness of his own opinions. Poole, twenty-one years Petrie's senior, was temperamentally cautious and deliberate, always mindful of avoiding giving offence to people on whom the continuance of the EEF depended.

Edwards was offended and angered when she learned, in 1886, that Poole – without consulting her – had promised Edouard Naville that he would be the Fund's choice for the next expedition to Egypt, in the coming excavation season. No one had bothered to discuss the decision with her. She was angry, too, on Petrie's behalf, that he had been passed over in favour of Naville. Not solely because Petrie was her protégé – it was not a matter of favouritism

– but because she appreciated Petrie's careful, methodical approach to excavation, and considered him the better archaeologist.

By way of trying to convince the EEF Committee, she warned them that Naville's rash methods, of valuing only large objects found on site, and discarding nearly everything else, risked leaving the Fund with no small artefacts to donate to museums in the provinces. It was a pragmatic argument, but it seems to have carried little weight with Poole and the rest. Amelia offered a second argument, based on fairness: 'Not to send out Mr Petrie would be very unjust. He has worked harder than Naville ever worked and brought home richer results'. But she was not a trained expert; and in the all-male environment of the British Museum, one suspects that her opinions regarding the choice of an archaeologist counted for little.[71]

Upset though she was, all the same, the needs of the Exploration Fund came first. When Petrie threatened public exposure of what he termed 'the waste and mismanagement' of the EEF, on the grounds that the publicity might 'clear the air', Edwards firmly dissuaded him: 'It would certainly clear the air', she wrote to him – but 'it would also clear the ground – of the Egypt Exploration Fund!'[72]

In another letter to Petrie, she poured out her anger and frustration. Although she had made nothing like his contributions to science, she told him, all the same, from a financial point of view, her work for the EEF and the time she gave to it, was 'worth a great deal more than yours'. For lack of time, she had turned down offers for novel-writing contracts, worth £600 each for the British newspaper serial rights alone, from the *Illustrated News* and *The Graphic*. She was conscious, too, of 'that literary position which I am fast losing before the eyes of the public'. In spite of it all – and although 'It is madness perhaps on my part to desire to preserve my chains unbroken' – she preferred to see the work of the EEF continue, even though it meant 'poverty and drudgery and obscurity' for herself personally.[73]

In the autumn of 1886, Poole resigned as joint Honorary Secretary – something he had been longing to do for some time, feeling that what he called 'clerk's work' was keeping him from his academic commitments.

Petrie, meanwhile, had drawn up a set of rules he believed should govern the future operations of the Fund. Edwards largely supported his proposals. It had long troubled her, for instance, that the de facto, self-appointed sub-committee of Poole and his assistant Barclay Head, made arbitrary decisions about the disposal of funds donated to the EEF by the public, without consulting others. Petrie printed out copies of his proposals and offered them to the EEF committee; but Charles Newton, who had become the Fund's President after the death of Erasmus Wilson, refused even to circulate them. Petrie was not, after all, a committee member. Seeking to direct the Fund's policies and practices from the position of an outsider was, it had to be admitted, highly irregular.

Petrie then – as he had long been threatening to do – resigned from the Egypt Exploration Fund. He wanted Edwards to resign with him – something she had no intention of doing. But she was deeply upset by the whole affair. She greatly admired Petrie's forthrightness, his innovative intelligence, and his conscientious approach to excavation work. She looked after his interests, as if he were her son. At the same time, she had grown fond of Stuart Poole. Even if frequently irritated by him, she confided in him, respected his opinions, and looked to him for support. His wife, Sophia, had become a close personal friend, and she was friendly with the rest of the family, too. It pained her to be pressured to take sides in a bitter quarrel.

In this unhappy time, she envied the archaeologists their freedom to travel to Egypt – the land she had fallen in love with once and for all, and would never see again: 'I am heartsick', she wrote – 'literally heartsick, sometimes, with the infinite yearning one has for the palms and sands and the wide rushing river.'[74]

She might have drawn a little consolation from a letter she received the following summer, from Edouard Naville. It might have reminded her that professional jealousies were, unfortunately, an all-too-common occurrence in academic circles. He had, it seemed, suffered a good deal from the jealousy of the late Samuel Birch, a revered senior figure at the British Museum (and the man Edwards had bombarded with requests for information, as she worked to teach herself about Egyptology). 'It is possible that since Birch is dead', Naville told her, 'his petty and mean jealousy may be extinct with him' – adding, 'It is the lot of every scientific discovery to be abused by somebody whose theories it upsets or contradicts'. He expressed his gratitude to both Edwards, and to Poole, for their support.[75]

Edwards was, indeed, a loyal colleague, and a loyal friend. Even after Flinders Petrie had resigned from the Fund, she stood by him; arranging for his later expeditions to be privately funded, through, among others, her personal connections with the wealthy manufacturer Jesse Haworth. Petrie went on to make finds in Egypt, at places that became household names in the history of archaeology: Fayûm and Hawara; the pyramid field of Meydoum; and Tel-el-Amarna, the royal capital of Akhnaten. (Edwards would refer to some of these later discoveries, in the public lectures that became *Pharaohs, Fellahs and Explorers*.) His (literally) ground-breaking discoveries in Egypt and Palestine, his prolific publication record, his distinguished professorial career, by 1923 had earned him a knighthood, and the informal title of 'Father of Modern Archaeology'.

By 1887, Amelia had a paid secretary, Hellier Gosselin, to assist her – replaced, the following year, on Poole's recommendation, by Emily Paterson, who she found particularly supportive, efficient and helpful. Edwards described the newcomer appreciatively as 'exceedingly apt, businesslike and methodical'. Emily, she said, took a real interest in the work of the Exploration Fund, and 'got through a large amount of correspondence daily'.[76] Paterson, for her part, expressed admiration for her employer. In her memories of Edwards, in a talk she gave in 1931, she described her as 'the most courteous person I ever met, no matter whether she spoke to a servant, a secretary or one of her friends. And she was the most delightful person to work for, as she gave full credit when one did anything to please her, and if she had to advise or correct, always did so in the kindest possible way'.[77]

The new arrangement freed Edwards to take full control of the publications work of the EEF. In spite of the stressful conflicts within the Fund, she had found time to translate Maspero's *L'Archeologie égyptienne* into English, for publication in 1887. With Poole no longer active on the EEF committee, Edwards actually began to find her role somewhat easier.

In June 1887, Ellen Braysher was ill – but so was Amelia, in August and September. 'I am very nearly done for', she wrote to Petrie.[78] All the same, she spent much of October preparing a series of lectures to be given in the north of England, the following month.[79] The following summer, she came down with typhoid, and took to her bed at Saville Villa. By June 21, however, she felt well enough to write to Petrie:

> I am wonderfully well considering what I ail and my doctor is never weary of wondering at my freedom from all sorts of canonical aches and pains belonging to typhoid – but he keeps me in bed, and this is the 7th day of it. He says I need not expect to be well under 21 days from that on which I fell ill.

As usual, it was the thought of neglected tasks piling up, the threat of unmet deadlines, that filled her with anxiety and impatience: 'This is despair – and my *Harper's* article, *Century* article, *Illustrated News* article and lectures all to write!'[80]

In her distress, she had the good fortune to receive help from a new, loyal friend. Kate Bradbury was the daughter of a businessman in Ashton-under-Lyne, near Manchester. While it is unclear how Amelia and Kate first came to meet, it seems likely they got to know one another during one of Edwards' Northern speaking tours. In a letter to Flinders Petrie, Kate reflected with some bewilderment on the intense and sudden attachment that Amelia conceived for her, a woman in her thirties, when Edwards herself was twenty-three years older:

> Her love for me, and her seizure of me – unwilling – almost at first sight, has always been to me one of the strangest things I have known – so strange that I dared not refuse it either, or its consequences . . . Of course I have grown to love her with a love as great as hers has always been for me, I think.[81]

In early July, learning of Amelia's illness, Kate came to be with her in Weston. Once her friend was strong enough to travel, she took her back to Ashton-under-Lyne, to finish convalescing at the Bradbury family home.

In October 1890, returning to her accustomed energetic multitasking, Edwards wrote to *The Times*, to tell the public of an important, and ambitious new project for the Exploration Fund's remit of safeguarding Egypt's antiquities. It was proposed to 'map, plan, photograph and copy all the most important sites, sculptures, and paintings and inscriptions yet extant, so as to preserve at least a faithful record of those fast-perishing monuments'.[82] This Archaeological Survey of Egypt, which had in part been suggested by Petrie, would be organized and overseen by Francis Llewellyn Griffith, who had been Petrie's assistant and co-worker on earlier expeditions to Egypt. Setting aside his differences with Poole and his associates, Petrie now gladly offered expert advice to the project team, which came to include himself, Edouard Naville and Naville's assistants, George Cowan and Riamo D'Hulst.[83]

If Edwards and the organization she founded had done nothing else to help in the protection of Egypt's ancient heritage, for this one EEF-sponsored project alone, her reputation would be secure.

7

A very private life

It was Kate Bradbury who said that Amelia, although she had many acquaintances, did not deeply love many people. It has even been suggested that Edwards suffered from a degree of emotional inhibition, due to some psychological block.[1] Yet, as we have seen in the case of Amelia's early attachments to Ellen Byrne and Marianne North, and in her loyal affection for Ellen Braysher, Amelia could, in her closest relationships, be both passionate and caring. She was reticent, however, with regard to her private life – in a way that people of the twenty-first century, where every detail of a famous person's life is open to scrutiny on social media, may find hard to understand. The few personal letters and journals of Edwards that have survived, and that were not intended for public view, along with letters that others wrote to her, call into question the notion that Amelia was emotionally inhibited.

For Kate Bradbury, the young Northerner who came to support her at a time of crisis in her life, and on whom, as her health declined, Edwards was more and more to depend, she clearly felt an abiding love. In letters to Kate, she called herself, 'thine Owl' – probably Kate teased Amelia about claiming to be wise and knowing? Amelia wrote to Kate from Saville Villa, eight months before her death:

> My own darling one, tomorrow will be thy birthday, and a little sketch is all a poo' owl has to send thee, but Owl thinks that perhaps a wee little sketch from Pompeii, done from the one made when Owl was such a very poo Owl, will please thee more than a valuable gift . . . God bless you my own one and I hope thou wilt have many, many birthdays, and happy years between each, and that thy owl may live to give thee less anxiety and more happiness for the future.[2]

To other good friends, Edwards wrote elegant and touching letters. Just before her last illness, she sent a scarab to an unidentified correspondent, with a verse:

> It was once the sacred token
> of eternity unbroken

And divine; Some long-vanished priest or king
Lord or lady owned the thing;
Now 'tis thine.'[3]

If she was emotionally reserved where most people were concerned, she
had a few very close friends, to whom she opened her heart – Kate, Marianne
North, Petrie – almost certainly, Ellen Byrne, while the relationship lasted;
Lucy Renshaw (although none of her letters to these last-mentioned two
women have survived). Given all the casual social relationships in her life,
the dozens of people she came to know – as fellow-writers and fellow-artists,
editors and critics, admirers of her work, supporters of her various causes,
collaborators on projects of all kinds, and people who wanted to get close
to her simply because she was famous – she could hardly become intimate
with all of them. Hers was the predicament of a 'celebrity', surrounded by
people who were fascinated by her, wanted to work with her, or wanted her
to do something for them. Inevitably, in her close friendships, she had to be
particular.

Throughout the latter half of the 1880s, Amelia kept in touch by letter
with the writer and artist Edward Lear. Their friendship seems to have begun
when, in May 1885, he wrote thanking her for her review of his work – a
'beautiful little criticism', he called it. He invited her to visit his home in San
Remo. But by September that year, Lear's health was failing, and Amelia
seems never to have made the visit. Lear did, however, send her two of his
paintings.[4]

She told Edward Lear about her tussle with cousin Matilda over the
matter of their names. He found her letter about it hilarious: 'Betham plus
Betham threw me into such a fearful fit of laughter, that my good Milanese
servant evidently thought I had gone out of my wits.' Lear explained he was
laughing at what 'La Signora del Nilo' had written; adding that probably
Edwards would retort, 'Things must B as they may B'. In the same letter, he
enclosed 'three small photographs' for Amelia.[5] He knew Lucy Renshaw,
Amelia's well-loved companion of the Dolomites and Nile, and asked to be
remembered to her. On learning Lucy had been ill with a cold, he told Amelia
to recommend drinking hot lemon.[6]

Amelia had a warm relationship with the artist Gustave Doré – who, in
between profuse apologies for his long delays in writing back to her, confided
to her his professional concerns as an artist, and his personal anxieties and
sorrows.[7] He had known John and Ellen Rice Byrne, and in 1869, when the
Byrnes were still living in Bristol, he sent them his greetings.[8]

In 1872, Doré wrote to her from Paris, as he, his family and the city, were
still recovering from the bombardment by the Prussian army, and the chaotic
and doomed popular uprising, the Paris Commune, that followed. His
brother, he told her, had been taken prisoner by the Prussians at Coblentz,
but was safe. He himself was safe, he assured Edwards – in spite of all kinds
of 'sufferings, fatigues and privations'. He had not been called upon to fight;

but the first floor of his brother's home had been totally wrecked by shelling, and the contents of two rooms reduced to fragments.

Later, he gave accounts of his travels, in Scotland – where he decided he had no aptitude for salmon fishing and would devote his time to painting instead – and in Switzerland, where he found peace in the tranquil beauty of the mountains: 'I shall return with an ample harvest of sketches and projects for pictures', he told Amelia. All the same, he envied her recent adventurous journey to the Dolomites, and her impending trip to Egypt. He felt sure her journey to Africa would result in a book that would do her proud. He foresaw that what he called her 'poetic spirit' would be, as he said, 'enriched and renewed' by her impressions of Egypt.[9]

As one artist to another, he discussed his work – his preference, for instance, for using watercolours, when painting out of doors. In 1877, he felt inhibited and was proceeding slowly with regard to bringing out new work. He did not feel ready, as yet, to publish new prints, for fear of attacks by the critics; but he hoped to bring his painting of Moses and the Brazen Serpent to London for the coming Season. There was also his image of Dante's Inferno, with which, he said, he wanted to 'disquiet peaceable visitors' to the exhibition gallery in Bond Street.[10]

When Edwards first met Doré, in 1869, he was both famous throughout Europe, and at the height of his powers as an artist. The last fifteen years of his life, however, Edwards observed, ended in 'disappointment, bereavement, death'. During this last period, although he continued to be successful as a designer, the critical rejection of his paintings, and his inability to sell them, hurt him deeply. When Amelia had first known him, he was almost 35, but she had thought he looked ten years younger. By 1868, she found him 'no longer boyish; no longer mirthful'. His attractive laugh, 'that 'rire étincelant et communicatif', was 'already silenced'.[11]

Doré 's letters, full of flowery compliments and warm appreciation of Edwards' work, are hardly boyish in style. They are respectful and quite formal – slightly impersonal, even. Amelia is always addressed as 'Chère Mademoiselle', and with the formal 'vous' form, never with the intimate, 'tu'. Only when Doré's beloved mother died, and in his desolate grief and loneliness, he reached out for comfort to his friend in England, did a more intimate and personal note break through.

Doré, who never married, lived his whole life under his mother's roof. Now, he found himself bereft, struggling to come to terms with this new solitary life without her. Edwards' condolence letter had been a great comfort, he wrote to her; he could hardly express how deeply it had touched him – 'combien j'ai été profondement touché de ta lettre affectueuse'. Unable to escape into work, he greatly valued her friendship. In particular, he thanked her for what she had written about his mother – 'the charming lines, so truly worthy of your pen', describing his mother's 'noble nature and her smile'. (It seems Edwards had met her, and he told Amelia how his mother recalled pleasant hours they had spent together.)

Even in the midst of his grief, Doré remembered to congratulate Amelia on the appearance in the *Graphic* of the serial version of *Lord Brackenbury,* and on its enthusiastic public reception: 'I've heard from quite a few people that your novel . . . has been a resounding success.'

Amelia could empathize with Gustave Doré's suffering, having herself lost a mother to whom she was intensely attached – like Doré, perhaps excessively so. Whatever she wrote to comfort him, clearly it meant a great deal.[12]

In the summer of 1881, he wrote to her that he felt unable to travel to London again, owing to what he called 'une lassitude', a weariness, that had made him 'très apathique'.[13] By January 1883, he was dead of a heart attack, at the age of 51.

In a brief posthumous biographical review of Doré's work, Edwards wrote a sensitive commentary on one of his last works, the sculpture titled 'Parque et Amour' (Fate and Love) – a meditation on love cut short by the inevitability of death. Edwards recognized the figure in the sculpture as a portrait of Doré's mother. Fate is represented as

> an ancient, majestic figure clothed in a heavy woollen robe, which covers her head like a hood, falls in broad folds over her arms and shoulders, and descends in rich voluminous drapery to the ground. She is seated on a rock, and Love stands between her knees. In her right hand she holds the shears, which in the triple sisterhood belong to Atropos; between the finger and thumb of the left hand she holds the thread of human destiny; the distaff and an hourglass lie on the ground at her feet, one of which rests upon Love's fallen quiver, whence the arrows are slipping. It is the fatal moment when those dread shears are about to close . . .[14]

It is a perceptive critical study; but also Amelia's meditation on grief, on the experience of the loss of a beloved parent, that Edwards and her friend Doré shared in common.

It may be true that in most of her public writings, Edwards gives us little in the way of disclosure about her innermost thoughts and feelings – certainly not in the form of autobiographical articles, or interviews with the Press. But to take such reticence for emotional repression, is to overlook the cultural context in which she functioned, in which uninhibited public displays of emotion were not encouraged. She was quite capable of giving vent to her feelings in interactions with close friends. And the account of her depressive episode while in Rome in 1871–2, confided to a private journal, is a harrowing piece of intimate reflection.[15] When it came to public disclosure, though, she was a well-bred Victorian lady, in a world where one sign of good breeding was a decent reticence. Excessive self-disclosure was considered 'bad form' – even shameful. Between the two spheres of the drawing room and the private study – let alone the bedroom – a great gulf was fixed. One simply did not bring private emotional matters out into the public sphere.

Edwards was skilled at retaining her privacy. A case in point, is the draft of an autobiographical article she sent in letter form to Edward Abbot, editor of the *Literary World* in Boston. Abbot had asked Amelia for some details about her life, that would be of interest to his American readers – they wanted to know more about the famous novelist than her books alone could tell them.

She begins her piece by insisting that there really is nothing to tell:

> The life of an author – what is it but a record of copy written and paid for, or not paid for, as the case may be? I feel abashed, now that I come to think about myself, that I have never performed any feat, or suffered any misfortune worth mentioning.

Edwards has lived 'the life of a cabbage', she tells the editor. She was born, she tells him, in 'the third decade of the present century' – carefully omitting a precise date: 'There is a poetic vagueness about this treatment of dates which commends itself to the feminine mind.'[16] There is something almost passive-aggressive about this seemingly coy statement. No one was normally more precise about details like dates, than Amelia Edwards. The rest of her letter is a bald summary of external facts: the childhood in Islington; the clever mother; the false start in the musical profession; her early literary successes. Nothing here, it goes without saying, about Ellen Byrne, Marianne North, Lucy Renshaw; or even about her shared life with Mrs Braysher.

Another proof Edwards knew how to keep at bay those who were too curious about her private life, is the piece she wrote for the American magazine *Arena*, published in 1891. Titled, 'My Home Life', it offers the magazine's readers an account of Edwards' day-to-day existence in England, at The Larches. She is pleased, she tells them, to be asked to write the article herself; thereby escaping the typical grilling to which she would be subjected by a reporter visiting her home, 'who cross-examines the victim like an Old Bailey counsel, and proceeds to take an inventory of his furniture, like a bailiff'.[17] Her opening statement as good as warns the reader, when it comes to self-revelation, not to expect too much:

> it seems to me that the conditions under which such a visit is paid and received are radically unsatisfactory. The person interviewed must be more or less uncomfortably self-conscious, and one cannot help doubting whether the interviewer ever succeeds in seeing his subject and his subject's surroundings in exactly their normal dishabille. It would ask more than Roman virtue not to make the best of one's self and one's house when both were sitting for a portrait; and difficult as it is to look natural and feel natural in front of a photographer's camera, it is ten times more trying vis à vis of a reporter's note-book. As for the temptation to 'pose', whether consciously or unconsciously, it must be well-nigh

irresistible . . . instead of receiving such a visitor in my ordinary working costume, and in a room littered with letters and papers, I should have inevitably put on a more becoming gown, and have 'tidied up' the library, when the appointed day and hour arrived.

In writing her own account of her home life, Edwards undertakes not to pose, but to tell what she does tell, truthfully – 'in my habit as I live'. Only the reader is not to expect any personal revelations.[18]

She takes two pages to describe the village of Westbury-on-Trym – of interest, possibly, to American readers with a taste for English rural 'charm' – the church with its medieval monuments; the bell-tower; the muddy little streamlet of the Trym; the 'romantic Coombe', much loved by artists; the elegant old houses. She then describes the house from outside – its walled garden surrounded by tall larch trees and a thick shrubbery, shielding the house from the public gaze, with the path where she imposes on herself 'the Draconian law', to walk two miles daily, winter and summer; the garden bird houses and bird-tables.

Next comes the house interior, with its oriental tiles and wooden Cairene latticework furnishings, and its rich abundance – some might say 'clutter' – of 'curiosities of all descriptions' – brass and pottery, ancient Egyptian funerary tablets, framed tiles. From this entrance hall, the visitor may (but probably will not, given that she is always busy, and that 'there are but twenty-four hours to the day'), be taken into Edwards' private study, where she works, seated at her writing table, with her back to the light from the window. The room is filled with books, showing, 'like geological strata', the studies she has undertaken at different times in her life. 'My life, since I have lived at The Larches, has been one of ever-increasing seclusion, and my books have for many years been my daily companions, teachers, and friends.' There are also huge Roman and Florentine jars, and 'stacks of pictures'.

There are ancient Egyptian artefacts, stashed away in nooks and crannies all over the house. She offers to make her readers flesh creep a little, with her collection of mummified body parts – 'fragments of spiced and bituminized humanity to be shown to visitors who are not nervous, nor given to midnight terrors'. A baby's foot ('some mother cried over it once'), three mummified hands; and, 'grimmest of all', 'the heads of two ancient Egyptians in a wardrobe in my bedroom, who perhaps talk to each other in the watches of the night, when I am sound asleep'.

Edwards refuses to describe her own physical appearance – her 'brethren of the press' have done that quite enough already, she says. She has no objection to describing her work habits, however. She has been 'a hard worker' since 'early girlhood'. She works, 'all the time when I am not either sitting at meals, taking exercise, or sleeping . . . I live with the pen in my hand, not only from morning till night, but sometimes from night till morning'. Night is the best time to work without distractions: 'for at least the last twenty-five years, I have rarely put out my lamp before two or three in the morning.' When she has an urgent deadline, she might work all through the night: 'The last chapter of every book I have ever written has been finished at early morning. In summertime, it is certainly delightful to draw up the blinds and complete in sunlight a task begun when the lamps were lighted in the evening.'[19]

What we are offered here, is a kind of showcase – a picture of the daily life of an English lady writer, to entertain the readers without venturing far into the realm of the personal. What is completely absent from the whole account, is the presence of other human beings. No maid or cook – above all, no hint of the turbulent presence of Mrs Braysher, that so dominated Amelia's life at this time.

While Ellen Braysher might not be mentioned in print, she was not at all a fact Amelia could ignore in daily life. With advancing age Ellen was becoming ever more difficult to live with. 'Old ladies and babies are bound to be vegetables', Amelia wrote to Stuart Poole, in 1883. 'My old lady is a most rampaging, vehement, political, belligerent, Gladstone-hating, boiling-over vegetable – quite uncontrollable and unmanageable.' She might confide such information to a friend like Poole. She was hardly going to share it with the world.

Edwards has been called a recluse, at least in later life. 'Habits of strict seclusion grew upon her with advancing years', said her cousin Matilda. 'Having from childhood arranged the plan of her daily life, she found it difficult indeed to diverge from routine.'[20] Towards the very end of her life, it is true, Edwards' world did tend to narrow to the small compass of The Larches, with occasional visits to Weston-super-Mare for Mrs Braysher's sake. Work for the Egypt Exploration Fund took so much of her remaining time, that she often found herself turning down social engagements. Poor health took a toll on her energies, too. Even so, she hardly lived cut off from the world. During the 1880s she was constantly travelling, either to London on Fund business or to see friends, or to Bristol to take part in public events there. Then there would be the five months spent touring and lecturing in America – with further lecturing trips in Britain, when she came back. It was not exactly the lifestyle of a recluse.

She did need privacy and free time in order to write. That a disciplined routine did obtain when she was at The Larches, there is no doubt. Without it – without the orderly habits acquired in her early home life, from her mother's careful home tuition and the example of her retired military father – she would hardly have been able to accomplish the huge volume of work she got through in a short lifetime. In the last decade of her life, she was not only writing and researching, but dealing with committee work, lecturing, supporting various good causes, dashing off letters on a dozen different subjects to *The Times* and the *Western Daily Press* – while also keeping in touch with friends.

Edwards herself is partly responsible for this myth of reclusiveness. When asked to describe her life, she was at pains to emphasize its regimen of discipline and routine. She disliked going into 'society', she said. As a young woman she had 'done my London seasons, and undergone the usual treadmill of dining, driving, dressing and the rest of it, till I became too weary of the wretched round to submit to it any longer'. She certainly refused to go into 'society' merely for the sake of seeing and being seen. There had to be a good reason for it – a suffrage meeting, or a lecture on ancient Egypt. She was always happy, though, to attend gatherings where people met for a common purpose, and where she might make a definite contribution.[21] Her task-oriented, driven, nature would not permit her to waste time on activities she viewed as meaningless.

The image of a reclusive, solitary existence was at least partly designed to keep off unwanted intrusions, whether from journalists, or from over-enthusiastic local secretaries for the Exploration Fund. One reason Edwards preferred Westbury and The Larches to Saville Villa at Weston was, that, as she explained to Stuart Poole, at The Larches, she could 'shut out the world and get enough air and exercise in our own bit of ground'. At Saville Villa, 'everyone pounces on me, and the terrible Tomkins comes at all hours, insisting on seeing me "for five minutes", and talking for an hour.'

The Reverend Henry Tomkins, a keen supporter of the Egypt Exploration Fund, was one person in particular, whose visitations Edwards most dreaded. On learning from Poole that the intruder was away in London, she wrote back: 'Oh yes, I know that Tomkins is in town. Blessed fact. If you love me, keep him there.' As in a scene in one of her early melodramatic novels, Poole ought to lure him down into the basement, 'and turn the key upon him'. 'Do this', Amelia promised Poole, 'and I will bless you and leave you something handsome in my will'.[22]

Towards the close of the 1880s, Edwards' health increasingly became an issue for her. Then she stayed at home, or was nursed in the home of a friend – not from choice, but because her ailing body refused to let her get on with all the things she wanted to do. Hers was a driven nature – she would push herself on to complete a task, never resting until it had been done to the limit of her ability. All too often, physical and emotional collapse would follow.[23]

Physical frailty brought with it a return of the periods of depression she had suffered from earlier in her life, when struck by emotional loss. Kate Bradbury described Amelia as 'prone to melancholia', believing the tendency to be hereditary.[24] It was a manic / depressive cycle characteristic of many highly creative people – in Edwards' case, coupled with a perfectionism that must always have left her feeling that her best was never quite good enough. Always, though, for as long as she was able – after a bout of flu, a bout of typhoid, even after the removal of a potentially cancerous tumour – even in periods of depression – she rallied her remaining energy and, for so long as she was able, set forth into the world again.

8

Novelist

The growing burden of work for the Egyptian Exploration Fund put an end to Edwards' novel-writing career. It was something she claimed not to regret, saying she was 'more usefully employed' struggling to guide the course of the infant, and growing, society she had brought into the world.[1] It is hard to believe, however, that she gave up novel writing without at least some sense of conflict. Whether she would feel the sacrifice to be justified – not only of earnings and literary reputation, but of the practice of hard-won accomplishments, just when her powers as a novelist had reached their height, only time would tell.

She had begun her writing career by learning to work within the often-constraining conventions of the then-fashionable 'novel of sensation', with its dramatic and violent incidents, mystery and suspense, improbable coincidences, breathless pursuits, tragedy and romance. She had, of course, handled similar material before, in her short stories; but to sustain the narrative pace while weaving complex plots involving many changes of scene and a large cast of characters, presented new challenges. In her first serious ventures into the novel form, credibility would at times be sacrificed to the urge to tie up loose ends in the plot. At other times, the narrative would stall, while characters indulged in long discussions of art, music, German legend, or medieval history, that did nothing to advance character development or plot.

Every writer, though, may be allowed their fair share of unsuccess before hitting their stride in a new genre; and it may be said of Edwards' early novels that, for all their faults, they have their excellences too; suggesting what might come to fruition in her later work.

Her first novel, *My Brother's Wife*, was published in 1855, when Edwards was twenty-four.[2] The title is somewhat misleading: the novel could more properly be titled, *My Brother's Mistress* – if Victorian proprieties had allowed.

When the novel begins, its narrator, Paul Latour, is hopelessly in love with his cousin, Adrienne. She, however, prefers to marry Paul's brilliant but feckless brother, Théophile. To Paul's distress, Théophile soon grows unfaithful to his wife, being hopelessly infatuated with a beautiful Austrian opera singer, Thérèse Vogelsang. The younger brother can only look on helplessly, as the destructive enchantress leads on the mesmerized Théophile to his doom.

Other plots intersect and interweave with this central story. An encounter with a drug-addicted and dying musician draws Paul into a paternalistic relationship with Margaret, the musician's friendless orphaned daughter, to whom he becomes guardian. Paul falls steadily in love with Margaret, who is working as a teaching assistant at a Brussels boarding school. All goes well between them, until he discovers her holding a secretive meeting with a mysterious man, who in turn seems to have some connection with the seductive opera singer, Thérèse.

With every scene the mystery now deepens, keeping the reader pressing on through the pages. The truth will not be revealed until the very last chapter. At last, the impending crisis in Théophile's marriage comes to a head, as he elopes from Brussels with Thérèse, along with her sinister companion Lemaire, a manager from the Brussels opera. After a dramatic chase across France, Paul finally catches up with his brother – but too late to save him from a tragic end.

My Brother's Wife is marred by some clumsy digressions – in particular a lengthy newspaper report of a murder trial, repeating in detail events already described far more dramatically by the narrator. The plot is full of absurdly improbable coincidences, in which half the characters, previously strangers, turn out all to be related to one another. Unexpected chance meetings take place all over Europe; so that a character who disappears in France unexpectedly turns up again, months later, on London Bridge. 'I have often wondered', says the narrator, 'whether a presiding hand had not led me to that eventful spot at that eventful moment'.[3] The presiding hand of the novelist is all too much in evidence. Invoking divine intervention for implausible coincidences does not let the writer off the hook; it only draws attention to clumsiness.

Though flawed in so many ways, however, this first novel exhibits some of the qualities Edwards would develop to good effect in later, more mature work. It has her gift, shown already in her short stories, for maintaining mystery and suspense; and her ability – that of a practiced artist and caricaturist, as well as a writer – to sketch a character in a well-turned phrase. So, an aged society lady, accompanied by her three unmarried daughters, has 'a face like the queen of spades'. The daughters, in their matching vermilion dresses, are said to resemble elderly flamingos. A taciturn police detective looks upon the world with a permanently impassive expression, 'as if he were counting the bricks in a dead wall'.[4]

Edwards' ear for dialogue is apparent, too, as she captures the Babel of disjointed simultaneous conversations at a society reception:

'in short, sir, the country is going to ruin . . . unless the military are immediately re-enforced and . . .'

'Stewed down with port wine and sugar. It is the finest thing in the world. I have tried it myself . . .'

PLATE 1 *Edwards as a young woman, in 1860.*

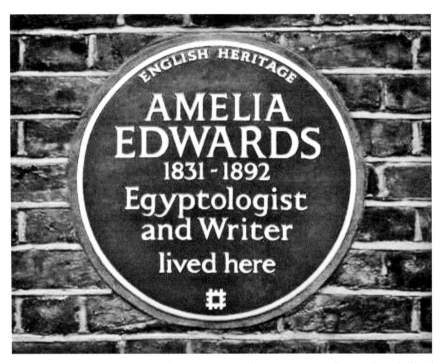

PLATE 2 *English Heritage plaque on 19, Wharton Street, where Edwards lived until the death of her parents in 1860.*

Westerfield Hall, Baylham.

PLATE 3 *Westerfield Hall.*

snf yurs
M Betham - Edwards

PLATE 4 *Matilda Betham-Edwards.*

PLATE 5 *'The Romans in Britain.'*

PLATE 6 *Park Place in 2018.*

PLATE 7 *Donnington Hall, childhood home of Ellen Webb Byrne.*

HELIOS,

ALEXANDRIE
& CAIRE.

PLATE 8 *Lucy Renshaw, from Amelia's photo album.*

PLATE 9 *Drawing by Edwards of Sasso di Ronch in the Dolomites.*

PLATE 10 *Edwards' sketch of Denderah.*

PLATE 11 *Karnak.*

PLATE 12 *Gustave Doré.*

PLATE 13 *Original seal of the EEF, 1882.*

The Larches. — Miss Edwards' Home at Westbury-on-Trym.

PLATE 14 *The Larches, Westbury-on-Trym.*

PLATE 15 *Flinders Petrie in 1886.*

DRAWN BY LUKE FILDES, A.R.A.

She got up, flushed and startled, and followed him to the window.

LORD BRACKENBURY: A Novel.

BY AMELIA B. EDWARDS,

Author of "Barbara's History," "Debenham's Vow," &c.

PLATE 16 *'She got up, flushed and startled, and followed him to the window.'* A *scene from* Lord Brackenbury.

PLATE 17 *Amelia B. Edwards in 1890.*

PLATE 18 *Kate Bradbury.*

PLATE 19 *Visiting Edwards' grave at St Mary's, Henbury, near Bristol.*

'And did you really come on purpose to see me, Charles?'

'You, and you only, my angel! You know that I live but in your smiles
. . . your glance alone has power to reduce me to . . .'

'Indeed, a most interesting experiment'.

'Possibly so; but I acknowledge that the present cabinet inspires me
with little confidence . . .'

'. . . the loveliest legs and ankles you ever beheld! They skim along the
stage, my boy, like . . .'[5]

Edwards' next novel, *The Ladder of Life,* is also very much in the
tradition of the novel of sensation. Its plot, full of unexpected twists and
turns, hairbreadth escapes and dramatic discoveries, takes the first-person
narrator on a journey from provincial Switzerland to the heart of London.
Natalie, a young orphan, raised by her governess Madame de Wahl, is
unexpectedly ousted from her adoptive home, after she falls in love with
Madame de Wahl's son. The mother separates the pair by sending Natalie to
England, where Mme de Wahl's sister is to care for Natalie till she comes of
age. No sooner has our heroine set foot on English soil, however, than she is
kidnapped by robbers, spending a terrifying night under the criminals' roof.
Her escape from this den of thieves – like a later kidnapping scene in the
novel – is vividly, dramatically narrated, with a capacity for depicting scenes
of action that will become even more evident in Edwards' later fiction.

Destitute, having lost touch with Madame de Wahl, and unable to trace
her new family, Natalie wanders helplessly, exhausted and hungry. She is
rescued by Vaughan, a gifted but impoverished musician, who takes her into
his home. Vaughan discovers Natalie has a remarkable singing voice. He
uses his theatrical connections to find her a place in the chorus at Drury
Lane; and her musical career begins.

This novel is as full of melodrama and unlikely coincidences as *My
Brother's Wife* – one of the most improbable being that the narrator, while
taking a holiday in the countryside, just happens to find herself staying next
door to Mme de Wahl's sister – the very person whose address she lost when
she first arrived in England. Like the earlier work, though, it contains a
number of effective scenes. One, certainly, is that where Natalie, a naive
young Swiss woman who has never seen a theatre before, explores backstage
at Drury Lane. It is a scene devoid of any romantic glamour. Natalie notes
the threadbare appearance of the chorus she is about to join as a new
member, as they gather for a daytime rehearsal. To her eyes, they have 'a
faded, sallow air'. 'The men look shabby and the women sickly, and they
have weak eyes and cotton gloves'. The empty, gloomy theatre backstage in
daytime is a mysterious place to her:

Faint lines of light and moted sunbeams fall here and there, like bright
arrows plunging into the gloom . . . Pale ghosts of white draperies hang
from box to box. There is dust, inches deep, everywhere and on everything.

Some pieces of scenery, lolling awkwardly together in a corner, look sad and strange . . . Now and then, when there is a momentary lull upon the stage, sounds of scrubbing and hammering are heard from the pit . . .[6]

In the same year *The Ladder of Life* appeared, *Home and Foreign Lyrics*, Edwards' own theatrical sketches set to music, were making a successful tour of the provinces. At roughly the same age as her heroine Natalie, the author was forced to give up any idea of a singing career, having had to cancel engagements after chronic illness affected her voice. If there is a certain amount of nostalgic wish-fulfilment, in the account of Natalie's operatic successes on the London stage, Edwards here describes a world she knows first-hand.

While stripping away illusions of glamour from the musical profession, the novel all the same acknowledges the musicians' love for, and dedication to, their art. The portrayal of Natalie's benefactor Keith Vaughan takes us beyond the conventional stereotype of the starving musician, to show us a man of strong tastes and convictions, and who cares for nurturing Natalie's talent as well as his own.[7] There is, too, an element of pathos in what *The Ladder of Life* has to say about the transient nature of the fame, of even a great musical performer. In an age before recording technology, the singer's reputation is 'but the echo of a sound', that 'dies away after a few seasons, and is utterly forgotten'. The fame of a musician 'is ever fugitive; and an opera reputation is the most fugitive of all'.[8]

As in earlier fiction, in *The Ladder of Life* Edwards once again shows her talent for capturing physical traits and mannerisms in a telling phrase. A man's head in a high collar seen from behind, resembles 'an egg in an egg-cup'. A suitor in a state of acute embarrassment, as he tries to pluck up courage to declare his love to a young woman, absent-mindedly twists the button off one of his gloves, and backs his chair into the fireplace.[9] Edwards' fiction now begins to explore unusual psychological states – particularly of male characters – in ways that bring a new depth and realism to her work. In the violinist Romani, who develops an obsession with Natalie, becoming convinced that she is destined to be his soulmate – she offers a compelling portrait of a sexually obsessed stalker before the term was invented. 'It was a mind that preyed upon itself', Natalie tells us; 'and he knew it'. Like many people with an obsession, Romani entertains the fixed notion that his infatuation with the young woman is predestined: 'My soul is prophetic, and has long foretold me of you. It is our fate, Natalie. It is our fate!'[10] He will not settle for the mere friendship the young woman tries to offer. Romani's grandiosity, his obsession with control of the object of his desire, are both apparent when, on visiting Natalie, he finds a perceived rival there before him: 'Leave the room! . . . This lady shall receive no visitors but such as are welcome to me.' Yet, Natalie insists, she does not think Romani insane: 'I honestly believed that his brain was only touched in a slight degree from excitement and over-study.'[11]

Edwards well understands the mechanism of projection whereby Natalie's resistance to Romani's overtures makes her, in his eyes, a persecutor rather than a victim: 'Natalie, you see how I love you. I believe, if you continue to treat me as you have lately treated me, I shall go mad.' Edwards appreciates, too, how the stalker's overbearing persistence can intimidate the victim and suppress her voice: 'When he spoke openly of his love, or treated me before people as his betrothed bride, I submitted in silence and terror.'[12]

Made ill by Romani's unwanted attentions, Natalie goes to the countryside to get away from him. Ruled by his obsession, however, he traces her even there, and tries to abduct her, before her friends sound the alarm, and rush to her rescue.

In the new element of psychological realism in this novel, in its careful depiction of obsessive behaviour and the impulses that drive it, we see Edwards working towards a greater maturity and complexity – elements that are apparent, too, in *Hand and Glove* (1858), the work that follows *The Ladder of Life*.

Amelia's cousin Matilda, who had many social connections in Germany, one day heard the story of an incident that took place in Frankfurt, at some time in the early 1850s. It concerned, as Matilda tells it, 'an elderly English clergyman, of noble presence and most winning manners', who was raising funds for a campaign in Jerusalem, to convert the city's residents to Christianity. This minister, who carried with him 'the very best credentials', was a charismatic preacher. When he made his appeal for the allegedly benighted souls of the Holy Land, 'Women wept, men were shaken by emotion, and gold pieces rattled into the collector's plate like hailstones.' 'Dr J.' became the idol of Frankfurt society – welcomed into people's homes and known for giving lavish gifts to his adoring host families. Women in particular, 'from the titled dame to the washerwoman', were completely infatuated with this irresistible clergyman. While some were a little dubious about a certain perceived worldliness and love of display in this otherwise 'gifted and godly' man, even his critics made allowances. Then, all of a sudden, the adored minister left Frankfurt in a great hurry – having squandered all the funds entrusted to him for the salvation of the heathen. In 1864, Matilda Edwards was to write a novel, *Dr Jacob*, based on this anecdote.[13]

Did Amelia Edwards know of the story, too? While it is unclear when exactly the tale was circulating in Frankfurt, or when Matilda came to hear of it, it does bear intriguing similarities to some of the events in Amelia Edwards' *Hand and Glove*, published five years before *Dr Jacob*, in 1859.[14]

Alexis Hamel arrives unexpectedly in the town of Chalons one day, to serve as Protestant minister for the little nearby community of Montrocher. He is, like Dr J. of Frankfurt, a charismatic figure with pretensions to piety, and far from being all that he seems.

Hamel is a vividly realized character, full of contradictions and complexities. He has hardly begun his ministry, when all kinds of wild rumours about him start to circulate. He is said to be a closet Jesuit. Or he is an ex-actor – a Spaniard, or a Creole. He is a disguised nobleman, fallen on hard times; a man disappointed in love; a former Italian revolutionary; or simply a man burdened with dark secrets. He dresses elegantly, but showily – inappropriately, murmur his few critics – unsuitably for a humble man of the cloth. He owns and races expensive horses, has a luxurious apartment in Chalons, plays cards for large sums, and keeps seemingly rather dubious company. But the people of Montrocher lead a mundane, not to say, boring existence; on the whole they are delighted to welcome Hamel into their homes to brighten up their lives. His lively, engaging ways, his knowledge of the world, his perfect manners, and his wit, make him a welcome guest almost everywhere.

The community's fascination with Hamel begins with his very first appearance in the pulpit, and his impassioned delivery of a controversial sermon, based on the Gospel text, 'I come not to send peace, but a sword'. A history of all the bloodshed in the name of Christianity, the sermon concludes that the supposed religion of peace has 'destroyed much, and it has reaped little', except for cruelty and violence. 'Despair all ye who follow this religion of peace, and salvation, and divine tenderness!' Hamel tells his hearers; for 'Where there is salvation for one, and perdition for ten thousand, there is woe for all!' A most peculiar sermon to be delivered from an orthodox Protestant pulpit; a thoroughly heretical, not to say, cynical, address. One may think that if the preacher's provincial Synod had ever come to hear of the sermon, it might have cost Hamel his job. As it is, the congregation are too enraptured by the preacher's style of delivery, to take much note of the sermon's actual content. They weep and break out in sweat, carried away by the flood of passionate rhetoric. With the exception of a few who dislike the rhetorical effects and would have preferred what they call a 'plain sermon', most people are mindlessly swept away by a wave of collective emotion. 'I feel just as if I had spent the morning . . . at the Comédie Française', one worshipper says.[15]

Among those who fall completely under Hamel's spell, is Marguerite, a lively but naive young woman from a local landowning family, who is engaged to marry her cousin. The attraction between herself and Hamel is mutual from the start. As Marguerite sits in the church looking at Hamel before he starts to preach, his gaze dwells intently upon her, making her intensely self-conscious. Edwards captures well the complex reactions of this well-bred young woman. She blushes; then feels the impulse, that she struggles to repress, to respond to his attention with 'the faintest trembling of a smile', at this older man in the gown of a clergyman who gazes at her so fixedly. At last, in confusion, she takes refuge in staring down at her prayer book.[16]

Marguerite's English governess Gartha, the narrator of *Hand and Glove*, watches helplessly as her pupil succumbs to Hamel's charm, and Marguerite becomes engaged to marry this man more than twice her age. There is little doubt that he genuinely loves her – even though, as Gartha notes, his tenderness towards her has 'something sultan-like and condescending in it'. Though many of his clever speeches to her are beyond Marguerite's comprehension, she is content to look up to him as a higher being. 'All that you say is beautiful', she tells him.[17]

As time goes on, however, darker aspects of Hamel's character emerge. Marguerite herself confesses that the longer she knows him, the less she feels able to understand him: 'There are depths in his nature to which I can never penetrate – there are moments when I almost fear him. With all his calm, he can be fierce and terrible.' Walking home late one night, she and Gartha witness Hamel pitilessly thrashing his dog. Gartha is revolted, turns 'sick and cold', on witnessing this cruelty. Marguerite weeps: 'How cruel!'

If readers imagine she will now break off her engagement in disgust, however, they are mistaken. Later, recalling the dog-whipping incident in conversation with Gartha, 'How pitiless he was', she says. But adds, 'and yet there was something fine about it, after all!' There is a sado-masochistic fascination in Marguerite's response to Hamel's cruelty, that does not bode well for a future as his wife.[18]

Not surprisingly, Marguerite's first fiancé Charles, to whom she had been betrothed since her early teens on the wishes of her family, feels a visceral dislike for Hamel. The animosity is partly a matter of temperament. If Hamel is articulate, extrovert and showy, Charles is precise in speech, reserved, even repressed, in his emotions. What he shares in common with his rival, is that he treats Marguerite as a child – in his case, one to be lectured and self-righteously instructed: 'He . . . stood looking down upon her with an air of lofty displeasure, as a proud father might look down upon a fretful child.'[19] When Marguerite fails to read a book on Roman burial customs he has given her, Charles punishes her by having her plunge her hand into a burial urn to discover its contents. The shock of finding herself clutching human ashes and charred bones, sends her into hysterics. Charles coldly justifies his behaviour – 'I meant it for a lesson' – only relenting when reproached for his unkindness by Gartha. He tears up a novel Marguerite has been lent by Hamel, self-righteously condemning the book as 'most unfit' for her to read. To Charles, his young cousin is sorely in need of 'restraint and guidance'.[20]

In Charles, Edwards gives us a perceptive study of a man who at first sight is not particularly likeable. Besides being emotionally repressed, he comes across as both intellectually snobbish, and self-righteous. It is only when he realizes that he may be about to lose Marguerite for good, that we see the deep emotional sensitivity and genuine emotion that underlie the cold exterior.

In the novel's final chapters, where Hamel is exposed and disgraced (as no doubt the reader has suspected might happen all along), there is a typical Edwards shift in attitude towards her character. Now that everyone is fully aware of his wrongdoing, and of how many people he has ruined, others show themselves capable of forgiveness towards him – even of compassion. Not least Gartha, who has been wronged more than anyone, but who regrets Hamel's tragic end, regarding him almost in the light of a fallen hero.

Over time, educated by suffering, Charles becomes more human, learning not only to feel deep love for Marguerite, but to show it to her. Social recognition of his intellectual attainments makes him less self-righteously didactic, as he becomes more secure about his place in the world. A character that at first sight appeared static and two-dimensional, over the course of the novel reveals an interesting complexity.

In general, Edwards does seem more interested in her male characters in this novel, than in her women. Some development in the character of Marguerite occurs, as she matures and grows less naive and flighty. But Gartha remains ever the wise, observant family friend; and her employer Mme Delahaye, is always the fond mother and adoring wife. It is Hamel and Charles, in *Hand and Glove,* who really hold centre stage.

A third interesting character in the novel, is that of Marguerite's Uncle Alexander. Although less fully developed than either Hamel or Charles, he too is capable of delivering surprises – and also a good deal of humorous entertainment. An uncouth, bearish man, who smokes in polite company, eats pasta with his fingers and peas with his knife, swears at the family pets, and kicks flowerpots, he is all the same far from being a fool. He is portrayed as a capable farmer and businessman, who manages his vineyard to make a profit. In comparison with others in *Hand and Glove,* many of whom conceal their true thoughts and feelings behind a mask of social politeness, Alexander is refreshingly blunt. He challenges Gartha, as to why she stays on as a governess with the Delahaye family: 'You are a dependant. You give up your country, your relations, your liberty – and all for what? For a paltry five hundred francs a year!'[21] His rough manners hide a generous heart; finding that Gartha has no warm outdoor clothing for winter, he buys her an expensive cloak. Readers will not be too surprised when, towards the novel's close, Alexander proposes marriage to Gartha, and she accepts him.

If there is a fair amount of melodrama in *Hand and Glove,* there is a good deal, too, of wit and humour. Much comedy is provided by the character of Marguerite's elderly father, the ridiculous Monsieur Delahaye:

'I will retire', said he, sentimentally. 'Polyhymnia, perchance, will prove less cruel to her votary! My talented guest, adieu'. He sighed, bowed, made an effort to see his back in the looking-glass, and took snuff with the grand air of Louis XIV. Finding that I was already sorting the bills, and quite heedless of these fascinations, he sauntered slowly to the door – paused – repeated in a mysterious whisper: 'Remember – not a word to Alexander!' – and withdrew.[22]

Edwards' next work of fiction, *Barbara's History,* which appeared in book form in 1864, marked the high point of her commercial and critical success up until then. After its first publication, the novel went through five more editions, and established Edwards' fame with the general public. Reviewers, too, were full of praise for *Barbara's History*: 'We have met with nothing of equal power or merit since the decease of Charlotte Bronte', said *Bell's Weekly Messenger*, when the work was serialized in December 1863, calling it, 'the best novel Miss Amelia B. Edwards has yet written'.

While later novels by Edwards are, in fact, arguably more original and more accomplished, *Barbara's History* is the literary work most often mentioned in connection with her reputation as a novelist. It was hailed as 'a stirring, original, and very amusing book, full of historical and topographical information, written in true and excellent English, and very rich in colour – the people in it are so wonderfully alive'. The novel's dialogues, *The Times* said, 'sparkle with repartee'.[23]

Inevitably, the critics drew comparisons with *Jane Eyre*, given that the plots of Charlotte Bronte's novel, and of *Barbara's History*, are quite similar. In both novels, we have love between a lonely, wealthy, eccentric older man, and a much younger woman. In fact, Barbara, Edwards' heroine, develops an adoring passion for her novel's anti-hero, Hugh Farquhar, in pre-adolescence. Barbara's devoted childhood friendship between herself and Hugh seems to have raised no eyebrows among Victorians but may provoke a sense of unease for a reader in the twenty-first century. (The *London Daily News*, while generally praising the novel, did remark on the child Barbara's love for a grown man as 'altogether too mature and conscious a passion for an English child of such tender years'.)[24]

As in *Jane Eyre,* the narrator and protagonist is an orphan, who is sent away from home to be fostered by relatives. Like Jane, she is later sent away again, to boarding school. And the man Barbara marries, has, like Mr Rochester, a dark secret hidden away in the old family mansion where he takes his bride to live.

Here the similarities end, however. Though Barbara has lost her mother, her coldly disapproving father is still very much alive. The great-aunt who fosters her is, if rough-spoken and eccentric, loving too; and Barbara returns her love. The school in Germany where the heroine is later sent is no penitential Lowood, but an idyllic creative centre for the arts, where Barbara makes friends, is encouraged by her tutors, and discovers and develops her talent as a painter.

Despite the superficial similarities to *Jane Eyre*, as a review in *The Spectator* noted, Edwards, by treating her story and characters with perceptive insight and originality, had made them 'thoroughly her own'.[25] Some reviewers actually preferred *Barbara's History* to *Jane Eyre*. The *Morning Post* found Edwards' novel to be free of what its reviewer termed, 'the rudeness' of *Jane Eyre*. Amelia Edwards had been properly ladylike, in her treatment of delicate topics: 'Nor has she approached subjects which are debatable ground for women's footsteps.' There was praise for her portrayal of the hero. Hugh Farquhar was 'as strong, as original, as truly living, and impressive as the black-browed gentleman who brought ugly men into fashion 15 years ago'.[26]

Like Jane Eyre, Barbara in time discovers that her beloved is already involved with another woman. Hurt and furious at his perceived unfaithfulness, she runs away from his home. Instead of wandering homeless across the moors, however, she decamps to Italy, in the company of a devoted old servant, and earns her living in Rome, by copying Old Masters for sale.

While in Rome, rather unexpectedly – since there has been no previous mention of any pregnancy – Barbara also gives birth to Hugh's baby. It is an agonizing birth, and she nearly dies while in labour; but, 'as the morning light poured in the window, a little tender blossom of life was laid in my arms.' The 'angels of life and death' have competed for the soul of the pregnant mother and her baby, and life has triumphed.[27] This is the closest we ever come in an Edwards novel, to a description of childbirth. As in all nineteenth-century novels, a great deal of the physical business of pregnancy is passed over in silence. No morning sickness, no dietary cravings; no swollen ankles, or unseemly bloating. (Edwards herself, of course – in common with many others among her fellow Victorian novelists – had no direct personal experience of giving birth, or of caring for a baby.)

Where *Barbara's History* really excels, especially in the early chapters, is in its depiction of a young child's eye-view of life – something Edwards could recall from direct experience of her own childhood. A lonely, bookish little girl, often disregarded and placed at the margins of social situations, Barbara constantly observes the adults in her world. She notes, for example, the affected mannerisms of her pretentious governess: 'Miss Whymper curtsied again, laid her head a little on one side, like a raven, and folded her hands together, as if she were expressing the letter M in the manual alphabet.'[28] Then we have Barbara's first experience of a grand dinner party, attended by all the local gentry:

> The ladies listened and chimed in; and the younger people spoke low, and flirted; the fat gentleman with the bald head took two helpings of everything; and the lady in the amber satin dress had the gravy spilt in her lap, and was so cross that she scarcely knew how to behave herself; and the clergyman at the opposite corner talked of hunting and shooting, and drank more wine than any other gentlemen at the table. All this I noticed . . .[29]

We have the child's impressions of Barbara's widowed great- aunt, Mrs Sandyshaft, a wonderful character in her own right. Outspoken, argumentative, kind at heart, devoted to her farm and her animals, she brings life to every scene she appears in. One of the best of these, between Barbara and her great-aunt, comes in the novel's early pages. Mrs Sandyshaft has accused little Barbara's father of sending his daughter to live with her, as a scheme to get hold of her money:

'He told you to cringe, and fawn, and pay court to me – to worm yourself into my favour – to profit by my death – to be a liar, a flatterer and a beggar! And why?

Because I am rich! Oh, yes! because I am rich!'

I sat as if stricken into stone; but half comprehending what she meant, and unable to answer a syllable.

Sternly, the aunt warns Barbara not to lie to her – implying that her great-niece might be in league with her father to gain control of Mrs Sandyshaft's fortune. For Barbara, this last accusation is too much:

My heart swelled within me – I shook from head to foot – I tried to speak, and the words seemed to choke me. 'I don't want!' I cried, passionately. 'I – I am not mean! I have told no lies – not one! . . .' Flushed and trembling in my childish anger, I sprang from my chair and stood before her, face to face . . . 'How dare you speak so of Papa . . .' [I] burst into an agony of sobs.

Contrite, moved by the child's obvious sincerity, Barbara's aunt takes the child into her arms. 'My anger was gone in a moment', Barbara tells us: 'Too deeply moved to answer her in words, I only clung the closer, and tried to still my sobs. She understood me. "Come", said she, after a few seconds of silence. "Let's go and see the pigs".'[30]

The unspoken bond created between the older woman and the child in this moment, is powerfully suggested in the 'few seconds of silence' that follow the angry words, more effectively than any more elaborate description could do.

As Barbara grows up, we continue to see the world through her eyes, and from a distinctly feminine perspective. Sometimes, it is no more than a tiny, but telling, observation, as when Barbara describes a pompous doctor visiting her bedridden sister: 'He closed the snuff-box with a click, glanced again at his watch, patted Hilda patronizingly on the head, and rose to take his leave.' For this self-important medical man, time is money, the incident suggests; but also, in the head-patting, how he feels his own superiority over his female patient. It is a detail a woman would be most likely to observe.[31]

In her descriptions of other women, Edwards can be cutting. Most often, her satire is directed at those who unthinkingly uphold the conventions of 'good' society. When Barbara's father decides to remarry, his daughter is none too impressed with his choice:

Mrs Churchill was what is generally called a fine woman. That is to say, she was large, well defined and of a comely presence . . . Her hands were small, her teeth admirable, her complexion well-preserved, and her taste in dress unexceptionable . . . She spoke seldom, always slowly, and never unless she really had something to say. That something, if clever, was not original; and if original, was not clever; but it was invariably judicious, and, like a paper currency, represented a value which was not intrinsic. Above all, she had studied the art of silence, and knew how to maintain a dignified repose ...

Mrs Churchill tries to discourage Barbara's artistic ambitions, telling her stepdaughter, 'I have heard that oils are sometimes bad for the chest'. (One of the arguments with which her family apparently discouraged the young Amelia Edwards from pursuing a career as a painter.) To which Barbara responds with spirit: 'Artists do not die so easily. When they love art, they have the good sense to live for it.'[32]

Barbara's History contains a number of images of female solidarity. The female art students at the German academy where Barbara and her sister are sent to study, help one another in preparation for their final assessment, almost to the point of cheating; so that one young woman, said to have no talent whatever, ends up winning a third-class medal. Then there is the faithful old servant who leaves her contented retirement in the English countryside to travel with Barbara to Rome; and Barbara's great-aunt Sandyshaft, who journeys across Europe to find her, even though she hates what she calls 'uncivilized' foreign countries.[33]

On the basis of *Barbara's History*, *The Athenaeum* accurately predicted Edwards' future celebrity; suggesting that if she went on writing books of such merit, she would, 'on some bright day of a lucky season wake up and find herself famous'.

With her next important novel, *Half a Million of Money* (1865/66), Edwards as a novelist really comes into her own.[34] She has paid her dues to the melodramatic fictional conventions of her day, winning a broad readership in the process. Now she branches out, writing about subjects and ideas of interest to herself. She broadens her scope well beyond the conventional romantic novel – bringing in themes of political commitment, and the price paid for idealism; attitudes to wealth and its potential for doing good; financial fraud, and the education of a gullible innocent. The choice to tell the story from the viewpoint of male characters, enables Edwards to describe nautical adventures and battle scenes, while also allowing some of the action to a heroic woman.

This is a highly original work. While it owes something in places to the romantic novel and depicts scenes that would not be out of place in a work by Trollope, at other times it takes the reader into worlds that few, if any, female Victorian novelists ventured to describe. *Half a Million* takes us from the drawing room of an English country house and the fashionable streets of London, on a dangerous secret voyage across the Mediterranean to the field of battle in Sicily, where the novel's main characters join Garibaldi in the fight for Italian independence. The event that sets all this in motion, takes place far away from such momentous historic events, in the sheltered, idyllic world of a remote Swiss alpine village. Here, Saxon Trefalden, a Swiss national of English descent, suddenly becomes heir to a vast fortune. By the somewhat peculiar terms of the bequest, Saxon alone inherits nearly everything. His cousin William, a lawyer, who is some years older than Saxon, receives nothing.

The innocent Saxon, who entertains nothing but goodwill to all the world, is unaware that, behind a facade of seeming helpfulness, William Trefalden has become the younger man's implacable enemy, determined to strip Saxon of his fortune. He also turns out to be robbing Saxon's friend Lord Castletown, by embezzling sums entrusted to him for paying off the mortgage on Castletown's debt-encumbered property.

Another strand in a fairly complicated story, concerns Giulio and Olimpia Colonna, father and daughter, fanatical republicans committed to the cause of freeing Italy from foreign domination. Devoting all their time, energy, money and peace of mind to the cause, they expect others to do the same. For the sake of Italy, Giulio 'would strip the coat from off his neighbour's back'.[35] He is quite ready to sacrifice his daughter's happiness by having her marry Saxon, whom she does not love, in order to gain access to his fortune. Olimpia, equally obsessed with the Italian cause, reluctantly agrees to throw herself at the wealthy young heir, even though secretly she dreams of marrying Lord Castletown. 'She believed that although it would be morally wrong to do these things for any other end, it would be practically right to do them for Italy.' Edwards' own view of Olimpia's intended sacrifice is made clear in the words of another of her characters. 'Virtues carried to excess become vices', says Castletown.[36]

In Olimpia, Edwards gives us a female character who is intelligent, resourceful and courageous. 'With 'a ring of authority' in her voice, she saves her injured father under fire, as he escapes from the battlefield.[37] She is certainly a more interesting character than the other, more conventional, heroine of *Half a Million,* Helen Rivière, for whom the Trefalden cousins become rivals in love. Many of Edwards' young heroines, it must be said, are equally vapid – Margaret, in *My Brother's Wife,* being another case in point. However, there is more diversity in Edwards' portrayal of women, than is sometimes acknowledged. Barbara, of *Barbara's History,* is a spirited, independent character; and so is her great-aunt Sandyshaft. In later novels, we will meet a professional poet, who continues to work and publish after her marriage (Hortense in *In the Days of My Life*); and a harassed, hard-working professional novelist (Mrs Pennefeather, in *Lord Brackenbury*).

To come back to *Half a Million* and the story of Saxon Trefalden and the Colonnas, the passages dealing with the Italian war for independence form one of the strengths of the novel. The battle scenes in southern Italy are simply, dramatically narrated, and utterly credible. We might recall that Edwards was a soldier's daughter. She neither glamorizes nor sanitizes what she describes, as she tells of hand-to-hand street fighting, of homes reduced to rubble, of corpses lying unburied in the streets, of nuns burned alive in their convent during a bombardment.[38] These scenes of carnage are contrasted with the festive atmosphere of a nearby street where, to Saxon's disgust, café-going civilians are noisily enjoying themselves.

By way of contrast, *Half a Million* contains a number of Edwards' lyrical evocations of place. She depicts nightfall in the countryside near Palermo, where Saxon and his friends have stopped to rest for the night: 'the magical dusk of an early autumn evening in south Italy, when the earth is folded to rest in a deep and tender gloom which scarcely seems like night, and the grass is alight with glow-worms, and the air kindling with fireflies, and the sky one vast mosaic of stars'. She gives us dawn over the sleeping volcano:

> The moon had paled and sunk long since, and the great mountain towered, ghost-like, with its crown of snow and smoke, high up against the cold grey of the sky. Presently the light in the east grew brighter and wider, and a strange, glorious colour – a colour compounded, as it were, of rose and gold – flushed suddenly over the snow-fields of Etna.[39]

This is Edwards' most mature and accomplished fictional work to date. Adoption of an omniscient third-person perspective, instead of a narrative tied to the personality of a single narrator, seems to free her authorial voice, and lend it confidence. There is a new lightness and liveliness in the telling.

An element of humorous irony, that appeared in occasional scenes in *Barbara's History*, here pervades the work as a whole. A clerk spying on his employer, secures an important piece of evidence – the employer's carefully concealed home address – by employing a private detective:

> 'Well sir, if the address is all you require – here it is'.
> The steely light so rarely seen there, flashed into Abel Keckwitch's eyes, and his hand closed on the paper as if it had been a living thing trying to fly away. He did not even look at it, but imprisoned it at once in a plethoric pocket-book with a massive metal clasp that snapped like a handcuff.

In another incident, a mediocre contemporary painting of 'Apollo and Daphne' has the erotically frustrated Apollo, 'in an attitude expressive of despair. Looking very like a fine gentleman in an amateur play, elegantly got up in the Greek style and rather proud of his legs'.[40]

Edwards gives full rein to her love of satire – for example, in the novel's comments on the fraudster William Trefalden. In his attitudes to his love affairs, she tells us, Trefalden 'had previously thought of women, as like horses, to be kindly treated, but to be held or changed at the pleasure of their owners'.[41] When, having robbed at least two people of their fortunes, he decides to become an honest man, we are told:

> Trefalden liked a clean conscience as he liked a clean shirt, because it was both comfortable and gentlemanly, and suited his notions of refinement.

So he fully intended to sin no more, but to cultivate all manner of public and private virtues and die at last in the odour of popularity.[42]

Edwards here captures the hypocrisy that is the hallmark of William's character. Like the clean shirt, the conscience must be 'gentlemanly' – in other words, socially acceptable. There is no thought of making restitution for his ill-gotten gains, so long as others think well of him. In the conventional phrase, 'odour of sanctity', the word 'popularity' is substituted. Public appearance is everything.

Toward snobbishness and triviality, Edwards is unforgiving. One target of her satire, in this regard is the haughty Lady Arabella Walkingshaw, 'one of that large majority who regard poverty as a crime'. Another target is the Eshers, who refuse to donate to the cause of Italian independence, because they view liberty as 'a vulgar institution', and 'patriots in general as doubtful characters'.[43] Then there is the case of Lord Castletown's mother. When Giulio Colonna and his republican comrades are frantically packing to rush back to Italy and join Garibaldi in the struggle, Lady Castletown is more concerned with the effect their departure will have on the dinner party she has planned:

It was nothing to her that Garibaldi had won a great battle . . . and was marching fast upon Palermo. She only knew that the Walkingshaws and Miss Hatherton were coming to dine, that Signor Montecuculi would make one too many at the table, and that the departure of her guests straight after dinner would spoil the evening.[44]

An alternative title for *Half a Million* could well have been, 'Paying the Price'. The novel is much preoccupied both with ethical dilemmas, and with the cost to individuals of their painful life experience, their ideals; and, at times, their bad decisions.

The central character is a case in point. Brought from his Alpine fastness, where ethical values, like the daily lives of the peasants, are stark and simple – plunged into the hectic round of English upper-class society, Saxon Trefalden has much to learn. Newly deluged with sudden wealth, he is at first delighted to be surrounded by so many new friends, all with ideas on how to help him spend his money. He must, he is assured, buy horses; gamble in exclusive clubs; acquire expensive London lodgings, where his friends can come to enjoy themselves; make loans to the allegedly needy, and grants to the supposedly deserving. Saxon is surprised to find how quickly his new fortune starts melting away. At this point, he begins nostalgically to compare the Swiss idyll he has left behind, with the false values, as he sees them, of English society: 'The world over here thinks a vast deal more of politeness than justice. It's not so in Switzerland.'[45] Given Saxon's naiveté regarding those who are out to fleece him in England, we may wonder whether he also entertains an overly idealized view of his homeland? But it is Saxon's innocent and growingly perceptive view of false values in England that compels our attention.

For Saxon personally, a greater threat than the rakes and spendthrifts – although Saxon for a long while fails to recognize the fact – lies in wait for him in the form of his conniving cousin. William offers to rescue Saxon from his own improvidence, by helping the young man to manage his finances. He is quite incapable of suspecting the cousin whom he loves and trusts: 'Saxon looked earnestly in his cousin's face. He fancied that no man could look another in the face and tell a lie.' Though, as the narrator tells us, the focused gaze into the other's eyes is precisely the most effective technique of a practiced liar, 'Saxon would not have believed this had an angel told him so.'[46]

When he finally wakes up to his cousin's duplicity – which involves not only his own potential losses, but those of a genuine friend, and of a young woman for whom he feels a protective affection – Saxon is implacable. The friendly, easy-going soul who parted with his money to anyone who asked, is no more. He will pursue his cousin to the end and force him to make good nearly every stolen penny. (He offers to allow William to keep a token amount – an offer the cousin contemptuously refuses.) Saxon's simplicity has very nearly cost him everything. A wiser man, thanks to painful experience, he is able to pull back from the brink just in time.

The same cannot be said of others in *Half a Million*. Giulio Colonna loses his life to a Neapolitan bullet, and Olimpia loses her father. After all the suffering and sacrifice, the goal they struggled for, of a republican Italy, is not fully achieved after all. Italy, although independent of foreign rule, becomes a monarchy.

The change in Olimpia after her father's death, as Edwards describes it, is a credible one, as she moves from grief and depression to a sad resignation, knowing that her republican dream has failed. She settles for marriage with Lord Castletown, who is busy involving himself in his own brand of – far less radical – British politics. There is no ideal resolution here – no conventional 'happy ending'. To the end of her days, Olimpia will go on 'mourning the great scheme unachieved', and 'learning that hard lesson of patience which all enthusiasts have to learn in this world, sooner or later'.[47]

Cousin William, who has swindled everyone, pays perhaps the heaviest price, losing his money, his (undeserved) good name, the respect and companionship of the only woman he ever genuinely loved – and finally, his life. As in *Hand and Glove*, there is compassion for the wrongdoer when in defeat. William Trefalden, deprived of everything he valued, becomes an object of pathos:

> Then he pressed his face against the bars [of the château fence] like a prisoner at the prison gate, and, sobbing, called upon her name. But his voice was borne away by the wind, and the pitiless rain drove in his face and mingled with his tears. [48]

This is in keeping with Edwards' view that – as for example in the works of Thackeray, whom she greatly admired – the novelist should show wrongdoing as meeting with fit punishment, but without disregarding the humanity of the doer.[49]

The final disillusionment in *Half a Million* concerns what the narrator tells us of the fate of the remaining sum from the original Trefalden inheritance – a portion of money not bequeathed to Saxon but set aside for the founding of a refuge for the poor and needy. Here, Edwards appears at her most satiric, and most cynical (or maybe simply most realistic). Why, she asks, has the noble project of the refuge not come to fruition yet? We need to give it more time:

> No intelligent and unprejudiced person can doubt, of course, that when the ground is bought, and the building is built, and the bills are all paid, and the dinners are all eaten, and the resident curator, clergyman, physician, secretary, housekeeper, and servants of the establishment are salaried on a scale befitting the splendour of the foundation, there will be something left to give to those insignificant persons, the intended beneficiaries.[50]

There were six editions of *Half a Million* in book form, brought out by different publishers, including a translation into French, as *L'Héritage de Jacob Trefalden*.[51] The novel was popular in America, where it was serialized in *Harper's Weekly*.

Reviewers made a few strange objections to the novel. For one thing, in the *Illustrated News*, Saxon Trefalden was said to 'parade his money on all occasions', which was thought 'indelicate' of him. In fact, Saxon's constant talk about his new-found wealth is shown to be, not because he wishes to boast, but because he is dazzled and confused by it, and constantly seeking advice on how to spend it. (The *Illustrated News* reviewer did, however, concede that *Half a Million* contained 'well-delivered, and well-deserved satire'.)

Another odd criticism was that Saxon is seen to do very little with his money. He actually is described as doing quite a lot, even if the activity is confined to his home village. He builds a road and a bridge over a dangerous river crossing. He commissions a new church for the village, establishes a cotton mill, breeds pedigree cattle – and is said to lead a 'busy and benevolent' existence, that makes a few Swiss peasants happier. We are being asked, no doubt, to contrast these modest achievements with the fraudulent greed of William Tredalden, or even the Colonnas' idealistic, but grandiose, dreams of revolution. Or the bureaucracy and opportunism that in England eats up the funds set aside to create a refuge for the poor.

In spite of a few criticisms, on the whole *Half a Million* received praise. The *London Evening Standard* praised Edwards' skill in developing a fictional plot within a framework of historical events, and her scenes of the war in Italy. In spite of 'some extravagances', *Half a Million* was said to be 'one of the pleasantest novels of the season', and 'full of clever, incisive sayings'.[52]

In 1869, Robert Browning started to take an interest in Edwards' work. He knew her personally but had until then been indifferent concerning her writing. 'Tell me something', he wrote that April to a friend, 'what has Miss Amelia Edwards written – novels or what? I know her and like her – but don't go to the extent of reading what you can tell me about'. Two years later, when he actually had read her new novel, *Debenham's Vow* (1869), he wrote to Edwards herself, praising what he called, 'your bright and beautiful story'.[53] Surprising adjectives to describe the work – for while scenes in the early chapters contain much that is indeed bright and amusing, taken as a whole this novel is surely the most sombre Edwards ever wrote.

The central character, Temple Debenham, while his doings as a man of action are constantly interesting, is, it must be admitted, often hard to like. He does have admirable traits – his resourcefulness, his driving energy and commitment to whatever he undertakes – his chivalry, too, to anyone who appears vulnerable or at his mercy. In his obsessive urge to undertake a project and follow it through, his portrait seems in many ways characteristic of the famous entrepreneurs of the Victorian age – Cunard, Bazalgette, Brunel. In this last-mentioned trait he could also be seen as a projection of Edwards herself, in her own unrelenting drive to make a success of her life and her projects, regardless of the cost to herself. At times, though, he comes across as disagreeably cold-blooded and arrogant.

Raised in poverty by his widowed mother, Debenham, who shows great promise as a pianist and composer, at first aspires to make a name for himself as a musician. Offered a professorship at his music academy in Germany, however, he considers that academic world too narrow for him. He must have 'a wider berth – more breathing space – some footing in that field where the race was really to the swift and the battle to the strong'.[54]

Returning to his native England to seek his fortune there, Debenham is disappointed to find himself confined to the role of an obscure church organist and music teacher. (Shades here, perhaps, of Edwards' own disappointments, in her early pursuit of a musical career?) He becomes bitter at the life of penury and obscurity, and contemptuous of the rest of the world in proportion to his disillusionment. When a friend arranges for him to perform for the guests at a wealthy London home, feeling snubbed by everyone from his hosts to the footmen, Debenham takes perverse revenge on them all by playing an obscure and difficult piece he knows will bore and alienate his audience.

On a walking holiday with the same friend, he meets, and falls deeply in love with, Juliet Alleyne, daughter of a society painter. It looks at this point, as if Miss Alleyne and Temple Debenham will quickly become engaged, following the conventional course of most Victorian novels, from romance into matrimony. The author, however, surprises us. Before his holiday is over, Debenham, and the reader, have been turned from this normally predictable outcome in romantic fiction, by an unsettling discovery. He comes upon the ancestral estate of the De Benhams, his forebears – now inherited by strangers, and largely gone to ruin – but still with the remains of a Norman castle, and a church where his illustrious ancestors lie buried. Inspired by a vision of returning his dynasty to its former glory; of not only claiming his aristocratic title, but of amassing a fortune to buy back and rebuild the ruined estate, Debenham becomes focused on this single goal, to the exclusion of everything else.

In case readers might find Debenham's obsession implausible, Edwards reminds us of 'the point from which Warren Hastings started as a boy' – namely the rise of Hastings from poverty and obscurity to eminence as de facto governor-general of India (and later privy counsellor), in a bid to restore his family's ancestral fortune and renown. We may also recall what we know of Edwards' own fascination with genealogy – in particular, with her maternal family connections to the illustrious Walpoles.

Convinced that restoring the family fortunes is his vocation and his duty, Debenham launches into a headlong pursuit of wealth, at any cost, in order to realize his dream. The quest begins to change him: 'A strange, hard look had settled on his mouth; when he smiled, it seemed less like an impulse than a deliberate effort of the will.' He feels the effort required to realize his ambition is ageing him. Yet, having 'taken up with the hardest of hard realities', he is resolved 'to pay the price, come in what form it might'.[55]

In his preoccupation with his new goal, Debenham gradually neglects, and then forgets all about, Juliet Alleyne – telling himself that he is a slave of necessity, of the imperatives of commercial business. It never occurs to him, as the narrator observes, that 'the stern necessity' he invokes, is entirely of his own making: 'He had no idea that he was ruled by a passion stronger than love.'[56] Edwards is too good a novelist to preach a moral here, on the ambiguous ethical choices in which Debenham's obsession involves him. She tells his story and allows readers to judge for themselves.

After he fulfils a commission from a London merchant, to rescue a grounded ship and its cargo from the southern Italian coast, Debenham has gained the merchant's confidence enough to propose a venture of his own. We are in the early 1860s, when the Union forces of the Northern United States were blockading the ports of the slave-holding Southern states, to force a Confederate defeat and bring the rebels back under the US flag. Debenham spots a commercial opportunity. He will charter a ship and, dodging the blockading Union warships, sail into Charleston harbour, there to buy bales of cotton at knock-down prices, for sale back in Britain. With the shortage of cotton imports from America pushing prices ever higher, the profits will be enormous.

Although she claimed to dislike historical novels, which she said were built 'upon radically unsound foundations', Edwards may have been thinking less of her own depictions of recent events – like the Italian war of independence – than of works like Bulwer Lytton's *The Last Days of Pompeii*, that dealt with periods in the distant past, where an author could only speculate about characters' thoughts and actions, always unsure of how credibly they represented a long-vanished world.[57] Now, in *Debenham's Vow*, she sets out to depict a piece of very recent history – the world of the American Civil War, that ended only three years before the publication of her novel. And she sets her main character down squarely in the centre of the action.

Although quite prepared to flout the Union blockade, Debenham still regards himself as a wartime neutral – even though his sanctions-breaking will benefit the slave-owners economically and contribute to prolonging the war. He tells himself that if he never gets drawn into taking up arms for the Confederate rebels, his hands remain clean: 'On the side of slavery we may not, and will not, fight.' All the same, his blockade-running ship carries munitions to Charleston, for sale to the Confederate army.[58]

Debenham further justifies his actions by claiming to be concerned for the mill workers of northern England, deprived of supplies of raw cotton, 'for want of which so many millions of workers must be thrown out of employment'.[59] Yet Debenham's compassion for the laid-off workers does not stop him hoarding his supplies of bootleg cotton, while he waits for its price in England to rise. 'A time must come, he argued, when there would be absolutely no American cotton in the market; and if prices were so high now . . . what would they be then?'[60]

Whether Edwards was aware of the desperate suffering of the English mill workers during the blockade, and the principled stand taken by a few of them in supporting a boycott of the imported American cotton, is unknown. Certainly, with typical thoroughness, she researched minute details of the shipping business in general, and of the cotton trade in particular, to write the blockade-running chapters of *Debenham's Vow*; even down to the weight of the average American cotton bale (480 lbs); the steadily rising price of cotton in the port of Liverpool in the first years of the American Civil War; the names of the beacons in Charleston Harbour – and the specifications for adapting a merchant steamer to the role of a camouflaged blockade-runner carrying contraband:

Her boats are lowered to the level of the gunwales. Her funnel, of the 'telescope' kind, lies low and raking aft. And her hull is painted of a dull, bluish, sea-green hue, which even by daylight is scarcely distinguishable from that of the waves . . . The *Stormy Petrel* . . . burns only anthracite coal, which yields neither smoke nor sparks; and her engines are so constructed that, in case of a sudden stop, the steam can be blown off noiselessly under water.[61]

The scenes of dramatic action in which Debenham and his ship evade the Union warships at the Southern harbour entrances, slipping across from the

Bahamas under cover of darkness, and making their way back with their valuable cargo, have often been justly praised. Equally dramatic and compelling, are the account of the fierce struggle on shipboard, between Debenham's men and the Union coastguard, for control of the vessel, and of the slow building of a storm that at one moment threatens to overwhelm the ship:

> At this moment a tremendous squall – swift, shrill, howling a wild war-whoop that seemed to cut the other thunders like a knife – hurled itself upon them from the North-West. The seas, checked in their running by this sudden shift of wind, struck the *Stormy Petrel* on her port quarter and broke over her decks … The good boat heeled over – a shriek of terror broke from the lips of all on board – and Archie and De Benham found themselves rolling together in the lee scuppers, drenched and breathless and half stunned.[62]

Returning home after his blockade-running adventures – after a fight with the Union coastguards in which he was injured, followed by a long bout of fever – Debenham is bewildered to discover he has suddenly become a public hero. Edwards takes this opportunity for a brief satiric riff on the unhappy fate of a media celebrity:

> What more could a sensation-loving public desire, except to persecute its hero with dinners and speeches … to waylay him on staircases; pin him up in corners of drawing-rooms; pester him for biographical materials for his autograph, his photograph, his monogram, and everything that was his, and lionise him within an inch of his life?

Debenham, who both disdains and shuns publicity, now finds himself under constant social scrutiny. When he walks into a drawing room, people are already gossiping about him, and his ordeal at sea:

> 'Raving in delirium!' echoed the lady in tulle, with infinite relish. 'Dear me, how dreadful!' … She indulged in a long stare at Debenham through her eyeglass.[63]

However questionable his means of acquiring wealth, Debenham's dream is not without its idealistic side. Like several of Edwards' characters, he cherishes a paternalistic vision of improving lives on a country estate: 'to pull down those miserable hovels, to build, to drain, to plant, to establish schools, to pay good wages, to make people healthy and happy!'[64] But his plans encounter a snag: he discovers that, even with the new wealth he has amassed through smuggling, he still cannot afford to pay the asking price for the former De Benham estate, or to rebuild the tumbledown ruin-cum-farmhouse that was once the De Benham castle.

After long indecision, Debenham makes a fateful personal choice. He thinks of Claudia Hardwicke, a snobbishly aloof woman, with 'about as much heart as a cricket ball', sister of the venture capitalist who backed his cotton trading enterprise. Debenham feels no love for Claudia. He admires her, 'as he might admire a fine statue'.[65] But he suspects that she yearns to have an aristocratic title, to add to her inherited mercantile fortune. A marriage of convenience, in which Claudia would make her wealth available to Debenham, in return for being called Lady De Benham would, he considers, be 'a fair bargain'. This proposed loveless trading of rank for money, is Debenham believes, 'one of mere self-sacrifice', entailing 'no kind of injustice towards anyone but himself'.[66]

About to propose marriage to Claudia, he steels himself with a quotation from Shakespeare: 'If 'twere well 'twere done ... then 'twere well it were done quickly.' Ominously, the words are those spoken by Macbeth, just before he goes to murder Duncan. Debenham makes the proposal without meeting Claudia's eye, all the while 'looking into his hat, as if the words were written there and he was reading them'.[67]

The engagement leads to a rift between Debenham and his closest friend, Archie. 'It was a part of the price he had to pay', Debenham tells himself. 'First his art; then his love; then his freedom; now his friend. What more had he to resign – except his life?'[68]

The novel's last pages vividly evoke the nightmare-like state in which Debenham goes through the wedding ceremony. As the newly-weds sign the parish register afterwards, the sight of Claudia's signature 'close against his own, with the ink yet wet upon both', causes him to start – as if he has only just registered the implications of the act. It now seems to him as if a bridge that linked him to everything in his past has 'suddenly given way, and crashed into the abyss behind him'. When his new bride is addressed by others as 'Lady Benham', the title 'jars unpleasantly upon his ear'. When, with a simulated affection he does not feel, he kisses her arm as they travel alone together to the wedding reception, he realizes that she feels he has 'taken a liberty'. On the honeymoon journey by train to Paris, the couple struggle for a while with banal small talk. 'And then they both gazed out of the window in silence.'[69]

'If she cared for me, it would be another matter', Debenham reflects, after his new wife coldly assents to his mother coming to join them on their honeymoon. Particularly ironic, is that Claudia *has* begun to care for her new husband, having nursed him safely through a sudden crisis, after the stab wound he received in the battle on shipboard re-opened, putting his life in danger.[70] Claudia's pride will not allow her to tell him that she wants to be alone with her husband, without the unwelcome company of her mother-in-law. When the mother does arrive and takes over care of her still-convalescent son, the wife suddenly finds herself shouldered aside, and surplus to requirements.

If Claudia is disappointed in her marriage, Debenham himself firmly rejects his mother's 'Love-comes-after-marriage' argument – that esteem between the couple will become love in the course of their journey through life: 'My journey', he said, 'lies through a desert.' In closing her tale of ambition, compromise, sacrifice and disillusionment, Edwards, as narrator, has the final word: 'To those whom the Gods chastise, they grant the desires of their hearts.'[71]

Debenham's Vow is the bleakest of Edward's novels – and, before the work of Thomas Hardy, possibly the bleakest in all Victorian fiction. Dickens, famously, bowed to his readers' demand to change the ending of *Great Expectations*, reluctantly allowing the hero Pip to find romantic happiness with his Estella. Regarding her own pessimistic ending, Edwards refuses to compromise. She knows many readers will find it, as she says, 'unsatisfactory'. They demand that 'the heroes and heroines of romance should either die or be happy'. Life itself, however, she replies, '*is* unsatisfactory'. Most human beings in their lives experience both happiness and pain, and sometimes more of the latter. 'Prosperity is not all success; conquest is not all triumph; love is seldom an unmixed joy or an unqualified evil.'[72] In short, she calls on her readers to grow up – to accept a mature vision of life in place of rose-tinted fables.

One person who apparently understood what Edwards was doing in *Debenham's Vow*, was Browning. In spite of his 'bright and beautiful story' remark, he wrote appreciatively of the novel's ending. While he thought the blockade-running chapters 'capitally done', he most liked what he called 'the delicater touches of the last volume'. He liked 'the abrupt ending too'.[73]

Anthony Trollope wrote personally to Edwards to praise *Debenham's Vow*: 'The character of Debenham', he wrote, 'is admirably kept up, and, as you no doubt intended, the pearl of the book'. He found the scenes set in America to be 'excellent . . . full of life'. He thought 'the only fault of the story – for there always is a fault – is the want of sympathy with Debenham'.[74]

Trollope was not the only reader to find the character of Debenham unlikeable. The *Examiner* called him 'the most improbable, un-lifelike hero – proud, priggish, selfish and disagreeable'. The reviewer for the *Pall Mall Gazette* found it hard to believe 'that this brilliant, dedicated musician, in love with a good woman', could become, by 'the paltry accident' of discovering his ancestry, 'so changed for the worse in one hour'. (In fact, the change is well prepared for, in the novel's account of Debenham's impoverished childhood, and the social humiliations he suffers as a young adult. The steady growth of his obsession is shown taking place gradually, not in a single hour, but over many chapters.) The *Northwich Guardian*, on the other hand, admired the portrayal of the novel's characters. The reviewer thought them sympathetically and vividly drawn and admired the naturalness of the dialogue. Like the *Pall Mall Gazette*, and *The Examiner*, this review praised the 'rare dramatic power' of the blockade-running scenes. Another reviewer was impressed by the accurate nautical and other technical knowledge displayed in *Debenham's Vow*: if not 'assisted professionally' in some of her descriptions, Edwards was 'a remarkable instance of female proficiency in masculine studies'. In the nautical episodes in particular, she was found to 'treat of intricate points of law with the cleverness of an equity judge'. The *Sunday Times* gave unstinting praise: 'Miss E. has produced a clever, exciting, and singularly powerful story'. A single novel like this was 'enough to place an author in a prominent position among writers of fiction, and the production of two or three such works ought to be enough to build a great and permanent reputation'.[75]

After *Debenham's Vow*, *In the Days of My Youth*, published in 1873, comes as a disappointment. Not only is there a retreat from the bold manifesto of the previous novel where facile 'happy endings' are rejected, but there is a return to the melodramatic events and contrived improbable coincidences, of Edwards' earliest fiction. Given her growing preoccupation with, and workload for, the study of Egyptology, it is quite possible that *In the Days of My Youth* is indeed an early novel, retrieved and given a new lease of life to meet a publisher's demand for a fresh production, at a time when Edwards found herself under pressure.[76]

In the Days of My Youth is a long, rambling, episodic tale – a concoction of many tales, in fact, with slight plots, and many digressions. The novel is narrated in the first person, by a young man sent to France to study medicine, under the tutelage of a friend and colleague of his father's. Young Basil duly travels to Paris, gets drunk, and has to be rescued by his new tutor. He falls in love with a fashionable lady, who jilts him; then with a shop assistant, from whom he quickly parts company, without hard feelings on either side. He neglects his studies and squanders his father's money, before settling down to study medicine in earnest, even though the subject bores him. He makes friends with an artist, Muller, a pleasure-loving, amusing, and not over-scrupulous character, and with an army officer named Dalrymple – the latter secretly married to a woman he loves, but who is wooed and bullied by her overbearing cousin. (A duel will be fought over this issue, before the story is done.) The novel describes student dances in makeshift garret ballrooms; a day out at a country fair; a visit to an all-male swimming club; the tracking, arrest, and attempted escape, of a convict on the run. In some parts there is a strong element of the tourist guidebook – where Edwards nostalgically evokes the Latin Quarter of bygone days, in an elegiac hymn to the 'dingy, delightful Arcadia' of the old bohemian Quartier Latin, long since 'improved off the face of the earth', but in happier times the haunt of artists, thinkers, novelists and poets.[77]

Towards the novel's close, we meet Hortense, a proud, independent-spirited woman, an accomplished poet, with whom Basil rather predictably falls in love. A series of preposterous coincidences, involving a family portrait in a deserted château, a travelling conjurer, a hidden drawer, leads us back to the English country town of Basil's youth, and to the restoration of Hortense's ancestral inheritance – whereupon the couple get married and settle down happily together.

Some reviewers were puzzled by the masculine perspective adopted in *Days of My Youth* – even more so, as the story is told in the first person.

Knowing that the book's author was female, one reviewer commented that the reader was therefore 'haunted by a sense of ambiguity'.[78] Others were intrigued by the novel's vivid depictions of exclusively masculine environments, like an all-male swimming baths, or an artists' drinking club. It has even been suggested that Edwards could have disguised herself to enter such establishments and gather material. Given what we know of her acting abilities, and the convincing way in which, as a young woman, she impersonated a man, the idea is not so implausible. A glance at the relevant scenes in *Days of My Youth*, however, makes clear that there is nothing she could not equally well have observed at an inn – or, in the case of the swimming-club scenes – at any European beach resort.

With all its flaws, the novel has some good comic moments. Muller's passing off of Basil as an aristocrat customer come to sit for his portrait, to impress potential middle-class patrons, is particularly well done. There is an amusing description of nineteenth-century home entertainment – a dramatic recitation from Corneille's *Horace*, which nearly ends in disaster: 'Ah heaven! My dear Mademoiselle, take care of the candles . . .' At which point the lead actor's wig catches fire, and he has to be rescued by being 'scalped' of his hairpiece by the quick-thinking Muller.[79] There is gentle satire on religious sectarianism, in a scene where various churches in an English parish compete for the right to bury a vagrant French gentleman, who has died unexpectedly there. Roman Catholics, Dissenters, followers of the Tabernacle, all claim the honour of burying the unfortunate man. In the end, the Anglicans win the day. Disregarding the glaring improbability that a Frenchman would be a member of the Church of England, the parishioners are content to celebrate the victory of the established Church, 'and the defeat of all schismatics'.[80]

Edwards' *Lord Brackenbury* – her last novel, and one of her best, was also one of her most popular with readers. Serialized in *The Graphic* in February 1880, before its publication in book form, it went through fifteen editions, including translations into German, Russian and French, and ran as a magazine serial in Australia and New Zealand.[81]

It was not therefore because of any failure, either artistic or commercial, that Edwards abandoned the writing of fiction, after completing *Lord Brackenbury*. Her commitment to Egyptology, and to the Egypt Exploration Fund, came to absorb all her interest and energy. There was, it seems, no more time for novels.[82]

Lord Brackenbury is the story of a man whose future life has been planned for him by his family from childhood. Heir to lands, a stately home and a peerage, he is destined, when he comes of age, to take his seat as a Conservative peer in the House of Lords. Even his future wife has been selected for him. Unsurprisingly, Cuthbert Brackenbury is unwilling to comply with the family programme. He has no interest in being a landowner, and his political sympathies lie not with the Conservatives, but the Liberals – a secret he feels unable to confess to his father. He suspects, moreover, that

Winifred, the young woman selected for his bride, is secretly loved by his younger brother, Lancelot.

Having pondered his predicament for years, Cuthbert comes to a fateful decision. He will disguise his identity and disappear, leaving his family to think him dead. He thereby secures his freedom, leaving his brother to inherit both the family estate and the peerage, and able to openly declare his love to Winifred.

Once happily married, Lancelot and Winifred embark on an ambitious plan to demolish the hovels of a gypsy-like society of 'dark folk' living on Biddulph Moor, and install them in model housing, in 'something like a community'. If their project comes across as autocratic and patronizing today, the idea of providing people with decent houses became a lifelong preoccupation with Edwards. Contrary to the belief that Lancelot is unique among Edwards' characters, 'in displaying public spirit and a social conscience',[83] the ideal of the benign and generous, if paternalistic, landlord, who strives to improve the living conditions of his tenants, was one she also imagined, as we have seen, in *Half a Million*, and in *Debenham's Vow*.

Cuthbert, meanwhile, now far from the ancestral home, is busy making a new life for himself, as a sea captain. Taking the name of 'Cesare Donato', he earns his living transporting people and goods around the coastal ports of Italy. He settles down happily with an Italian wife. But the longing comes over him, to see his brother again, and the friends of his childhood. He travels back to England; exposes the fraudulent designs of his former servant, who is caught trying to claim to be the long-lost Lord Brackenbury, and announces his intention to be reunited with Lancelot. His lawyers, however, advise Cuthbert that to do so would be to disinherit his brother, and to deprive him of his seat in the House of Lords.

Cuthbert makes a painful decision. He will go away from England, without ever having seen his brother's face. This, he reflects, is 'the hardest sacrifice of all'. As the ship sails out of harbour, carrying him back to Italy, 'The night is dark, and there are none to see his tears'.[84]

For the illustrations for *Lord Brackenbury*, Edwards worked closely with a well-known artist, Luke Fildes. A few of Fildes' letters have survived, where the artist consults Edwards on details for his drawings. In particular, he wants to avoid any of his pictures becoming 'spoilers' for the reader. Where he has done a drawing of Cuthbert putting an engagement ring on Winifred's finger, for instance, has he inadvertently revealed to the reader something readers were not supposed to know till much later in the story? In another scene illustrated by Fildes, Cuthbert is shown rescuing someone from a burning house. Fildes writes to ask Edwards, should Cuthbert be carrying an adult, or a child? A child 'might pictorially be better', he suggests – particularly as Cuthbert is described in the novel as 'pointing back' to the house – difficult to manage, if he had been carrying the weight of an adult. In another letter, written early in 1880, he asks Edwards for a sketch plan of the moor, based on Biddulph Moor, around the Brackenbury ancestral home.[85]

'I like your *Lord Brackenbury* very much', Marianne North wrote to Amelia from New Zealand. Edward Lear liked it too and told Edwards so in a letter.[86]

The *Pall Mall Gazette* praised the novel for its skill in weaving together several different plot lines. But while the novel was a best-seller with the public, other reviewers were inclined to pick holes. 'A great deal of plot, but not much mystery . . . the reader sees very plainly what Lord Brackenbury is up to from the beginning', was one criticism. It was also said that 'Miss Edwards indulges too much in description of places familiar to everybody'.[87] For many readers, though, Edwards's descriptions of Verona, Rome and Naples no doubt formed part of the attraction of the novel, in an age before filmed travel documentaries, and when relatively few could afford to go abroad. And her extraordinarily vivid first-hand description of the eruption of Vesuvius is not exactly clichéd, either.[88]

By 1880, Edwards could have looked with pride on a substantial literary achievement – dozens of short stories in popular magazines, and eight substantial, well-received novels, printed in multiple editions, some of which had been translated into other languages.[89]

As a novelist whose work circulated widely, she was a household name. When, in 1867, a daring theft of gold bullion occurred on a ship moored in the Thames, the best way one newspaper could convey the drama of the robbery, was to call it 'worthy of the pen of Amelia Edwards'.[90]

Whatever the reasons why she gave up writing novels in the 1880s – whether owing to lack of time, physical exhaustion, or because she found her work for the Exploration Fund more compelling – her imaginative gifts were still very much a part of her. She would deploy them now in the service of Egyptology, for fascinated audiences, who, it seemed, could not get enough of her fact-based tales from the land and times of the Pharaohs. Though dismissive of most historical fiction per se, she would invoke and bring the remote past to life, in what Maspero called, 'fiction about things and people that did actually exist'.[91] Having honed her story-telling skills in the writing of novels, she had begun to apply them to the narration of history, in Egyptology lectures all over England. Now, it was time to move onto a wider stage. She would take her gifts across the Atlantic.

9

America

For several years, the Reverend William Copley Winslow had been urging Edwards to come over to America, for a lecturing tour he would organize for her. His invitation was backed up by others, from the presidents of Columbia and Northampton colleges.

Edwards loved to travel – and in this case felt, too, that she needed the lecturing fees the tour would bring her. As she wrote to Flinders Petrie in the Spring of 1888:

> The truth is that I want the money very much. The house wants repairing, much renewal of furniture, etc. – and I want to build out a little snug room which shall serve as a museum, and be warm for me to write in winter.[1]

The proposed journey was delayed by her illness that summer. Finally, though, by the following year, she felt well enough to accept Winslow's invitation. What seems finally to have decided her and given her the confidence to embark on what she knew would be a challenging undertaking, was that her new friend Kate Bradbury had offered to come with her. As she said, Kate was: 'a very clever, energetic, capable friend . . . one who would really look after me, and take care of me if I were ill – and who would even be capable of herself reading a lecture for me, if I . . . lost my voice from cold, and had an engagement to fulfill'.[2]

She still worried, however, about leaving Ellen Braysher, who in her old age had grown ever more frail physically, and more temperamental and demanding. She even considered cancelling the American tour for Ellen's sake, worried what might become of the older lady while Amelia was away on her travels. But the doctor assured her that, given what he called Mrs Braysher's 'marvellous constitution', she could safely be left behind in Westbury for a few months. Reassured, Amelia got ready to travel. On October 26, 1889, Amelia and Kate journeyed together to Liverpool, where they went on board the RMS *Etruria*, and sailed for America.

It was the consensus in the British press, that Edwards was going to have 'a thoroughly good time' in America. A gossip columnist in one paper, wrote that Amelia Edwards was 'enjoying a holiday' there.[3] Whatever else the gruelling lecture tour of northern American states was to be, it was definitely not going to be much of a holiday. A substantial workload had been arranged for her, before she even sailed from Liverpool. The Reverend William Copley Winslow had suggested Edwards might prepare half a dozen lectures to give in America, 'of a popular sort', but also appropriate for 'cultured people' in New York and Boston. Would she feel able, he asked, to give about sixty lectures in the space of thirty days? Before leaving England, Edwards was said to have already received over 300 requests to speak.

Her reputation in America, and in Britain, was enhanced by the honorary degrees she had been awarded by American institutions three years before – an LLD from Smith College; a PhD Diploma from the Episcopal Church College of the Sisters of Bethany, in Topeka, Kansas (1886); and an LLD from Columbia, in 1887. The PhD was among the first doctorates – honorary or otherwise – to be awarded to a woman in America; and the first for a woman from Britain.

The awards were largely due to the recommendations of Winslow. Edwards, with less success, tried to reciprocate, using what influence she had to gain similar awards for Winslow in England. She did succeed in securing him an honorary degree from the University of St Andrews.[4]

The reactions in the press to Edwards' academic honours were, on the whole, supportive. The *Pall Mall Gazette* thought Edwards deserved to have a degree from some more prestigious institutions than those granting the awards – from Harvard, for example. Noting that the PhD was 'the first distinction of the kind ever bestowed upon a woman', the *Dublin Daily Express* demanded to know why women should be denied doctorates from British universities: They deserved recognition 'at least as often as men do', in the opinion of the Dublin newspaper, 'and they would become the robes considerably better'.[5]

The American speaking engagements and the itinerary had been thoroughly prepared beforehand. Edwards' lectures – later reprinted in *Pharaohs, Fellahs and Explorers* – would be largely based on talks she had given during her lecturing tours in England and Scotland. Buried cities; the influence of ancient Egypt on the art and literature of other cultures; the status of women in ancient Egypt; Egyptian beliefs about the afterlife, formed the themes. She would travel through the towns and cities of the East Coast, and around the Midwest – often, by prior arrangement, giving a series of lectures in a single place. Her contract was with the Redpath Lyceum Bureau, who would supply her with stereopticon equipment to show her slides, and a projectionist to accompany the stereopticon. She would be paid $500 a week, plus weekly expenses of up to $125.[6]

She had invitations to stay in a number of Americans' homes. Many of them were old friends. She was invited by friends in Hartford, Connecticut; by the painter Frederick Church and his wife, and by a Mrs Fields in Boston. Warmly welcoming her to stay at his home in Brooklyn, was the civic reformer and former mayor of Brooklyn, Seth Low. In 1902, Low would become mayor of New York city, after running for election on a manifesto to clean up corruption. Whether Edwards took Low up on his offer of hospitality, is unclear.

Edwards had often declared her liking for Americans. She had socialized with American artists and theatre people, while staying in Rome in the 1860s and early 1870s. In *A Thousand Miles Up the Nile,* she had written in praise of 'our American cousins, ever helpful, ever cordial':

Their flag stands to me for a host of brave and generous and kindly associations. It brings back memories of many lands and many faces. It calls up echoes of friendly voices, some far distant; some, alas! silent . . . my heart warms to the stars and stripes whenever I see them.

As she had pointed out to Anne Brewster, she had dedicated *Untrodden Peaks and Unfrequented Valleys* to 'My American Friends in Rome' – amended, with the publication of the second edition, in 1890, to 'My American Friends in All Parts of the World'.[7]

Edwards and Bradbury arrived in New York on November 1, 1889. It had been a rough Atlantic crossing on the *Etruria.* Never a good sailor, Amelia had been violently seasick. Never again, she swore, on landing. 'Miss Edwards', Kate Bradbury wrote, 'declared she would be naturalized rather than re-cross the Atlantic'. Despite her misery, Amelia had found time and energy while on shipboard, to get her lecture notes into shape, copying them out 'in a round black hand, that she might be able to read them at a glance', even in the dim lights of lecture halls.[8]

Although outspoken in her opinions on Italy and Egypt in her travelogues about those places, Edwards gives little information on what she thought and felt about her American tour. For much of what we know about it, we are indebted to newspaper reports, and to the journal kept by Kate Bradbury. Kate's Journal – based on her letters home, and clearly designed for public consumption – contains nothing introspective or particularly intimate. (While she and Amelia were intimate friends, in the journal, Amelia is always referred to as 'Miss Edwards'.) All the same, we learn a great deal from the journal about how Edwards and her lectures were received in America, and something about her impressions of places and people.

They were met outside the New York customs by eager reporters; and by Edwards' publisher, Richard Bowker. After giving interviews to the press, they drove to the George Hotel in Brooklyn, their base for the first stage of their tour.

Like other British visitors, used to the more Spartan conditions in English houses, Amelia and Kate found it difficult to adjust to what felt to them like the overheated rooms in American hotels and private homes.[9] Moving between these warm interiors and the chilly streets of New York in early November, Edwards quickly came down with a chest infection, and lost the use of her voice. Exhausted from the sea crossing, still tired out from her work in England for the Egypt Exploration Fund, and now in her late fifties, she no longer had the stamina that had taken her trekking on muleback up the Dolomites, seventeen years before. It was hardly a propitious beginning to what was going to be a strenuous speaking tour.

The sheer intensity of human interaction could be demanding, too. Almost from the hour of landing, and the first meeting with reporters, people wanted to see and talk to Miss Edwards. (Winslow's public relations work had been most efficient.) In her journal, Kate remarked on the 'piles of newspaper notices' that quickly arrived in their hotel room, 'few of which we have time to read'.

Kate, (and no doubt Amelia too), were amused by the reporters' capacity to make up what they didn't know – or what they thought their readers wanted to hear. 'They make Miss E. short and tall, stout and thin! Plain and not plain', Kate remarked. Her clothes were a constant source of fascination. There was surprise that Edwards wore no jewellery. When she appeared to speak at the Detroit Opera House, a local newspaper lovingly detailed her black silk dress, adorned with 'a corsage bouquet of yellow roses', her brown fur-trimmed wrap, her black bonnet 'trimmed with yellow pom-poms'. Another Detroit journalist impertinently speculated that her bonnet was home-made.[10] One reporter later described Edwards as 'bronzed by the suns of the Nile'. (She had been nowhere near the Nile for years, and by the time this report was written, had been journeying for days through the deep snows of a Midwestern winter.)[11]

Edwards had been assigned a business manager, a Mr Whittredge, to deal with expenses and fees, and keep the tour running smoothly. Day-to-practicalities – helping deal with correspondence, making sure they caught trains on time, making doctors' appointments – and, when necessary, acting as gatekeeper to guard Amelia's peace and privacy – were seen to by Kate Bradbury.

Amelia's chest infection persisted, and a doctor was called to attend to it. He forbade Edwards to talk until she was fully recovered, and sent her to bed to eat grapes, while Kate kept both well-wishers and reporters at bay. In the intervals of nursing Amelia, she dealt with the constant stream of letters and press cuttings. Two days later, Amelia went to the doctor's surgery, to do breathing exercises; and began to feel a great deal better.[12] But she continued to be plagued by bronchial and throat problems throughout the tour.

By November 7, she was well enough to begin her first lecture, in the hall of the New York Academy of Music, to a crowd of expectant listeners. The hall seated 2,400. 'There was not a seat to be had for love or money', Kate Bradbury noted.[13] The success was repeated a few days later, at Vassar College in Poughkeepsie, a short train ride from New York. After it, Edwards returned to New York, to speak again there. She was able to exit the building after her lecture only with difficulty, surrounded as she was by hundreds of well-wishers, who competed to present her with flowers.

As they travelled, public attention was, if anything, growing. 'Miss Edwards carried them all captive', Kate reported triumphantly, as her friend began a series of lectures in Boston. 'She is, and is increasingly, phenomenally popular.'[14] Amelia and Kate attended a reception given for Amelia by the New England Women's Press Association, at Boston's Parker House Hotel, attended by two hundred distinguished guests. Everyone wanted to speak with her; so that the 'breakfast', scheduled for noon, did not begin until an hour later. Edwards, of course, was the guest of honour. The meal, Kate noted, 'was gorgeous, but bad, and there was no wine'. But the menu carried Edwards' portrait, on a background of coloured silks. Edwards' own menu was decorated with lotus flowers shading an image of pyramids and sphinx – the sphinx bearing an image of her face. A ribbon pinned to the menu read, 'To Dr Amelia B. Edwards'. It was one of the few occasions on which her honorary PhD was publicly recognized.[15] A poem by one Henry Austin was read, hailing her as 'A queen and a pioneer'.[16] The veteran suffrage activist Lucy Stone, spoke of the changes that had taken place in the situation of American women during her lifetime.[17] Edwards, too, spoke on matters dear to her heart, that also would be of interest to the progressive-minded members of the Women's Press Association: the need for women's colleges, like Vassar and Wellesley, in Britain, and for technical schools, where young people could learn a useful trade; the greater scope women in America had for doing different types of journalism; the role that female journalists might play in helping bring an end to what she called 'the great crime' of war.[18]

Also attending the reception was Dr Winslow, who sat beside her. It was a rare moment during Edwards' travels in America, when he was actually able to meet her personally. Winslow was deeply hurt that he saw so little of her. 'Miss Edwards has closed a wonderfully successful course of lectures here . . . I deplore that I have seen, and shall see, her so little', he wrote to Emily Paterson. 'It is cruelly hard for me to bear, and I feel she does not realize it.'[19] Winslow seems to have developed what might be called a 'crush' on Amelia. After he had her send him a photograph of herself, he wrote back to her:

> Is it you? You, one of the truest of all women since Eve began? [The photograph] is less than two feet from my pen, and I look upon it just as I say this. Are those eyes chestnut or hazel? They are gazing on, on, on, like those of the Sphinx. Tell me . . . of thy eyes, complexion, hair and *smile* . . .

It was a telling instance of Edwards' charismatic attractiveness, a quality of which she was largely unaware – what Matilda Betham Edwards called 'the perilous dower of personal fascination', with which her cousin unwittingly affected others. 'No one ever exercised stronger influence', said Matilda; and it was hardly her fault if she at times awakened interest or affection she could not return'.[20]

The press continued to interest itself in the Amelia Edwards story. 'Egyptology has become the very latest Boston fad', reported Jean Kincaid, for the *Boston Daily Globe*, 'and attendance on these lectures is one of the most popular social events of the season'.[21] Other reporters could hardly restrain their sarcasm, as they questioned the motives of female Bostonian socialites in attending Edwards' lectures. 'It has been a subject of some wonder', one reporter wrote, 'that so many Boston women had made a profound study of Egyptian art, and had been waiting for years for such a course of lectures. Nothing could be more absurd than much of the balderdash talked about art by many of Dr Edwards' attentive auditors, but, in Boston, one may as well not exist as not to be up to the topic of the hour . . .'[22]

Others were more appreciative of the chance to hear Edwards speak about ancient Egypt. According to one newspaper, it was 'An Intellectual Treat'. 'Honors to a Talented Lady', ran a headline in the *Boston Herald*.[23]

Edwards and Kate Bradbury continued to meet eminent New England intellectuals. Their hostess in Boston, Mrs Annie Fields, invited the poets Oliver Wendell Holmes and James Russell Lowell, then elderly men at the height of their fame, to have noontide 'breakfast' with her visitors. The meeting seems to have been a success. 'We were all very happy, and playful, and pleasant together', wrote Bradbury in her journal.[24] While staying with Mrs Fields, Amelia and Kate also sometimes had the company of her black servant William, who dropped in on errands, and stayed to chat.

Amelia and Kate stayed in Hartford, Connecticut, for several days, at the home of the essayist and novelist Charles Dudley Warner and his wife. There, they met Mark Twain (Samuel Clemens), who had attended one of Edwards' lectures. Warner and Twain/Clemens were close friends,[25] and Clemens visited the Warners' house several times during Edwards' visit. He stayed long enough to tell several long, entertaining anecdotes. A week later, Amelia, Kate and their hosts returned the visit, and met Clemens' wife. Their neighbour, the novelist Harriet Beecher Stowe, author of *Uncle Tom's Cabin*, by now sadly confused by the dementia that had attacked her in later years, wandered in and out of the Warners' home, her odd behaviour apparently accepted and accommodated by all her Hartford neighbours.

Kate and Amelia would see the Dudley Warners and the Clemenses again, several times during their trip. The Warner home in Hartford became a welcome refuge for Edwards, when her tour became too stressful.

For both the English visitors, New England, with its cultural inheritance from Puritanism, delivered something of a culture shock. The rarefied atmosphere of New England 'good society', at once devout, high-minded and intellectual, often went with a certain austerity regarding the comforts of life. The New Englanders believed in 'plain living and high thinking'. Edwards, who did not much take to American food at the best of times and liked a glass of wine with her meals, was not impressed. At one New England college, where the piety was intense, but supper consisted of bread and a couple of apricots, she remarked privately to Kate that she could do with a little more in the way of 'high living'.[26] She was deeply shocked to learn, when in Massachusetts, that alcoholics there might by law be confined in asylums. 'Miss Edwards', Bradbury wrote, 'is horrified at such interference with the liberty of the subject'.[27]

By early December, they were in Philadelphia, where, on the 7th, Edwards lectured to an appreciative audience, on 'Egypt as the birthplace of Greek art'. On December 8, Kate Bradbury wrote of what she perceived as Edwards' increasing confidence as a speaker. Apparently, Amelia no longer experienced what Kate termed 'attacks of woodenness' during her lectures, when she failed to engage with an audience.[28] In view of Edwards' long track record as a performer and a public speaker – from amateur theatricals and singing engagements in her late teens, to her highly popular public lectures in more recent years, when observers often commented on her ability to hold an audience's attention – Kate's mention of 'attacks of woodenness' is somewhat puzzling. Perhaps Edwards was, at times, simply tired and ill?

While in Philadelphia, they visited the University of Pennsylvania, where the provost gave them a tour of the campus. He had hoped to persuade Edwards that the university, which had its own museum, could establish itself as a separate branch of the Egypt Exploration Fund, rather than remaining a 'mere subscriber' to the Fund's main American branch.[29]

They caught the train back to Boston, and on to New York. Then to Baltimore, and an evening dress reception, with 1,500 guests. The Peabody Institute altered its constitution, which excluded women from lecturing there, to enable Edwards to speak.[30] Here, she came down with another throat infection, and again consulted a doctor. She was unable to speak to an audience, and Kate Bradbury read part of her lecture for her.

There was another lecture on December 21 – back in Philadelphia again. (By this point, Edwards and Bradbury might have begun to wonder whether whoever designed the convoluted itinerary, might not have devised something a little more linear, and hence less wasteful of energy.) Christmas was spent in upstate New York, at the home of the painter Frederick Church and his wife, old friends from Edwards' time in Italy.

After Christmas, it was Providence, Rhode Island; New York, and Columbia University; small towns in upstate New York; Connecticut, with another visit to Hartford at the end of January, and a stay back at the Dudley Warners. Mark Twain again called in, and held the company spellbound with his singing of African-American spirituals, and telling of folk tales he had learned as a child from the blacks in his home town of Hannibal, Missouri.[31]

Edwards continued to receive warm hospitality wherever she went, and adulation from audiences and well-wishers. At Mount Holyoke Female Seminary, in South Hadley, Massachusetts, when she visited and spoke there at the end of January, they made Edwards an Honorary Member of the graduating class of 1891.[32]

Amid all the flurry of travelling from town to town, and speaking engagements, they even found time for a little tourism. In February, they went to Niagara Falls, and, twelve days later, visited a native American encampment near Mendota, in Illinois. But, after a rare 'day off', and the Niagara Falls excursion in early February, Edwards fell ill again, and spent a day in bed, gathering her strength for the long train journey into the Midwest.

Reporters followed them in Chicago, where one of them, according to Kate, accompanied them across the town; and the interviewer 'fastened on Miss Edwards until our train left'. In Milwaukee, Wisconsin, Mr Whittredge managed to keep Edwards' arrival from the public, giving her a little respite from the unending public attention.

Back at the end of December, while they were still touring New England, Kate Bradbury had been required to hold up a handkerchief towards the end of one lecture, 'to signal to Miss Edwards that she must be done in 10 minutes, or miss the train to Boston'. In Aurora, Michigan in February, the railway company staff were a little more considerate. It was arranged for the train to be delayed for twenty minutes, so that members of Edwards' two audiences there – at the Fortnightly Club, and at the town's Art Institute – could say their goodbyes and shake her hand before she left town. (At the latter venue, 1,800 people had wanted to attend Amelia's lecture; but the room was able to accommodate only three hundred.)[33]

In New York and New England, where people were more used to British visitors, Edwards' manner of speaking would not have attracted much attention. Now they were in the Midwest, however, it became more conspicuous; and one journalist in Illinois was struck by Amelia's 'broad English accent'. He found it 'not unpleasant'. The *Macon Telegraph*, more complimentary, described her 'lovely and very English' voice as 'a charming gift', as attractive 'in low social converse as when brought out more fully on the platform'.[34]

People continued to send flowers, to wherever Edwards and Bradbury were staying. Their arrival in Detroit was not untypical: 'Miss Edwards has had five interviews, two poems and wheelbarrow-fulls of flowers from her ardent admirers here today', Kate wrote. While the floral gifts expressed the warm admiration of the Illinois citizens, they sometimes made it hard for Edwards to move around freely indoors, in the cramped space of hotel rooms, or the dorm of some college. 'So many flowers drive her wild with the room they take up', Kate noted.[35]

After Detroit, they moved on to Indianapolis – and another luncheon with the city's 'prominent women'. On the night of February 26, Edwards was due to give her eighty-ninth lecture in less than four months – twenty-nine more than Dr Winslow had proposed in his letter before she left England.[36] And there were still another three weeks of the tour to go.

Both Edwards and Bradbury were impressed by the thirst for knowledge, wherever they went, among American men and women of all social classes. It was not only those like the provost of Penn University, with his hope that the university might establish a separate branch of the Exploration Fund;

but people without academic connections, like the audiences from small towns in rural Minnesota, who gladly came sixty miles in the dead of winter, for the sake of hearing Edwards speak.[37] In Connecticut, she had lectured both at Miss Porter's School for Young Ladies, and at the Mechanics' and Tradesmen's Educational Association. 'What a nation this is, for desire after learning, and intellectual communion!' Kate Bradbury wrote in her diary. But she came to tire of so much enthusiasm for intellectual socializing – of what she complained of, as people's 'everlasting meeting together to improve themselves'. Why could they not quietly read books at home on their own?[38] Edwards, though, even when tired out by the effort of touring and speaking, was clearly in her element. She thrived on the interaction with a curious and lively audience.

To American women at this time, when they were increasingly forming professional associations, campaigning to gain the vote, leaving the small towns to train for skilled occupations in the cities, Edwards, a self-confident, dignified woman – a novelist, an international traveller and erudite Egyptologist – must have appeared as a role model, an example of what an aspiring woman might achieve.[39] She was not shy about doing a little agitation for Votes for Women, as she travelled around. At the end of January, while still in New England, she wrote to the Women Suffragists' Convention then being held in Boston, expressing surprise that women in Britain had more opportunities to be elected to school boards and municipal councils than in the otherwise seemingly more 'progressive' United States:

> I have learned with surprise that the women in America are not privileged to vote on so many local, parochial, municipal and educational matters as the women of England, seeing how influential the social position of women in the United States is. I am amazed at this anomaly, which I earnestly trust will soon be swept away, by the advance of public opinion in the right direction.

Whether or not they had any effect on the delegates at the Suffragists' Convention, her words resonated with the British press. Possibly because they seemed flattering to British readers, her letter was reproduced in the *Sheffield Independent*.[40]

By December, after roughly ten thousand miles of railroad journeys, the strain of travelling was telling on Edwards quite heavily. In upstate New York, they had ridden in overcrowded, unheated trains, to remote places that might take two days to reach. If she found some respite from talking and writing while on the train – she enjoyed reading Thackeray's *The Virginians*, instead – still, the railroad travel drained her of energy. If Winslow, to his disappointment, saw hardly anything of Edwards during her time in the States, looking at her punishing schedule, it is not difficult to see why. (How much of the revised timetable was due to Winslow's adding further engagements for her – how much to her eagerness to use the time in

America to the maximum; how much to her inability to refuse invitations and offers of hospitality – is impossible to say.)

On the evening of March 3, in Columbus, Ohio, Edwards had an accident. Falling down a flight of steps outside her hotel bedroom, she landed heavily, breaking her left arm just above the wrist. A surgeon was sent for, who arrived in half an hour, and strapped up the injured arm. Kate Bradbury cut open the sleeve of Edwards' dress – she had been fully dressed when she fell – and tied the sleeve up with ribbons, so that she could take it on and off more easily. Although in intense pain, Amelia bravely undertook the five-mile carriage journey, to her scheduled evening lecture. She got up and left for Philadelphia, at six o'clock the following morning.

She was still in pain when she got up to speak at her lecture in Philadelphia. She made light of her injury, telling her audience that 'she had indeed had the misfortune to break her arm but had not broken her word', to come and speak. Her stoical army officer father would surely have been proud of her.

Two days after the accident, she had not fully recovered from the shock of the fall and was still in pain. She went to rest briefly at the home of their friends the Warners, in Connecticut. Mark Twain/Clemens called in to see her; but would not stay – even though Edwards urged him to, saying, 'But you will do me good'. 'I know I should', said Twain, 'but Mrs Clemens would not believe it'. He went away.[41]

A report on the accident that appeared in the *Kansas City Star* expressed 'warm admiration' for what the article called 'her plucky endurance' in carrying on with her speaking engagements after the accident; 'as well as for her great ability and charming manners'.[42]When she arrived in Wilmington, Delaware, on March 9, Amelia's considerate hosts helped her in and out of the lecture venue in a wheelchair.

By the time Amelia and Kate arrived in Washington, where they had hoped for an audience with the US president, they spent so much time going out to see a doctor, that they saw hardly anyone – let alone President Harrison, who had previously expressed a wish to meet Edwards.[43]

By March 1890, they were coming to the end of the long tour. They went back via New England, to Boston. They were again feted by members of the New England Women's Press Association, who gave Edwards a bracelet made of Californian gold, set with stones mined in different parts of the US. It was inscribed, 'from grateful and loving friends – the women of Boston'. Kate Bradbury was presented with a pendant. In thanking her hosts, Edwards said she had met with 'the utmost kindness everywhere in America', and would long remember it – adding wryly, as she touched her damaged arm, that she was now 'an ancient Egyptian relic – fragmentary, but genuine'. Her words drew sympathetic applause.

Events like these, at which Edwards was the guest of honour, were described in a number of British papers, both during her time in America and upon her return, suggesting the interest with which her doings in America were followed in England. Reports appeared in, among other papers, the *Derby Daily Telegraph*, the *Eastern Daily Press*, the *Worcestershire Chronicle*, and the *Northern Whig*.[44]

Back in New York at last, on March 18 Edwards attended yet another breakfast in her honour, at the Sorosis Club. It was the final social engagement in America, and the members gave her a splendid farewell celebration. They presented her with a model canoe containing flowers and the flags of the United States and Britain, and voted her an honorary member of Sorosis. A well-wisher gave Edwards some claret in a cream jug (allegedly for medicinal purposes), which she drank discreetly from a coffee cup, to avoid offending the teetotal members of the club. A slightly awkward incident occurred, when the veteran activist Lucy Stone, a lifelong teetotaller, on reaching for what she took to be cream, was shocked to discover the jug full of wine.

Otherwise, the reception was a great success. Edwards made 'a very good speech' in the opinion of Kate Bradbury, who added, however, that Amelia had harped a little too much on Americans' Anglo-Saxon heritage. 'A little trying to German members of Sorosis', Bradbury thought. More acceptable, no doubt, to all the members, was when Edwards said how impressed she was, 'with the opportunities set before American girls for a new development of womanhood'. She noted that the Sorosis president, in her welcoming speech, had listed Edwards' honorary academic titles. 'I owe them all', she said, 'to the American nation'. She went on to describe the mockery of women's situation at Oxford and Cambridge, where a female student who might well have performed in her final examinations 'more creditably than men' would all the same be awarded only a certificate 'setting forth that if they had been born men they might have had a degree'. She praised the more egalitarian policies of American co-ed colleges.[45]

There was still one more lecture to give that evening, at the Nineteenth Century Club, where Edwards would speak on, 'The Romantic Literature of Ancient Egypt'. A report in the *Brooklyn Daily Eagle* noted that those attending her lecture made up 'the most scholarly audience the Metropolis could have contributed'. She debated with professors of literature from Cornell University and the University of Pennsylvania, in what the *Eagle* judged to be a capable defence of her argument that ancient Egypt had produced the world's earliest fiction. Her talk had proved, the *Eagle* reported, 'a delightful revelation of the learning, grace, versatility and strength of thought of one of the most remarkable women of modern times'. She was a role model to others of her sex.[46]

After a final visit to their friends in Hartford, Amelia and Kate said their goodbyes. Edwards had covered thousands of miles by train, and given 120 lectures – addressing, one English newspaper estimated, a hundred thousand people.[47] Though the tour had been an undoubted triumph, and a high point of her career, it had burned her out, physically and mentally. It was time to turn for home.

10

A quiet activist

'She never dabbled in politics or philanthropy', Matilda Betham Edwards wrote of her cousin, in an obituary published in the *Bristol Mercury*.[1] That was not quite true: Amelia Edwards 'dabbled' in both. As if her activities as essayist, Egyptologist, correspondent and organizer, lecturer, traveller, were not enough for one life, she was often busily engaged with one or more of several causes, a few of which she had supported since her twenties.

Emily Paterson, secretary to Edwards in the 1880s, noted the seeming contradictions in her employer's social attitudes, that extended even to her choice of clothing. 'Although very conservative in some ways', Paterson wrote, 'in others Miss Edwards was in advance of her time. She was one of the most ladylike women I have ever met, and yet she dressed in advance of her day in coat, skirt and waistcoat.'[2] Edwards' social attitudes exhibited similar complexity. While far from being a political radical, she had a strong sense of fairness. She hated cruelty, believed in even-handed justice, and the need to alleviate human (and animal) suffering. Her rational mind was keenly aware of social anomalies – such as the denial of voting rights to women.

In the later part of her life, Amelia Edwards was a 'joiner'. By her mid-fifties, besides her position as honorary secretary of the Egypt Exploration Fund, she had joined the Society of Biblical Archaeology, the Society for the Promotion of Hellenic Studies, the Anti-Vivisection Society, and the Bristol and West of England Society for Women's Suffrage. She was a member of the General Committee of the Association to Protect the Rights of Authors (with Robert Browning, Thomas Hardy, George Henry Lewes, Algernon Charles Swinburne). Through public talks and letters to the press, she supported, if she did not join, the Society for the Protection of Ancient Buildings,[3] and the Society for Protecting Birds. For a short time in the late 1870s, she chaired an all-female board of directors, of a social enterprise aimed at helping working-class women to make an independent living. Contrary to a common perception – that she took little interest in campaigns, charitable works, or politics – she was, at various times in her life, committed to all three. She campaigned, not only to preserve the treasures of ancient Egypt, but, to a modest extent, for the rights of women, and for better treatment of animals.

The image of Edwards as an apolitical figure, shut away in her study, absorbed in her work, shunning direct involvement even in causes she supported theoretically, calls for re-examination: not least, in the years after she came to live near Bristol. The city, then, as now, was a centre for groups of independently-minded people, and for radical thought on all kinds of topics. Unitarians like Mary Carpenter campaigned for educational and penal reforms, and explored comparative religion. Local Quakers and Socialists were active in the cause of women's rights. Members of the Quaker Sturge family, among others, were committed supporters of work against cruel experiments on animals, and by the early 1880s, there was an active Bristol branch of the Anti-Vivisection Society.

The second half of the nineteenth century saw national legislation to regulate vivisection, with an amendment to the Cruelty to Animals Act, in 1876. The new legal provisions did not go far enough for those, like Frances Power Cobbe, founder of the Anti-Vivisection Society, who campaigned for a total ban on animal experiments; but still, it was indicative of a new and growing public sensitivity to animal rights issues in general.

Women's rights were another keenly debated issue, all through the 1850s and beyond, with reforms in married women's entitlement to control of their property, and, over decades, limited extension of the suffrage in elections for local government. There were repeated, if abortive, efforts too, to introduce bills for granting women the vote in national elections.

As a well-read woman with an interest in social change, Edwards followed all these developments. There is no evidence that the radical political ideas that circulated in the salon of Samuel Laurence she had attended as a young woman, remained with her into her later years. She continued for a while to correspond with the democratic socialist politician Louis Blanc, who had been a member of the French revolutionary Provisional Government of 1848 and was a keen supporter of the co-operative movement. While still living at her parents' house in Islington in the 1850s, she invited him to visit the family, and Blanc apparently accepted the invitation.[4] Her politics in later life, however, would more accurately be described as those of a reform-minded liberal. Edwards is on record as attending meetings of reforming campaign organizations in Bristol, sometimes making public statements there, on causes she believed in. She may not have given more than a small percentage of her time to such activities, but the commitment was very real.

The issue of women's rights is one in which she was involved from her mid-twenties. Given Edwards' sustained commitment to the woman suffrage cause, why her cousin played down this involvement, in her account of Amelia's life, is puzzling. In her own later years, though, Matilda had become thoroughly sceptical about the fitness of women to hold public office, which possibly made her somewhat dismissive of the suffrage campaigning of others.[5]

Edwards herself left a contradictory impression about her involvement with women's rights, by a statement she made to an American reporter, while on her speaking tour in the States. Asked whether she considered herself 'a woman suffragist', Edwards replied, 'I am one of those suffragists who believes the present condition of affairs is outrageous, but I am too much occupied with my studies to be interested in politics . . . The ballot is something I don't want but think I ought to have'.

If in disclaiming interest in 'politics', Edwards meant *party* politics, she was telling no less than the truth. She would not involve herself in campaigning for the advancement of any organization seeking to form a government, whether Liberal, radical or Tory. She would never – unlike her beloved Ellen Byrne – have had any interest in joining the Primrose League, or even some liberal equivalent of it. She supported – and indeed at times made modest efforts to campaign for – the vote for women, and similar reforms, for the principle of the thing. Denying the suffrage to intelligent people on the grounds of their anatomical structure was not only unjust – it made no sense. She would back any effort to correct that absurd injustice. In an interview with *Boston Daily Globe*, at the end of her American tour, she made her position explicit: 'I am earnestly in favour of woman suffrage . . . I am vice-president of the West of England society for the promotion of that movement.'[6] If her statement that she did not want the vote for herself, has given the impression of someone who was passive or quietist, that impression is mistaken. It was simply that, as she added, her life was 'so much absorbed by Egyptological and archaeological work', that she was unable to dedicate as much time to suffrage activism as she would have liked. 'The ladies of the west of England refuse to allow me to resign, and are content to take me as I am – though I fear I am a very unsatisfactory vice-president.'[7]

The reporter for the *Boston Sunday Herald* who asked Edwards if she was a suffragist, was at least aware that her lectures on ancient Egypt, and indeed her mere presence as a female role model, might of themselves carry a feminist agenda. The journalist supposed that in this respect, Edwards was unaware of her influence. In her work to promote 'the advancement of Egyptian exploration', she had 'wrought better than she yet knows in enlarging the sphere of American womanhood', the reporter believed.[8] As Edwards' after-dinner speeches in America, her visits to women's colleges, her talks on the status of women in ancient Egypt, her letter to the Boston suffrage conference, amply testify, in fact she knew very well what she was doing. Much of her public work for Egyptology might be construed as, with a small 'p', highly political in the cause of women's rights.

Regarding her true attitudes towards women's rights issues, others who knew Edwards were aware of her commitment. 'She was an ardent advocate of the enfranchisement of women', said one anonymous tribute, at her death in 1892.[9]

Edwards' first recorded involvement in a women's rights campaign occurred in 1856. In British law, a married woman was considered a *'femme couvert'* – a woman protected by her husband, from whose identity she was inseparable: according to the judicial expert William Blackstone, the 'legal existence of the woman is suspended during marriage, or at least is incorporated or consolidated into that of her husband' – meaning that, once wed, a woman lost control over her earnings, investments and property. A petition to Parliament that year, calling for the abolition of the husband's control over his wife's finances, was launched in the press, with the signatures of twenty-three women. The name of novelist Elizabeth Gaskell appears, along with those of the poet Elizabeth Barrett Browning, the feminist social thinker Harriet Martineau, and of Amelia Edwards. A supportive article in the press, pointed out that for married literary women, the issue of control over their earnings had become of increasing relevance, as more and more married women turned to writing as a means of supporting their families. For widowed or deserted working-class women supporting their families on meagre wages, and for those at the mercy of violent husbands, access to their own finances was a matter of even more urgent concern.[10] As Edwards herself remarked, it was ironic that the vows of the marriage service in theory promised the bride, 'With my goods I thee endow'; while in practice relieving her of whatever goods she might have brought to the marriage in the first place.[11]

The petition launched by Bessie Rayner Parkes, Millicent Fawcett and others in the newly-formed Married Women's Property Committee, eventually gathered 26,000 signatures, and was duly presented to Parliament. However, the parliamentary bill that resulted was set aside in favour of an alternative piece of legislation, the Matrimonial Causes Bill of 1857 – a less comprehensive piece of legislation, that provided for control of their property only for women separated from their husbands. Married women still lost control of all property or earnings upon marriage, if they stayed in the marital home. This outcome must have been a disappointment to Edwards, as much as to other signatories to the petition. Although, unlike some who signed it, as an unmarried woman she was not directly affected by the unjust laws on wives' property – as with the right to vote, it was the principle that mattered to her.

In 1866, a small group of women activists, including Matilda Betham Edwards' friend Barbara Bodichon, approached the social thinker and newly-elected Liberal MP, John Stuart Mill with a new request. If they could collect at least 100 signatures, would he present a petition to Parliament calling for the granting of the right to vote to women?

Mill would be the first MP to call in Parliament for women's suffrage at national level. Thanks to the work of Bodichon and others, he was able to do so with a petition containing 1,521 signatures. Amelia Edwards had signed, along with many who were friends of hers, or who would become political fellow-campaigners in the Bristol community. Ellen Braysher signed, and Ellen Rice Byrne (who gives a London address on the petition – 22 Seymour Street, suggesting that she and her husband still retained a connection with the capital). Other signatories were the Bristol suffrage activist Agnes Beddoe, and the animal rights campaign Frances Power Cobbe. Edwards would come to know both of them well over the next two decades. Matilda Betham Edwards signed, too, indicating that she had not yet become disillusioned with the idea of votes for women.[12]

In July 1889, two thousand women signed a public statement in favour of female suffrage, that circulated widely in the national and regional press. It was an initiative designed to counter an anti-suffrage declaration of a few weeks earlier, organized by the Women's National Anti-Suffrage League and published as an advertisement in the *Nineteenth Century* for June, that had gathered a similar number of signatures. The pro-suffrage statement read, 'The undersigned desire to express their approval of the proposed extension of the Parliamentary Franchise to Women, which they believe would be beneficial both to them and to the State'. Both Amelia Edwards and Matilda Betham Edwards appear as signatories to the statement (under the professional heading of Literature).

By the late 1880s, Edwards had been elected honorary vice-president of the Bristol and West of England Society for Women's Suffrage. If, for much of the time, other commitments kept her from more than token participation in the organization's work, the prestige of her name would in itself have been valuable to the Society. She did occasionally attend meetings and spoke at them. In December 1886, when she was at her most burdened with administrative work for the Egypt Exploration Fund and struggling to deal with the after-effects of the resignation of her co-worker Stuart Poole, she still found time to attend an important women's suffrage conference held in Bristol, at the Clifton Down Hotel. In order to mobilize for a new parliamentary initiative, it was proposed to petition the then prime minister, Lord Salisbury, calling on him to voice his support for the impending Parliamentary Franchise (Extension to Women) Bill. Amelia Edwards spoke at the conference. She was applauded as she expressed 'cordial sympathy with the movement, the objects of which had been set forth with so much thought and research by those who had studied it'. A year later, on March 27, 1887, Agnes Beddoe, founder of the Bristol Suffrage Society, hosted a meeting at her home, Manor House in Clifton, at which Edwards gave a public lecture on women and the vote. According to the *Western Daily Press*, 'a large number of guests' attended.[13]

Two months later, she was busy circulating a copy of a new suffrage petition among her friends. When she asked Stuart Poole, he, and all the women of his family, refused to sign. Poole said he was put off by 'the last utterances of the party', which he considered 'wild'. (What he meant by this statement, is unclear. Poole could hardly have been referring to the Conservative Party, who were in government at that time. Did he mean the National Society for Women's Suffrage?) Whatever he meant, the Pooles were not interested in supporting Edwards' petition. In the end, only their son, Reggie, signed.[14]

Then Amelia wrote to the Petries:

Will you, and your father and Mrs Petrie sign the enclosed petition for me? Mrs Petrie signed one paper for me a month or so ago. I consider the vote of immense importance now, as women need protection and are on the side of conservatism, law and order, as a rule – and this measure would add about 200,000 votes to the safe side.[15]

The appeal to conservatism and 'the safe side' seems a little disingenuous on Amelia's part. Though she no doubt believed in 'law and order', she was hardly an entrenched conservative. Perhaps she calculated what arguments would be most persuasive to Flinders Petrie.

She spoke again to the Suffrage Society the following February, when she was joined by the prominent suffrage activist Millicent Fawcett, who would later become president of the National Union of Women's Suffrage Societies. A notice announcing the event appeared in the *Bristol Mercury*: 'The annual meeting of the Bristol and West England Society for Women's Suffrage will be held on February 11th, when Mrs Fawcett and Miss Amelia B. Edwards will be amongst the speakers.'[16] The main topic on the meeting's agenda was yet another attempt to bring a suffrage bill before Parliament. At this point, optimism prevailed. Edwards, like others present, agreed that, with 355 MPs supporting it, 'the suffrage bill would pass easily'.[17] Once again, though, the campaigners were doomed to be disappointed – which did not deter Edwards from continuing to speak up for giving women the vote. From the 1880s onwards, she seldom lost an opportunity to speak publicly about women's rights.

Her confidence to do so seems to have grown, as campaigns for legal reform gathered momentum, and the possibilities for genuine change grew more apparent. When a limited number of British women won the right to stand in elections for local government, the significance of that development was not lost upon her. As we have seen, while in America, she wrote to the delegates at a suffrage convention there, challenging them to fight for similar reforms in the United States.[18]

Even Edwards' talks about ancient Egypt, seemingly quite remote from the concerns of the late Victorian era contained elements of feminism, as she informed her audiences about the social and legal rights enjoyed by women living thousands of years ago but denied to American and European women of the nineteenth century; and about the power wielded by Egypt's great queen, Hatshepsut. While on her travels through Egypt, in 1873–74, she reflected on the situation of Egyptian women of different classes – the degree of freedom, or lack of it, available to them in their particular situation in life. These observations were likely to resonate with her female readership in Britain.[19]

When Edwards left money in her will for the furthering of Egyptological studies in Britain, a feminist agenda once again played its part. The new professorship she endowed would be established at the one British university that at the time awarded a full degree to both women and men, on equal terms. Women were to have equal opportunities, also, to apply for any scholarship funding offered by the new programme.[20] It seems fitting that in the twentieth century the Egyptology programme at University College London has produced so many distinguished female scholars and archaeologists.

Some of Edwards' activities for women might be regarded as an extension of the charitable work she had undertaken while with Ellen Byrne, in Bristol in 1870. In October 1877, readers of the *Belfast News-Letter* learned that Amelia Edwards and 'Miss Annie Thomas', another novelist, had recently set up a laundry business. The Great Western and Parisian Laundry Company had been registered under the Companies Act since the previous October. 'A remarkable institution', the *Belfast News-Letter* called the new firm – remarkable principally, it seemed, in being overseen by an all-female board of directors, of which Amelia Edwards was chair.[21]

The laundry was sited at the back of Paddington Green, at an old manor house set in three acres of grounds, where the washing could be hung out to dry. The new firm had a motto: 'Fragrat, delectat, sanat' ('Perfumes, delights, sanitizes').[22] 'This company', the *Belfast News-Letter* explained, 'claims to have made the sanitary requirements of the present age the objects of its especial solicitude'. The washing of each household was to be done individually, preventing the risk of any spread of disease. The project was envisaged as a social enterprise, providing work for women in need, 'orphan girls or widows', who were required to produce references to be employed in the new laundry. By working there, they might learn a trade and have a means of becoming economically independent.

The *Paddington Times* for July 21, 1877, reported on a garden party the Great Western Laundry held for its staff, in the grounds of the Old Manor House, where it was hosted by the laundry's 'lady-manager'. Some seventy employees, 'many of whom are French blanchisseuses *en fin*', sat down to enjoy a 'substantial meal', at tables under the trees. A number of distinguished writers, musicians and artists also attended the party – among them, Edwards' old friend Gustave Doré.[23]

While it was a noble philanthropic vision that inspired the founding of the laundry company, the project may have proved difficult to implement in practice. What became of it in the long term, or why it ceased to exist, is unknown – only that, like many such idealistic (or, for that matter, mercenary) enterprises, the Great Western Laundry seems to have quietly faded away.

It evidently exhausted Edwards' personal funds in the process. When, in 1878, she received a letter asking for a donation for a different cause, she felt obliged to refuse: 'I am so sorry not to be a subscriber to the Fund you campaign for so ably – but my purse is washed clean out. I have put all my pennies into the Laundry, and all my precious working time too, for the past eight months, and now I have neither days nor pennies to spare.'[24]

Edwards herself could be a role model to many women, simply by being who she was – in her self-education and obvious intellectual accomplishments, in her adoption of elegant but practical clothing – the long skirt, blouse and jacket that would become popular among professional women in the early 1900s – even in her very ladylike demeanour, that seemed so non-threatening, in spite of some firmly held progressive opinions. Her reputation as an independent traveller, and as an erudite Egyptologist – a 'clever lady' – all sent other women unspoken signals of possibility. It is hardly an accident that a popular women's magazine in 1894 singled out the late Amelia Edwards as a pioneer in contemporary women's achievement, and an example to others.[25]

She was involved in some aspects of what today would be called Animal Rights. In 1888, Frances Power Cobbe, founder of the Anti-Vivisection Society, wrote to Edwards, inviting her to become an honorary member. Edwards wrote back, apologizing for the long delay in responding to the invitation – emphasizing how busy she had been, as 'secretary and slave' of the Egypt Exploration Fund, but thanking Cobbe for selecting her: 'It is an honour I prize very much indeed.' She once, she said, knew an army officer who was more proud of being voted a member of the Humane Society, than of all his military medals – because that organization, like the Anti-Vivisection Society, was dedicated to saving, rather than taking, life. Like that officer, 'In truth', Edwards wrote, 'I may say much the same of this honour which I owe to your suggestion. It is especially dear to me – and it has given me more real pleasure than many others'.[26]

In the rest of her letter, she was not above making fairly strenuous efforts to enlist Cobbe in a campaign of her own – delivering her a lecture on her favourite pharaoh, Queen Hatshepsut, and urging her to take part in promoting the Egypt Exploration Fund. Cobbe, Edwards knew, had a casual interest in Egyptology, having studied the genealogy of the pharaohs; which encouraged Amelia in urging her to become a local honorary secretary in north Wales, where Cobbe had gone to live. 'I assure you, it is not your money or your life that I want', Edwards insisted – 'but your name'.

Four days later, Edwards wrote again. Cobbe had agreed to become a subscriber to the EEF; but drew the line at becoming an honorary secretary, protesting that, in the depths of Wales, she would be her own 'only subscriber', and the secretary title would therefore be a 'barren honour'. Edwards, though, persisted:

Oh! that I could have your name down in the list of Hon. Secs – for the glory of it? . . . Can an honour be barren? Is it not its own exceeding great reward? Yea – though you took one of the tops of Snowdon or Cader Idris for your district, would we not be the richer for having you – not silent, on a peak, but advocating the cause of our diggings now and then in print?

Any letter to the press signed with Cobbe's name would, Edwards calculated, be more valuable than one from a less-well-known hon. secretary, even if that anonymous person organized the work of twenty members or more. Perhaps Amelia hoped that if she kept up the pressure, Cobbe would finally give in for the sake of peace. At last, however, she let the matter drop: 'I leave the subject for your consideration.'[27]

Like the movement for women's rights, campaigns for the ethical treatment of animals had been building throughout the century – from the passing of the Cruel Treatment of Cattle Act of 1822, and the anti-vivisection movement that Frances Cobbe had been instrumental in founding, in 1875; through the previously mentioned Cruelty to Animals Act of 1876, and the publication of Anna Sewell's *Black Beauty* (1877), a story for children that was also an impassioned appeal for an end to the mistreatment of horses. The nineteenth century was an era of growing awareness that animals should not be treated as insentient objects but were capable of pain. Part of civilized human behaviour, it was recognized, consisted in treating them with consideration and compassion.

Edwards was more than a mere 'sleeping member' in the Anti-Vivisection Society. She supported its branch in Bristol; where, in 1889, she took part in a debate at its annual meeting, where the keynote speaker was the anti-vivisectionist physician, Dr Edward Collis Berdoe.[28]

Two years later, the issue of vivisection was still enlisting her concern. When the opening of a new Institute of Preventive Medicine was planned for London, the plan attracted intense public opposition, as it was expected that horrific experiments would be conducted on live animals without anaesthetic, as had already been done in similar, already-extant facilities. A petition of November 1891, against the new institute, addressed to Home Secretary Henry Matthews, gathered 41,315 signatures. It read:

> your memorialists view with disapproval and alarm the establishment of an Institute of Preventive Medicine, one of the objects of which (as stated by its advocate, Dr Farquharson in Parliament) is 'to carry out the operations of Pasteur in this country'. Your memorialists urgently request you to avert the evil of this design by refusing to license for vivisection the institute in question, or any place in connection therewith.

Edwards signed the petition, along with Tennyson, Ruskin, Cardinal Manning, and fifty medical practitioners. She is recorded as, 'Miss Amelia Edwards, LLD'. The possession of an academic degree, if not one in medicine or science, may have added credibility to her name. Although the planned institute was eventually established, that it had aroused such opposition was another sign of changing attitudes towards cruel animal experimentation – and one more evidence of Edwards own' commitment to yet another progressive campaign for change.[29]

It has to be noted, however, that Edwards' attitudes to the treatment of animals – particularly wild animals – were far from straightforward. When it came to hunting with guns, she had few qualms. As a young woman, she had owned a gun herself. One of her fictional characters – Saxon Trefalden, in *Half a Million of Money* – is proud of his skill in hunting chamois in the Alps and talks about it without any sense that others might disapprove. On her journey up the Nile, Edwards learned about the shooting of crocodiles – the desperate rush of the wounded animal to escape back to the water, where, she explained, the animal dives, and dies on the river bottom, 'in agony'. Yet she had no objection to someone killing a single crocodile – and even seemed to favour the idea of having a dead crocodile at the mast, as a trophy on their boat. What she did really object to, was that each 'sportsman' should kill not one animal, but a dozen or more of them – an indiscriminate slaughter she called 'mere butchery'.[30]

She cared deeply for the protection of birds. 'Her love of birds amounted to a veritable passion', Matilda Edwards said.[31] Edwards wrote several letters to the press, appealing for people to feed birds in winter. 'These most innocent, beautiful, and helpless of living creatures', she wrote in one letter, 'are dying at our doors by tens of thousands, from cold, hunger and thirst'. With typical practicality, she told readers what to do: put out soaked bread, scraps of cooked potato, scraps of fat. Provide water. Open a shed, to allow the birds to shelter.[32] After her death, her initiatives on behalf of bird life were not forgotten. A few days after she died, a letter appeared in the *Western Daily Press*, from Mrs Robert F. Sturge, secretary of the Bristol branch of the Society for Protecting Birds. The writer recalled how deep Edwards' 'sympathies were with all animals and birds, especially when the cruelty and selfishness of human beings brought suffering, misery and needless death upon them'.[33] Another local letter writer, in deploring the slaughter of birds for decorations to adorn women's hats, wished Edwards were still alive to speak up for wildlife: 'The death of Miss Amelia Edwards deprives [the birds] of another eloquent advocate.' He remembered how she wrote to the local papers, pleading 'for their nests to be spared and their lives saved in the winter by timely food'.[34]

Edwards' 'own child', the product of her own intelligent thought, love and commitment, the Egypt Exploration Fund, was, as its name indicates, an organization primarily dedicated to new excavation and research. At the same time, the Fund was necessarily committed to publicizing the findings of its archaeologists and scholars – as indeed the Egypt Exploration Society is to this day. Education thus also became part of its remit – explaining to a wide public why they should take an interest in the world of ancient Egypt; and what relevance that remote time might have to their own lives in the nineteenth century. The dozens of public talks Edwards and others gave, as well as the scholarly publications of the Fund, were a means to this end. Hence Edwards' endowment of the Chair of Egyptology at University College, London. She was, in this different kind of campaigning, a consciousness-raiser and a skilful fundraiser – a talent that, on behalf of the EEF, she exercised to the limit.

As for other causes with which she was involved, she wrote occasional letters to the press on subjects related to Egypt. She wanted people to know about Auguste Mariette's work, for instance. In a letter of 1880 to the *Morning Post*, she pointed out that, thanks to Mariette's oversight of excavations and his subsequent conservation work, a museum 'that had no existence twenty years ago' had created a collection in Egypt, 'one of the richest in the world'. Ever scholarly and thorough, for the interest of those who would like to know more, she accompanied her letter with a copy of Mariette's report of April 1880, on the rebuilding of the museum to protect its treasures from the seasonal Nile floods.[35]

Less obvious in its motivation, is the letter Edwards wrote in September 1882, at the time of the British invasion of Egypt. In it, she informed readers of *The Times* and *The Star*, that the valley where the invading British troops were fighting their way from Ismailia on the Suez Canal, to Zagazig on the eastern side of the Nile Delta, 'anciently formed part of the land of Goshen'. The town of Tel-el-Kebir, where the British army was about to rout the defending Egyptian forces led by Ahmad Orabi, lay on the site of an ancient city, also with Biblical associations.

It is unclear from that bald statement of fact, whether Edwards' intention is simply to inform – to raise awareness of links between ancient Egyptian, contemporary and Biblical history, since this opportunity presents itself. Or is there an oblique criticism here? – akin to the shocked comment of a friend, when told that the US and Britain were about to attack Iraq in 2003, with possible consequent damage to the ancient sites of Mesopotamia: 'Do you mean they're planning to bomb the cradle of civilization?'[36] While Edwards often did support large public campaigns for causes she believed in, she would have been careful, at this sensitive time, not to directly criticize British foreign policy in ways that might have put a stop to the work of the Egypt Exploration Fund. There were more subtle means, though, of making her point.

An extended version of the 'Goshen' argument appeared anonymously in the *London Daily News* for August 17 and was reproduced two days later in the *Wiltshire and Gloucestershire Standard*. Although the *Daily News* article is unsigned, the detailed, erudite exposition, and indeed its exact similarity to the wording in Edwards' letter, suggest that the piece can only have been written by her. Though the article deals at length with likely Biblical associations for each site along the route traversed by the invading army – an analysis which at first glance seems to be the main point of this fairly lengthy piece – one passage in it strikes a different note. Edwards cites a passage from Exodus, 30.7, where, 'It is stated that "the young men of Aven and of Pi-beseth shall fall by the sword: and these cities shall go into captivity".' 'If this should chance to be an unfulfilled prophecy', she adds, 'it is not likely to remain so very long.' Hardly an outspoken protest; but it hints, perhaps, at what Edwards really thought about the British intervention in Egypt.

In 1891 Edwards, in her capacity as secretary of the Egypt Exploration Fund, was contacted by Justin Ross, a former superintendent of ancient monuments, and inspector general of irrigation in Egypt. Ross warned her that the temples on the island of Philae, five miles downriver from Aswan, were threatened with inundation by a new British irrigation scheme, to dam the Nile and create a reservoir. Edwards at once contacted Edward Poynter, a socially well-connected Orientalist painter, later to become president of the Royal Academy, who was one of the principal founders of the Society to Protect the Monuments of Ancient Egypt. She urged him to join the Egypt Exploration Fund in lobbying the Foreign Office and the British occupation administration in Egypt. The response that came back from the officials they questioned, was reassuring: a way would be found to build the dam and develop the irrigation scheme without harming the temples. Edwards, however, experienced by now in the plausible words, and devious ways, of politicians – not least when, as in this case, profitable investments in cotton cultivation were at stake – was unconvinced. This was one occasion on which – unusually for Edwards – she thought a public outcry in Britain would be the best way of halting the Nile scheme. She failed, however, to persuade Poynter, who was afraid a mass campaign would be unsustainable. He suggested instead that a report-cum-petition – a 'draft memorial', be circulated to selected 'eminent persons' for signature.

Edwards would not live to see the matter of the Philae temples settled; but she had done her part during what remained of her lifetime, to raise the alarm. After her death in April 1892, the Philae dispute rumbled on for almost another decade. The matter was finally resolved by a vote of the British cabinet to modify the original irrigation scheme. The water level of the proposed reservoir behind the dam would be lowered, leaving the island and its temples safe from harm. Construction was finally completed in 1902.[37]

'Your rebel', Edwards' says, in *Debenham's Vow*, 'is generally a man who dares to think for himself'.[38] Or a woman, for that matter. She often went very quietly about it – but Edwards' active involvement with campaigns and causes she believed in – some of them in her day fairly controversial – was very real. It is an aspect of her life that demands fuller recognition.

11

Reputation

When Amelia sailed back from America on March 29, 1890, her imminent return and her actual arrival back in Liverpool, were announced in the press across Britain. First to report was the *Pall Mall Gazette*, of March 5. The story was taken up by the *Bradford Daily Telegraph*, the *Croydon Chronicle and Surrey Advertiser,* the *Derby Daily Telegraph, The Globe.*[1] Even before her American triumph, Edwards had been a household name. Now everyone was talking about her.

Her accident in Ohio, turned out 'to have been exaggerated', *The Globe* had reported, while Edwards was still in America; 'She is getting on as well with her lecturing tour as if it had never happened.' The *Derby Daily Telegraph* concurred. Miss Edwards was said, upon her return, to be 'none the worse' for her fall. Fascination with her daily doings now extended even to her physical appearance: 'She has a strong, handsome face, and a finely-shaped head, and carries herself with dignity and ease', opined the *Croydon Chronicle*. To another reporter, she was 'tall and portly, with a somewhat florid, kindly face', from which her grey hair was 'drawn severely back'. On this occasion, 'She wore a black silk dress with a long train beneath her fur-lined cloak'.[2]

Inevitably, celebrity attracted gossip – some of it bizarre. In 1872, for example, the *Belfast News-Letter* had claimed that Edwards was about to marry her friend Gustave Doré.[3] In the previous year, rumours had circulated that Amelia B. Edwards was actually someone else. She was really 'Mrs Freund', and the mother of John Christian Freund, who edited the Oxford-based literary magazine, *Dark Blue*. Alternatively, she was a 'lady who holds advanced views on political and social questions' (which she was); but who also used the *nom de plume*, 'Amelia Lewis', and had written a novel called *The Silvestres*. (That work was actually by Amelia's cousin, Matilda Betham Edwards, and titled *The Sylvesters* – the old confusion once again rearing its head.)[4]

The mix-up between her own and Matilda's names had dogged Amelia all her life. In June 1880, she wrote an uncharacteristically irritable letter to *The Academy*, demanding that the editors get the matter straight:

Will you kindly grant me space to say – for perhaps the tenth time within the last twenty years – that my name is neither Betham nor Betham-

Edwards; and that I am not related to the Betham family? . . . In an article, for instance, which appears in the current number of *The Academy*, Miss Betham-Edwards is repeatedly styled Miss Edwards; whereas I believe I am the only writer to whom that name can be correctly applied.

To make matters clear once and for all, Amelia Edwards went on to list examples of the novels written by herself and Matilda respectively. The confusion annoyed her sufficiently, for her to reproduce her letter to *The Academy* as a notice on the frontispiece of the first edition of *Lord Brackenbury*.[5]

Along with the rumours and confusions, there had in the past been accusations of plagiarism – not against Edwards herself but directed at other people. In 1870, it was said that Benjamin Disraeli, at that time leader of the opposition, had stolen the plot of his novel *Lothair* from Edwards. (In *Lothair*, as in her *Half a Million of Money*, a young English lord follows the daughter of an Italian independence leader to Italy.) Disraeli's friend Lord Houghton, the author and politician Richard Monckton Miles, came to his defence: 'Lord Houghton . . . denies the assertion that some of the incidents in Mr Disraeli's novel *Lothair* are taken from . . . *Half a Million of Money*.'[6]

One plagiarism charge, according to a report in *Lloyds Weekly*, was well-founded. A magazine serial story, titled 'Home Sweet Home', was said to be a faithful reproduction of *Barbara's History*. Such close imitation might be taken as a perverse kind of compliment. It is unknown whether Amelia Edwards took it that way.[7]

In 1890, the overall achievements of Edwards' life still continued to defy easy classification. She was the author of eight successful novels, and numerous short stories. She was well-known as a travel writer. She was a famous Egyptologist – celebrated, too, for her gift for public speaking and for publicizing the work of the organization she had founded. How to define such an intellectual chameleon? 'Probably one of the most versatile writers of the day', was what a writer in the *Croydon Chronicle* settled for.[8] Others grappled with the question: 'Sometimes Miss Edwards is described as a writer on Egyptology, sometimes as a novelist, rarely as both.'[9]

One thing it seemed, everyone could agree on: in whatever she turned her hand and her mind to, Miss Edwards was 'clever'. She wrote 'clever stories' said *The Examiner*, in 1858. Her novel *Debenham's Vow* was 'decidedly a clever book', noted *The Morning Advertiser*, reviewing the novel in 1869. When she lectured on ancient Egypt, she was 'the clever lady'; or, 'the learned lady'. Others wrote of 'clever artistic touches', and the 'clever' sayings in *Half a Million*.[10]

Is there perhaps just a touch of patronage in this repeated epithet? As if some of these reporters and reviewers were even a little surprised that a lady could indeed be both feminine and 'clever'?

On her return from the American speaking tour, Edwards' work for Egyptology was far from done. For as long as her failing health would allow, she went on lecturing. And she still attracted audiences; although at one lecture in Nottingham, where the audience was small owing to bad weather, she clearly was unwell. That did 'not affect her sympathetic delivery', said the *Nottingham Evening Post*, of her talk, on 'The Origin of Portrait Sculpture and the History of the Ka'. (The journalist was appreciative, too, of the speaker's patience with 'trying questions' from the audience.)[11] In November the following year, the *Western Daily Press* covered Edwards' talk in Bristol on 'Literature and Religion of Ancient Egypt', given at the Museum on Queen's Road. Her lecture was said to exhibit, 'in a marked degree, concentrative power, lucidity, and eloquence'.[12] The *Western Daily Press* would remember, for many years afterwards, Edwards' gift for bringing the past to life. In 1896, an anonymous writer for the paper recalled how:

> Miss Amelia Edwards, in one of her interesting discourses about Egypt, pointed out how difficult it was to get people to regard the Ancient Egyptians in any other light than that of dried mummies rolled in many wrappings . . . To remove this misconception the clever lady talked and wrote of their life, their legends, their poems, until in place of the mummy the living person, full of hopes and affections and activities, was pictured by the mind's eye.[13]

In 1890, as she gave her inspiring talks, it must have seemed that Amelia Edwards was at the height of her powers. But the reporters who had thought she looked 'all the better for her visit to America', were unaware of a painful reality, that she largely managed to conceal from the public. To the casual observer, her dignified bearing and neat, elegant clothes, her faultless courtesy, and the coherent, compelling manner in which she delivered her lectures, would have suggested that nothing was amiss. Only those closest to her knew that after her fall and breaking her arm in America, there had been other repeated falls – once on shipboard, on the voyage home, when the rolling of the *Etruria* during a gale had flung her violently against the cabin furniture; and again, after arriving in England. This third fall caused a new fracture in her left arm. A bone splinter had pierced a vein and an artery. She was forced to rest up at home. 'This is rather a bad job, and promises to be a long one', she wrote to Petrie; I can do nothing for myself – a miserable, helpless, one-handed cripple; and I suffer great discomfort'. She tried to be stoical. All the same, though, she complained, 'The worst of it is, it stops my work'.[14]

As if the fractured arm was not enough, in July that year, Amelia was advised by a surgeon to have a growth removed from her left breast, in case it turned cancerous. Kate Bradbury went with her to a London hospital, to have the operation. Afterwards, she went to Saville Villas to convalesce.

Whether Edwards ever fully got over this drastic operation, is questionable. She continued to suffer from exhaustion and chest infections, most probably brought on by the shock of the operation. Kate Bradbury, certainly, believed that this post-operative shock, and the loss of blood during surgery, were effects from which Amelia never really recovered.[15]

A further source of stress arose from the demands for work she continued to make on herself. While convalescing in Weston-super-Mare over the summer, she was still meanwhile having daily massage for the after-effects of the broken left arm. The injury healed slowly and, she complained once more, slowed down her usual productive output.[16] By October, though, she was back at work at The Larches on behalf of the Exploration Fund – writing letters, editing – even from a distance, keeping a careful watch on the doings of the Fund's committee in London, and preparing her American lectures for publication. In November, accompanied by Kate Bradbury, who had been looking after her at Saville Villa, she set out for a lecturing tour in northern England and Scotland.

Bradbury watched over Amelia, and worried about her constantly. On Christmas Day, 1890, she wrote to Petrie, telling him of her intention to go and stay with Edwards in the New Year: 'I shall go to her in a week. She is very weak, and entirely helpless, and the weight of my heart about her wakes me at nights.'

Edwards had stayed with Kate at Ashton-under-Lyne while giving a new northern lecture tour, by which she earned enough to pay for the breast surgery. She had gone back to Westbury, though, to spend Christmas with Ellen Braysher – 'that she might do her Xmas duty to Mrs Braysher's threadbare and exacting life', Kate wrote to Flinders Petrie. Kate was more than ambivalent about Edwards' decision, feeling, no doubt correctly, that Christmas spent with Mrs Braysher would be stressful. 'Could she have remained here for a long rest, unharassed by domestic worry, the lecturing would have done her no harm, but actually good. Travel always pleases her, and to be doing something, one among the living again.'

Kate had other concerns: it appears that Edwards' emotions were under strain, and that her mental health was fragile. She had become very dependent on Kate: 'She does not like me out of her sight for five minutes', Kate wrote to Petrie. As if to reassure herself – or possibly to avoid troubling Petrie, Kate added, 'But it was right that she should spend Xmas day with Mrs Braysher, and right that I should spend it here'. In March, Bradbury told Petrie that she found Edwards 'very aged and weakened, and very helpless. Yet I am thankful to say, that the depression is less . . .'[17]

It seems likely that an element of self-doubt always underlay Edwards' public image of self-possession and confidence. A classic 'over-achiever', all her life she drove herself towards success and completeness, in whatever she undertook. Only the best she could do would ever be good enough – and would even that best suffice?

The devoted Kate Bradbury was with her when, in early January, a letter came, notifying Edwards that, on the recommendation of Arthur Balfour, she had been awarded a Civil List pension of £75 a year – for services both to literature and to archaeology.[18] Amelia, who had been kept awake, coughing all night with bronchitis, was lying exhausted in bed while tea was brought to her. The letter 'lay at the top of the pile, and she opened that first. I gave my attention to her tea, but suddenly looking up, I saw her holding a half sheet in her hand, and crying, with a very white face . . .' Amelia showed the letter to Kate: 'and then – we both cried'.[19]

The pension was well-earned recognition for Edwards' obvious intellectual achievements. Yet, even after her death, the award would stir unexpected controversy. Why had Amelia Edwards stooped to accept charity? demanded the *Glasgow Evening Post*. The *Kinross-shire Advertiser* went further: 'The Civil List pension is awarded to those who are *both* deserving and destitute'. How, the editor wanted to know, did these conditions apply to the late Amelia Edwards, who had left 'a substantial endowment' for the founding of a Chair of Egyptology?[20]

Others did her more justice. In the *Montgomeryshire Echo*, an editor wrote: 'Objection has been taken to the pension granted to Miss Amelia B. Edwards, because she left enough money in her will to found the Chair at London University.' The 'excellent work done by Miss Edwards', however, remained 'the best claim that could be made', for a Civil List pension. A commentator in a West Country paper pointed out that Edwards had never asked for the pension, and had not known it would be awarded to her: 'If she had thought for a moment that the annual sum had been offered on the grounds of poverty, she would have refused it.' The *Norwich Mercury*, too, found it necessary to point out that the award had been 'well earned by painstaking and conscientious work'.[21]

From March 17 to the August of 1891, as her health continued to deteriorate, Edwards accepted that she needed to take a long rest. On the advice of her doctor, who recommended convalescence in a warm climate, she went to Italy; where, in fact she became even more exhausted and ill. Only when she and Kate reached Switzerland, on their homeward journey, did she find herself really starting to recover some of her health. 'So much for the doctors!' she exclaimed.[22] On her return from continental travels, she was racing to complete the editing of her American lectures. In October, she found herself drawn into the campaign to save the island of Philae from submersion by that 'great scandal' as she called it, the proposed British irrigation scheme.[23] In early December, she went on preparing lectures, to be given in January and February, in the north of England – in spite of ongoing bronchitis, and having contracted influenza, while overseeing a consignment of antiquities at the Millwall Docks.

Edwards' published collection of lectures came out at last at the end of that year, as *Pharaohs, Fellahs and Explorers*.[24] It was a bright spot in an otherwise grim year.

By the end of December, it became clear that Edwards would have to cancel her planned New Year lecture tour. She continued to suffer with chest infections. Presumably from writing so much, she was also unable to use her right hand.[25]

On the 9th of January, Ellen Braysher, Amelia's friend and companion of thirty-five years, died. As Amelia sat at her bedside, Ellen – who had suffered for a long period from what Kate Bradbury called 'brain failure' and had been wandering in her mind – briefly recovered lucidity, long enough for Amelia to bid her a loving goodbye.[26]

Miss Edwards would not be coming to speak in Scotland in February, the *Glasgow Herald* now had to tell its readers. She had been forced to cancel all her lecture engagements for the month. She was 'slowly recovering' from a serious illness.[27]

The claim that she was getting better turned out to be overly optimistic. In spite of brief periods when she seemed to recover, her health continued to decline. On the 15th of April, at Saville Villa in Weston-super-Mare, Amelia Edwards died.

The news was carried in reports and obituaries, in newspapers across the land. (Kate Bradbury collected over two hundred of these, pasting them in a scrapbook.) In one tribute, Ernest Wallis Budge, by now Assistant Keeper of the Oriental Department at the British Museum, wrote of Edwards as 'large-hearted, kind and sympathetic, a delightful companion and a good friend'. Matilda Betham Edwards, in a piece that appeared in the *Bristol Mercury*, offered an improbably idealized version of her cousin's last days. She had ended her life, 'In the midst of fame, friends and fortune, surrounded by everything to make her happy'.[28] In fact, Edwards' closest friends had either died, or were far away. Lucy Renshaw was in a Sussex nursing home. Ellen Braysher had succumbed to dementia, and Amelia had had to witness the death of this companion of over three decades. If it had not been for Kate Bradbury, she would, at the end, have been very alone.

If Flinders Petrie had once criticized a tendency Edwards had to dramatize her feelings and to exaggerate, Kate Bradbury was honest about this, but also understanding. In a letter to Petrie she reflected on 'what a heavy weight of herself' Amelia had to carry, and 'how near insanity, with its many miserable connotations, she often was'. We have to remember, however, that Kate only knew Amelia in the final years of her life, when her health had already begun to give way. In her last months, particularly, she clearly was no longer the person she had been in stronger, healthier days. She was always worrying Kate with, 'If there is a next world, will you stand by me in it?' She would do so, Kate had promised Amelia. 'But it was all so strange and intense . . .'[29]

Amelia was buried in the churchyard of St Mary the Virgin in Henbury, in the same grave where Ellen Braysher's body had been laid to rest only weeks before. Her funeral was, if anything, more widely reported than the fact of her death. The *Pall Mall Gazette* remarked on the 'very large concourse of friends' who followed the coffin to the grave, 'many of whom had come a long way'.[30] The Egyptologist Percy Newberry attended, as a representative of the Egypt Exploration Fund. Agnes Maitland came, to represent Somerville College. The one family member present was Captain Gerald Fitzgerald, one of Amelia's cousins.

Mourners laid piles of flowers around the grave. Lucy Renshaw, from her nursing home, was unable to come to the funeral, but sent a wreath. Kate Bradbury laid an ankh – the ancient Egyptian Key of Life – made of pansies, on the coffin. Later, she and Flinders Petrie would arrange for a large carved ankh to be placed on top of the tomb.

There was already an obelisk at the grave – a common ornament in Victorian cemeteries – that had been by erected by Ellen Braysher for her daughter. It carried inscriptions in memory of Ellen and Sarah. Now a new inscription was added: 'Here lies the body of Amelia Ann Blandford Edwards, novelist and archaeologist, born in London on the 7th June 1831 – died at Weston-super-Mare on the 15th April 1892 – who by her writings and her labours enriched the thought and interests of her time.'[31] (If Edwards had never actually been an archaeologist, as opposed to an Egyptologist, no one seemed too troubled by the anomaly.)

Edwards' will, signed and witnessed on March 8, 1891, and revised with only minor alterations on January 22, 1892, gives a fair indication of who, and what, had been important to her at the end of her life. The principal beneficiaries were named, firstly, as Ellen Drew Braysher – who, besides being Edwards' close companion of thirty-five years, had been elderly and frail, and seen as in need of regular financial support; and, secondly, the devoted, caring Kate Bradbury, who had done more than anyone to ease Amelia's physical sufferings and keep her company in her last years. Bradbury, with the solicitor Edmund Kell Blyth, was named as executor of the will, in which Edwards left a total of £8,446, 15 shillings and 5 pence.

Edwards left Kate a lump sum of £500. Ellen Braysher had been intended to receive an annuity of £200 a year; the income to be derived from Edwards' £2,415 worth of stock in the Great Eastern Railway Company. This arrangement had been designed to assure Mrs Braysher a regular income, while allowing others more physically and mentally capable, to manage her money for her: 'Having regard to her great age and state of health', Edwards had written, 'I think this is a better way of providing for the said Ellen Braysher if she survive me than bequeathing her the said annuities absolutely'. Since Ellen had died before Amelia, making this provision irrelevant, in March 1893, the will had to be 're-sworn'.

There were other, smaller, personal bequests. To her cousin Matilda Betham Edwards, Amelia left £100. To Emily Paterson, her personal secretary, who had done so much for the Egypt Exploration Fund, £20. To her cousin Captain Gerald Fitzgerald, £100, 'and my Roman gem ring'. To her friends Jesse and Marianne Haworth, benefactors to the cause of Egyptology, her album of water colours, and an oil painting of Venice, by Tilton. To Lucy Renshaw, her old love and the companion of her travelling days, Amelia had at first left 'my collection of Etruscan and Roman antiquities', and some jewellery. Later, she changed her mind, leaving the Etruscan and Roman antiquities to Kate Bradbury instead, and substituting another piece of jewellery to bequeath to Lucy. The lawyer, Edmund Blyth, would receive a painting by the American landscape artist Frederick Church. To her neighbour, Mrs St Vincent Ames, Amelia left 'my gold pendant of Etruscan design'. The will bears witness to Edwards' usual careful attention to small details; and to her care in considering what it would be most useful, most practical, most pleasing, to offer to each of those close to her, to remember her by.

There was no question of leaving anything to Marianne North, who had died in 1890, or to Gustave Doré, who had died seven years before that. One notable omission, however, is any mention of John Addington Symonds (whose life would end almost exactly a year after that of Edwards herself). Perhaps there was an issue about the propriety of a woman leaving property to a male who was neither an executor (like Blyth the solicitor), or, like Captain Fitzgerald, a relative?

The other name that does not appear, is that of Ellen Rice Byrne. She was no longer a part of Amelia's life.

The third chief beneficiary was not a person, but a new institution – the Chair of Egyptian Archaeology and Philology, to be established in Edwards' name, at University College, London, and for which £1,600 in shares were to be used to establish a trust fund. With typical meticulous precision, Edwards stipulated which of her possessions were to be donated to UCL, for the use of the new professor and his students. She listed everything – all books, photos, artefacts relating to Egyptology – even down to 'jewellery, scarabs, amulets, sculptures of Deities . . . writings on linen and papyrus'. She asked either Flinders Petrie or Francis Griffith to label and catalogue the scholarly books. (Her books of a more general nature, she left to Kate Bradbury, to pass on to the Ashmolean Museum in Oxford.)

The will required the university to devise rules and regulations in keeping with her aim – 'the teaching of Egyptology with a view to the wide extension of the knowledge and the history, antiquities, literature, philology and art of Ancient Egypt'.

Particular conditions attached to the actual professorship. No officer of the British Museum was to be considered eligible for appointment to the Edwards Chair of Egyptology, and the successful applicant for the position must be under forty years of age. These rules were the subject of some puzzlement in the British press – one editor noting that they might 'modify the advantages' of the endowment.[32] In fact, they were designed by Edwards to do just that – to ensure that only Flinders Petrie, of all potentially qualified applicants in Britain at the time, would be eligible for the post.

The terms of the will went on: all classes, and any scholarships that might be offered, were to be open 'to students of both sexes'. The donated books and artefacts were to be kept in glazed bookcases in a designated room, where the collections could be added to from time to time. The entrance to the room would bear a plaque, with the words, 'The Edwards Professorship of Egyptian Archaeology and Philology', with a tablet stating that both the materials and the professorship were 'the bequests of Amelia B. Edwards, with the dates of my birth and death'.

With Edwards' death, the question once again arose, of how to define her achievements – whether to privilege the novelist, or the Egyptologist? The *York Herald* recalled that Edwards' 'light and sketchy novels' had 'amused one generation', while a younger following was astonished by 'her profound acquaintance with Egyptian archaeology, and the interesting manner in which she was able to treat of this abstruse subject'. (One might take issue with the description of Edwards' fiction as uniformly 'light and sketchy'. Certainly, neither *Half a Million* nor *Debenham's Vow* deserves to be dismissed so lightly. But at least the author of this piece took the trouble to recall Edwards' work as a novelist.)[33] There would later be an admiring assessment of her fiction by a fellow-novelist, Katharine Macquoid: 'Miss Edwards appears to have gone about the world open-eyed and with notebook in hand, so vivid are some of her portraits.' Macquoid also noted Edwards' democratic sympathies, and her ear for dialogue.[34] Another tribute recalled Edwards' early career as a musician, remarking that 'In dealing with musical matters' in her novels, 'she never makes a mistake'. There were 'not too many novelists of whom this can be said'.

Editors, for more pragmatic reasons, remembered Edwards as 'a model contributor – never declining a request, punctual to her promises, writing in a clear, bold hand, and considerate of the conveniences of printer as well as editor'.[35]

A tribute in the *Western Morning News* was inclined to privilege the work for Egyptology over Edwards' contribution to fiction. Although her novels were still readily available, 'Her best work, and that which she herself most valued, was given to Egypt'. Edwards had performed the difficult task of making Egyptology popular. Others chimed in: 'Egyptian antiquarian lore', according to one obituary, had lost 'one of its most devoted students'.[36] It was this consensus, no doubt – that Miss Edwards was to be remembered as an Egyptologist – that doomed her fiction to undeserved obscurity.

After her death, she continued to be an inspiration to many. In particular, she was remembered as a feminist role model. The Woman's Building at the Chicago World's Fair of 1893, had a frieze in gold lettering with names of famous women – Queen Victoria, Christina Rossetti, Florence Nightingale, Elizabeth Barrett Browning – Amelia B. Edwards.[37] The Egypt Exploration Fund, that would not have existed without Edwards initial inspiration, and her dogged determination to see it succeed, along with the Chair of Egyptology she had founded, empowered a new generation of scholars and archaeologists.

After Edwards' death, Emily Paterson became Exploration Fund honorary secretary, assisted by Kate Bradbury, and by the man Kate later married, the Egyptologist Francis Llewellyn Griffith. In 1919 the Fund was renamed the Egypt Exploration Society.

Today, the society draws its membership from all over the world. With an office in Egypt, based at the British Council premises in Cairo, along with the centre in London, the EES trains and funds scholars and excavators –

and conservationists – to carry on the work of Egyptology for generations to come. As Edwards had intended, the new department of Egyptology she had endowed at UCL, with Petrie as its first professor, would educate the scholars and diggers of the future – women as well as men.

The new department in time trained and enabled the work of a whole new generation of female Egyptologists, beginning with Mary Brodrick (1858–1933), who became the first woman to undertake excavation work in Egypt. Brodrick was followed by Janet Gourlay (1863–1912), a student of Flinders Petrie best known for her excavations at the shrine of the goddess Mut at Karnak. Margaret Murray (1863–1963), who began her studies at UCL in 1894, was four years later appointed by Petrie as a junior professor at the university.

In the next generation, there was Julia Samson, who joined the Egypt Exploration Society in 1924, aged fifteen, and remained a member and supporter for over seventy-seven years. Samson became known for her scholarly writings on Akhnaton and Nefertiti. Her near-contemporary, Joan Crowfoot Payne (1912–2002), would become curator of the Ashmolean Museum. Another scholar and hands-on archaeologist, and keeper of the Petrie Museum, was Barbara Adams (1945–2002), who became an Honorary Fellow of UCL.[38] In the twenty-first century, the university gave undergraduate training in Egyptology to the energetic, charismatic Professor Joann Fletcher, whose scholarship has focused on the women of ancient Egypt to a degree that surely would have delighted Amelia Edwards. Known to a wider public than Edwards could ever have dreamed of, through her more than twenty TV presentations, Fletcher is a prolific author of both scholarly publications, and articles in popular magazines.

In the work she did to foster the pursuit of Egyptology, Edwards is unlikely ever to be forgotten.

For a time in the twentieth century, however, her reputation waned. For many decades after her death, all her works were out of print – even the ever-popular travel books. After a few disparaging appraisals from critics more interested in newer, more fashionable writers, for a time she faded from popular memory. The put-downs began, in fact, even in the year of her death; when, in an article in the *Paisley and Renfrewshire Gazette* of December 1892, her achievement as a novelist was slightingly dismissed as that of a 'favourite writer of women's stories'.[39] By 1924, in a piece in the *Western Daily Press*, Edwards had dwindled in stature to 'a local lady who was a keen Egyptologist, at a time when few devoted themselves to the study of Egypt'. (An eccentric spinster, in other words, with an obscure antiquarian hobby.)[40] Although in 1915, the Bristol Naturalists' Society visited Edwards' grave, presumably to pay homage to this woman who had championed animal rights, and cared for wildlife, most Bristolians by this time probably had no idea who she was.[41]

A hundred years would go by, before, on March 19, 2015, English Heritage placed a blue plaque on the house at 19 Wharton Street Islington, where Edwards lived in her twenties, and began to make her name as a novelist. The Larches, home to Amelia Edwards and Ellen Braysher for so many years, was destroyed by bombing during the Second World War; but another plaque, on the surrounding wall of a new house built on the site, proclaims that Amelia once lived there.

In September 2015, Historic England named Edwards' grave in Henbury as a Grade II Listed monument. Their reasons: the unusual nature of the grave, with its ancient Egyptian symbolism; but also what was described as a 'poignant memorial' to Amelia Edwards and Ellen Braysher, 'with the relationship unusually described in the inscription'. Historic England noted the significance of Edwards' grave to the LGBT movement. Edwards was to be 'remembered as an unconventional, dignified woman who had lasting relationships with women', who is buried 'beside her beloved long-term partner Ellen Braysher'.[42] Last, but certainly not least, Historic England recalls Edwards' own remarkable 'life and accomplishments', and her 'legacy to Egyptian studies'.[43]

A small sculpture of Edwards, by Emma Jean Kemp, has recently been erected outside the Amelia Lodge retirement living complex in Westbury-on-Trym, not far from the site of The Larches. The National Portrait Gallery has four separate photographs of her, and a portrait bust of her in marble, done by Percival Ball in 1873.

In more recent years, Amelia Edwards has become a somewhat legendary figure. In Stephen Medcalf's 2012 production of *Aida*, Edwards appeared as a non-singing character, in a stage set representing a Victorian archaeological site. Her presence there was imagined as awakening the ghosts of Aida and Radames, to re-enact the tragic drama of their lives.[44]

Her novels still make good reading, and are available in print-on-demand versions online. All her major works, both fiction and non-fiction, are now available as e-books, from the University of Pennsylvania Digital Library. There have also been reprints of her travel writings in recent years – notably by Kegan Paul (who brought out a new edition of *A Thousand Miles Up the Nile*, in 2003). The Egypt Exploration Society aims to publish a full-colour reprint of the original edition of the book, for Edwards' 130th anniversary in 2021.

To Edwards personally, the price of her many achievements was high. Relentlessly self-driven from her youth, she would never be able to pace herself. What if she had allowed herself a little more respite – time to recover her strength between tasks, before embarking on the next one – would she have lived on beyond the relatively young age of 61? Could there have been more books of travel, more novels? Might she have founded another useful institution, to enhance the world's cultural life? We shall never know. As matters stand, her legacy abides. This complex, enigmatic, multitalented woman gave what she had in her to give, within the short span of her lifetime; and did so to the limit. The work consumed her, and left us her achievements:

Whatever flames upon the night
Man's own resinous heart has fed.

Appendix 1

Amelia Edwards, biographical timeline

June 7, 1831	Amelia Edwards born, in Islington, London.
	Shows talent for writing, drawing, music. Prevented by illness from following a singing career.
January 1851	Engaged to be married. Breaks off the engagement after a few months.
1852	Edwards gives up the idea of becoming a musician or composer. All through the 1850s, she writes for newspapers and magazines. First short stories published.
1853–57, 1862, 1864	First trips to continental Europe give her a lifelong passion for travel.
1855	Her first novel, *My Brother's Wife*, is published.
1856	*The Ladder of Life*.
1858	*Hand and Glove*.
1860	Death of Edwards' father and mother, within days of one another.
1863	*Barbara's History* appears, in monthly serial form. Published in book form, 1864.
***c.* 1864**	Edwards moves to Westbury-on-Trym, to live with Ellen Braysher at The Larches. Her *Ballads* are published.
1865	*Miss Carew* is published.

Half a Million of Money is serialized. (Published in book form, 1866.)

Meeting with Ellen Byrne and her husband, the Reverend John Byrne. Clandestine marriage to Ellen.

1869   *Debenham's Vow* is published.

1871   To Edwards' grief, Ellen and John leave Bristol. Amelia offers a wedding ring to her friend Marianne North, who makes fun of the idea.

1871–72   Edwards leaves England to travel on the Continent. She spends the winter and spring in Rome. Love letters to Anne Brewster. In Italy, she meets Lucy Renshaw, with whom she will have a long-term, loving relationship.

April 1872 Amelia and Lucy are together in Salerno, where they witness the eruption of Vesuvius. In July, they begin their trek through the Dolomites.

1873   Return to England, where she prepares work for publication. *Untrodden Peaks and Unfrequented Valleys* published – also *In the Days of My Youth,* and *Monsieur Maurice.*

December   Edwards and Lucy begin their journey up the Nile by
1873   sailing barge.

1874   Edwards returns from Egypt through Syria, Lebanon and Greece. In Athens, she meets with the archaeologist Heinrich Schliemann.

1874   Reads a paper on 'Recent Excavations in the Necropolis of Abydos', at the Oriental Congress in Vienna.

1876   *A Thousand Miles Up the Nile* first appears in print, with a publication date of 1877. (A more affordable version appears in 1888.)

October 1877 With fellow-novelist Annie Thomas, Edwards founds a charitable enterprise – a laundry business to give employment to women in financial need.

1880   *Lord Brackenbury* is published.

Edwards writes letters and articles to promote the idea of an organization for funding excavations and preserving Ancient Egyptian monuments and antiquities.

1882   With a group of distinguished scholars, she founds the Egyptian Exploration Fund. (Later named the Egypt Exploration Fund.) She serves as honorary secretary of the Fund, until 1889.

1886–87   Edwards undertakes lecture tours in Britain, to raise awareness about Ancient Egypt. She writes dozens of articles on Egyptology at this time, both academic and popular.

                First meeting with Kate Bradbury.

1886–   Vice-president of Bristol and West of England Society for Women's Suffrage. Public speeches in Bristol – and later, in America – on the subject of women's social and political rights. Makes appeals against vivisection, and for the protection of birds.

1889–90   Speaking tour of America, accompanied by Kate Bradbury.

July 1890   Edwards undergoes a breast cancer operation, from which she never fully recovers.

January 1891   Award of a Civil List pension, for services to literature and archaeology.

March–   Travelling across Europe to Italy, in a bid to recover her
August 1891   health.

October   Edwards takes part in a campaign to save Egypt's Philae temple from inundation by an irrigation scheme.

                Publication of *Pharaohs, Fellahs and Explorers*.

                While at Millwall Docks to oversee unpacking of a consignment of artefacts, she contracts influenza.

January 9,   Death of Ellen Braysher.
1892

April 15   Amelia Edwards herself dies, at her home in Weston-super-Mare.

Appendix 2

Maps

MAP 1 *The Dolomites, from* Untrodden Peaks

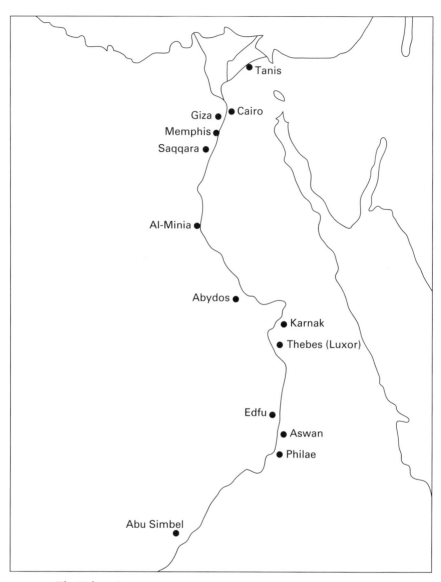

MAP 2 *The Nile in Egypt*

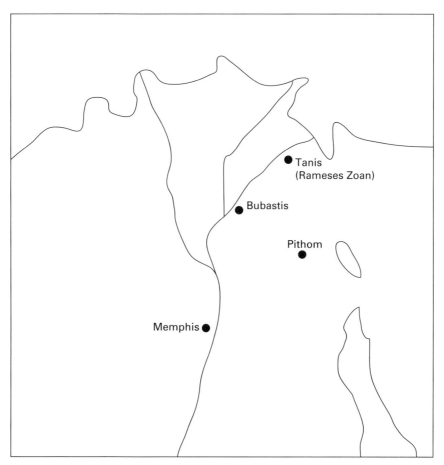

MAP 3 *The Land of Goshen*

NOTES

Preface

1 'Egyptology': *Norwich Mercury*, April 20, 1892, p.2; 'novels . . . a generation'. *York Herald*, April 19, 1892, p.5.

2 *Freeman's Journal*, April 19, 1892, p.5; *Preston Herald*, April 23, 1892, p.4.

Chapter 1

1 Somerville College Library Archives, Oxford, [hereafter SCO] Edwards 351.

2 John Gardner Wilkinson, *Manners and Customs of the Ancient Egyptians*. London: John Murray, 1837 (6 volumes, 1837–41). Between first publication and 1878, the book went through five more editions.

3 Matilda Betham Edwards, 'Amelia B. Edwards, Her Childhood and Early Life'. *New England Magazine* 7.5, January 1893, pp. 549–64: p. 549.

4 'Amelia B. Edwards, Her Childhood and Early Life', pp. 549–64: p. 560.

5 'Childhood', pp. 549–64: p. 560.

6 'Childhood', pp. 549–50.

7 'Childhood', pp. 549–64.

8 Draft autobiography, written in letter form for Edward Abbott, editor of *The Literary World*. SCO Edwards W22, 351.

9 It was previously assumed that the Edwards family moved from 1 Westmoreland Place while Amelia was still a child. Recently, from an examination of census records, it has been established that she and her parents were still living at Westmoreland Place at least until 1851, when Edwards was over twenty. My thanks to Alan Boyle for making this discovery; and for drawing it to my attention.

10 'Childhood', p. 560.

11 'Childhood', pp. 549–64; p. 553.

12 SCO Edwards 439.

13 'Childhood', pp. 555–6.

14 Autobiographical letter to Edward Abbot, editor of the *Literary World*. SCO Edwards 351.

15 *Barbara's History: A Novel*. New York: Harper, 1864, vol. 1, p. 60. All references in the present work are to this edition.

16 'The Two Dromias', in *Reminiscences*, London: George Redway, 1898, p. 133. 'Amelia Blandford Edwards', *Mid-Victorian Memories*. London: John Murray, 1919, pp. 110–18.

17 'Childhood', p. 562.

18 'The Two Dromias', p. 121.

19 'The Late Miss Amelia Edwards', *Bristol Mercury*, April 25, 1892, p. 6.

20 *The Young Woman*, December 7, 1894, p. 95.

21 'Childhood', pp. 548–9.

22 'Childhood', p. 562.

23 'Childhood', p. 553.

24 'Childhood', p. 562.

25 'Childhood', p. 562. Either Matilda or Amelia got the quotation slightly wrong. The lines are from *Endymion*: 'O magic sleep! O comfortable bird, / That broodest o'er the troubled sea of the mind / Till it is hush'd and smooth'.

26 'Childhood', p. 563.

27 *The Young Woman*, December 7, 1894, p. 95; and Amelia Edwards' letter to *The Academy*, of September 1878.

28 SCO Edwards 351.

29 SCO Edwards 439. Ann Sheppard Mounsey Bartholomew (1811–1891), was a pianist, organist and composer. She wrote an oratorio, *The Nativity* (1855), and over a hundred songs and part-songs, as well as pieces for keyboard. She was known as a gifted teacher.

30 SCO Edwards 439.

31 SCO Edwards 439.

32 'Childhood', p. 562.

33 SCO Edwards 439.

34 SCO Edwards 60.

35 SCO Edwards 351.

36 SCO Edwards 439.

37 'One of my best'. See Brenda Moon, *More Usefully Employed: Amelia B Edwards, Writer, Traveller and Campaigner for Ancient Egypt*. London: Egypt Exploration Society, 2006, p. 20; SCO Edwards 439. See also Moon, p. 29, n. 9.

38 SCO Edwards 438.

39 The tale first appeared in 1864, in the Christmas issue of Charles Dickens' magazine *All the Year Round* (pp. 35–40). It has been reprinted several times in anthologies. See, for example, Richard Dalby, ed., *The Phantom Coach: Collected Ghost Stories* (1999); *The Phantom Coach*, ed. Ruskin Bond, Rupa: New Delhi, 2018. The story has also been reproduced in Kindle versions, and as an audiobook.

40 See Eliza Lynn Linton, *My Literary Life*. Ed. Beatrice Harraden. London: Hodder and Stoughton, 1899, pp. 19–32.

41 SCO Edwards 351.

42 SCO Edwards 439.

43 SCO Edwards 515.

44 SCO Edwards 351, 439.

45 *My Brother's Wife: A Life-History*. London: Hurst and Blackett, 1855. (All references in the present work are to the edition published in New York by Harper and Brothers, 1865.)

46 *Dundee, Perth and Cupor Advertiser*, February 5, 1856, p. 4. For a full discussion of Edwards' work as a novelist, see Chapter 8 of the present work.

47 By Harper in 1865, and by Lovell in 1889. In 1877, Munro in New York brought out a collection of extracts from the novel.

48 'The author, were it not for the name . . . a young man . . .' Review in *The Globe*, August 1855. SCO Edwards 434.5.

49 'Books of the Week', in *The Examiner*, May 15, 1858, p. 5.

50 'Books of the Week', p. 5. *Il Guanto Fatale*. Milan: Emilio Croce, 1872.

51 In Matilda's obituary tribute to her cousin: 'The Late Miss Amelia Edwards', *Bristol Mercury*, April 25, 1892, p. 6.

52 *Etiquette for Gentlemen: being a manual of minor social ethics and customary observances*. (London: Knight, 1857); *A History of France from the Conquest of Gaul by the Romans to the Peace of 1856*. (London: Routledge, 1858.) *A Lady's Captivity among Chinese pirates in the Chinese seas*. (Fanny Loviot, transl. Amelia B. Edwards. London: Routledge, 1858); *Sights and Stories: being some account of a holiday tour through the north of Belgium*. (London: Victoria Press, 1862); *The Story of Cervantes*. (London: Routledge, 1862.)

53 SCO Edwards 213–20.

54 SCO Edwards 36.

55 SCO Edwards 213–20.

56 *Reminiscences*, p. 180.

57 'My home life', *Arena*, 4, 1891, pp. 299–310.

58 Letter to her neighbour, Miss Worrall, December 1, 1883. University College London Special Collections [hereafter UCL] Ms Add. 181.7, quoted in Moon, *More Usefully Employed*, p. 195.

59 Her 'List of Remarkable Persons' had 92 names of artists, writers, and Egyptologists. See SCO Edwards 565.32. A letter of February 2, 1873 shows Edwards donating specimens from her autograph collection to a Mrs Grove for a charity bazaar – 'I enclose another scrawl – Please put a good price on them' – and offering to swap autographs. For this information I am indebted to William Joy, curator of the Peggy Joy Egyptology Library, Michigan, who kindly shared his original MS copy of the letter with me.

60 Letter from Browning to Edwards, July 16, 1882, SCO Edwards; Letter from Browning to Edwards, July 1, 1869.

61 *Ballads.* London: Tinsley, 1865. By way of thanks, Symonds gave Amelia a copy of his own volume of verse, *Many Moods* (London: Smith, Elder and Co.,1878).

Chapter 2

1 'Love . . . of all stimulants the most powerful': *Debenham's Vow.* London: Hurst and Blackett, 1870, vol 1, p. 137. The novel had previously been serialized in *Good Words*, between December and January 1869.

2 University College, London: Mss Add 182.3, n.d.

3 'The Correspondence of John Addington Symonds and Havelock Ellis on the project of sexual inversion.' Sean Brady (ed.), *John Addington Symonds and Homosexuality: A critical edition of sources.* London: Palgrave Macmillan, 2012, pp. 239–41, p. 240.

4 See Joan Rees, *Amelia Edwards: Traveller, Novelist and Egyptologist.* London: Rubicon, 1998, p. 93.

5 'Grand Amateur Concerts at Westbury-on-Trym', *Bristol Daily Post*, December 16, 1870, p. 3. The *Bristol Times and Mirror*, December 16, 1870, p. 3, carries a fuller version of the same article.

6 A 'death-blow': SCO Edwards, 251. See also Moon, *More Usefully Employed*, p. 62.

7 Ellen Byrne's London concert was held at the Poplar Mission to Seamen Institute. Like her benefit concert in Westbury, the event was covered in the local press. (*Norwood News*, March 14, 1896, p. 5.)

8 Marianne's invitation to Amelia: undated letter, SCO Edwards 236.

9 SCO Edwards 236, n.d; 'Wednesday', SCO Edwards, 241.

10 'Saturday', SCO Edwards 237; n.d., SCO Edwards 241.

11 'When the Byrne bullies you too much, come here': North to Edwards, June 3, 1871, SCO North 237. Brenda Moon thought that the bully in question might be Julia Clara Byrne, editor of *The Morning Post*. In *More Usefully Employed*, p. 63.

12 In describing Ellen Byrne as 'a mother figure', Joan Rees seems to have confused her with Ellen Braysher. In *Amelia Edwards: Traveller, Novelist and Egyptologist,* p. 23.

13 July 19, 1871, SCO Edwards 244.

14 North's letters: SCO North 245–253 (1871–1884).

15 'Friday', SCO Edwards, 228. This correspondence took place between May 13 and July 19, 1871. There are 19 letters, in all.

16 May 26, 1871, SCO Edwards 230.

17 'Reminiscences and Notes of a Tour in Germany, Bavaria, Tyrol and Italy', SCO Edwards 515, p. 68.

18 'Reminiscences and Notes of a Tour', SCO Edwards 515, p. 68.

19 Letters to Anne Maria Hampton Brewster, Library Company of Philadelphia. Box 1, folder 17, 1871–73.

20 University of Chicago Special Collections Research Center, Gerald N.Wachs Collection.

Chapter 3

1   SCO Edwards 428.

2   *Untrodden Peaks and Unfrequented Valleys: A midsummer ramble in the Dolomites*. London: Longmans, Green, 1873, p. 28.

3   *Untrodden*, p. 29.

4   *Untrodden*, p. 45.

5   In the preface to *Untrodden*, the edition of 1873, p. xii.

6   *Untrodden*, p. 30.

7   'paw like a Bengal tiger': *Untrodden*, p. 99. Alan and Susan Boyle tell of meeting Marco Ghedina, the great-grandson of 'Old Ghedina', when they visited Cortina a few years ago. In their evocative and thoroughly researched work on Edwards and Renshaws' Italian mountain journey, *Spirits of the Dolomites* (London: Leannta, 2018, pp. 36, 38).

8   *Untrodden*, pp. 95–97.

9   *Untrodden*, p. 117.

10 *Untrodden*, pp. 192–5.

11 *Untrodden*, p. 238.

12 'a single bound . . . gulf below': *Untrodden*, p. 184.

13 *Untrodden*, pp. 231–2.

14 *Untrodden*, p. 214.

15 *Untrodden*, pp. 244–5.

16 *Untrodden*, pp. 115–16.

17 *Untrodden*, pp. 54–55.

18 *Untrodden*, pp. 82–83.

19 *Untrodden*, pp. 107–8. Matilda B. Edwards once said that as a young girl living under her parents' roof, Amelia never did any housework or cooking. Her mother 'forbore to give her the domestic training she had herself received'. ('Childhood', p. 550.) Amelia's basic culinary skills had evidently improved since her youth.

20 *Untrodden*, pp. 237–8.

21 *Untrodden*, p. 133.

22 Traditional greetings: *Untrodden*, p. 95.

23 *Untrodden*, p. 337.

24 *Untrodden*, p. 217.

25 *Untrodden*, pp. 344–5.

26 *Untrodden*, p. 200.

27 *Untrodden*, p. 23.

28 *Untrodden*, p. 162.

29 *Untrodden*, pp. 204–5.

30 *Untrodden*, pp. 144, 147.

31 *Untrodden*, p. 354.

32 *Untrodden*, pp. 274–5.

33 *Untrodden*, pp. 364–5.

34 *Untrodden*, pp. 338–9, 345–6.

35 *Untrodden*, p. 389.

36 *Untrodden*, p. 251.

37 Letter from Edwards to Brewster dated November 15, 1873.

Chapter 4

1 *A Thousand Miles Up the Nile*. London: Longmans, Green, 1877.

2 For Jenny Lane and her diary, see Moon, *More Usefully Employed*, pp. 112–32.

3 George: *Thousand Miles*, p. 74.

4 *Thousand Miles*, p. 3; SCO Edwards 351.

5 *Thousand Miles*, p. 58.

6 *Thousand Miles*, pp. 61, 64.

7 *Thousand Miles*, p. 241.

8 *Thousand Miles*, p. 62.

9 *Thousand Miles*, pp. 105–6.

10 Andrew McCallum (1821-1902) was a popular and fashionable landscape painter. His painting, 'The Rock Temple at Aboo Simbel, Egypt' (1874), now hangs in the Field Museum of Natural History in Chicago. See, Beth L. Asbury, 'Pitt-Rivers, the Painter and the Palaeolithic Period', Pitt-Rivers Museum, University of Oxford. *Birmingham Egyptology Journal*, 2014.

11 *Thousand Miles*, p. 134.

12 *Thousand Miles*, p. 251.

13 *Thousand Miles*, pp. 219–20.

14 *Thousand Miles*, p. 605.

15 *Thousand Miles*, pp. 595–6.

16 *Thousand Miles*, p. 215.

17 *Thousand Miles*, pp. 276–7.

18 *Thousand Miles*, p. 21.

19 *Thousand Miles*, p. 370.

20 *Thousand Miles*, pp. 528–9. The Sheikh-el-Beled, a statue dating from the 26th century BC, is now in the Egyptian Museum in Cairo. He is an imposing figure, slightly stout but authoritative and upright, walking with a staff of office.

21 *Thousand Miles*, pp. 678–9.

22 *Thousand Miles*, p. 122.

23 *Thousand Miles*, pp. 608–9. J. Gardner Wilkinson's *Manners and Customs of the Ancient Egyptians*: See Chapter 1 of the present work.

24 *Thousand Miles*, pp. 194–5.

25 *Thousand Miles*, p. 94.

26 *Thousand Miles*, pp. 307, 318–20.

27 *Thousand Miles*, p. 445.

28 *Thousand Miles*, p. 386.

29 *Thousand Miles*, pp. 224, 392.

30 *Thousand Miles*, p. 76.

31 *Thousand Miles*, p. 60.

32 *Thousand Miles*, p. 487.

33 *Thousand Miles*, p. 232.

34 *Thousand Miles*, p. 61.

35 *Thousand Miles*, pp. 357, 450, 61, 163.

36 *Thousand Miles*, p. 245.

37 *Thousand Miles*, pp. 296, 374.

38 *Thousand Miles*, p. 374.

39 *Thousand Miles*, pp. 557–8.

40 *Thousand Miles*, pp. 564–5. Jenny Lane says the child was hit in the face by the shotgun pellets, which would have been a great deal more serious. See Moon, *More Usefully Employed*, p. 127.

41 *Thousand Miles*, pp. 566–9.

42 *Thousand Miles*, p. 347.

43 *Thousand Miles*, p. 368.

44 *Thousand Miles*, p. 108.

45 *Thousand Miles*, p. 132.

46 *Thousand Miles*, p. 174.

47 *Thousand Miles*, p. 702.

48 *Thousand Miles*, p. 274.

49 *Thousand Miles*, p. 545.

50 *Thousand Miles*, p. 298.

51 *Thousand Miles*, pp. 684–5.

52 *Thousand Miles*, pp. 263–4.

53 *Thousand Miles*, p. 246.

54 *Thousand Miles*, pp. 196–7.

55 *Thousand Miles*, p. 559.

56 *Thousand Miles*, p. 107.

57 *Thousand Miles*, p. 295.

58 *Thousand Miles*, pp. 573–5.

59 *Thousand Miles*, pp. 241–42.

60 *Thousand Miles*, p. 28.

61 *Thousand Miles*, pp. 41–44.

62 *Thousand Miles*, pp. 118–19.

63 *Thousand Miles*, p. 168.

64 Esna: *Thousand Miles*, p. 237; Amada, p. 363. Edwards would have been glad to learn that the Amada temple was eventually rescued from the desert sands. When, in the 1960s, the building was threatened by the rising waters of Lake Nasser during construction of the Aswan Dam, the temple, with its beautifully preserved bas reliefs, was moved, stone by stone, to higher ground. Today it is a popular tourist site. Edfu: p. 587.

65 *Thousand Miles*, p. 97.

66 *Thousand Miles*, pp. 181–2.

67 *Thousand Miles*, p. 328.

68 'The Arabs were breaking up and selling piecemeal priceless specimens . . .' *The Buffalo Commercial*, June 31, 1890, p. 3; 'Is it wonderful that ignorance should follow?' *Thousand Miles*, p. 520.

69 The Khedive at the time of Edwards' Nile journey was Ismail Pasha, who ruled until 1879. Ismail was succeeded by Tewfik (who ruled from 1879 to 1892). The debts incurred by Tewfik to European creditors were part of the pretext for the de facto British occupation of Egypt.

70 *Thousand Miles*, pp. 481–2.

71 *Thousand Miles*, pp. 657–8.

72 *Thousand Miles*, p. 708.

73 *Thousand Miles*, pp. 450–52.

Chapter 5

1 *Belfast News-Letter*, April 18, 1876, p. 4.

2 'A delightful gossiping book': Review in *The World*, February 6, 1877. 'A woman's view', *Saturday Review,* February 13, 1877, pp. 58–59.

3 *The Globe*, January 4, 1877, p. 6. 'A labour of love': review of *A Thousand Miles* in *Pall Mall Gazette,* January 19, 1877, p. 12.

4 'Your Egyptian book': Edward Lear to Edwards, July 14, 1883. SCO Edwards 98.

5 'Signora del Nilo': SCO Edwards, October 1885.

6   Publishing his own diaries: SCO Edwards, December 17, 1885. If he never published a written account of his own travels in Egypt, his delicate sketches – preparatory work for planned oil paintings – can still be enjoyed at the National Maritime Museum, Greenwich.

7   Letter, Frederick Church to Edwards, September 2, 1877, SCO Edwards 32.

8   Edwards to the Countess of Ballestran, autobiographical notes, 1881. SCO Edwards 351: 4.1.

9   Gustave Doré (1832–1883): engraver, illustrator, artist. Edwards' review of his work was published as, 'The Doré Gallery', *Morning Post*, May 4, 1869.

10 Letter, Doré to Edwards, August 23, 1877, SCO Edwards 452.

11 Letter, Maspero to Edwards, October 17, 1878, SCO Edwards 142.

12 Unaffordable edition. Reported in *Warminster and Westbury Journal*, October 13, 1888, p. 3.

13 SCO Edwards 351.

14 See Moon, pp. 136–40.

15 August 22, 1876, British Museum (BM), Oriental Antiquities 1868–81, 1704.

16 Oriental Congress: See, *The Graphic*, November 14, 1874, p. 3; *The Examiner*, September 19, 1874, p. 6. Edwards would read again at subsequent Congresses, in 1886 and 1887.

17 *Pharaohs, Fellahs and Explorers*, New York: Harper and Brothers, Franklin Square, 1891, p. 11.

18 *Morning Post*, April 21, 1892, p. 2.

19 *North London News* January 23, 1892, p. 2.

20 'Books of Eastern and Colonial Life: Egypt and its Explorers', *The Graphic*, April 9, 1892, p. 22. (For reasons unknown, the reviewer was using the American edition published by Harper, that came out at the same time as the British edition, published by Osgood, McIlvaine. The latter might have been found less distracting.) *Athenaeum*, 3357, February 27, 1892, pp. 274–5.

21 'Bubastis: An Historical Study', appeared in *The Century*, prefaced by a note about the author. (Quoted in *The Graphic*, January 11, 1890, p. 10.)

22 *Pharaohs, Fellahs*, p. 11.

23 *Pharaohs, Fellahs*, p. 142.

24 'Lying in State in Cairo', *Harper's New Monthly Magazine* 65.386, July 1882, pp. 185–205, 190.

25 *Pharaohs, Fellahs*, p. 222.

26 'Lying in State in Cairo', pp. 185–205, 202–3.

27 *Pharaohs, Fellahs*, p. 197.

28 'The Story of Tanis', *Harper's New Monthly Magazine* 73.437, October 1886, pp. 710–73.

29 *Pharaohs, Fellahs*, pp. 98–99.

30 *Pharaohs, Fellahs*, pp. 111–13.

31 *Pharaohs, Fellahs*, p. 134.

32   *Pharaohs, Fellahs*, p. 130.

33   *Pharaohs, Fellahs*, p. 135.

34   Edwards was, moreover, writing almost half a century before the discovery of the 20,000-year-old cave paintings at Lascaux, France.

35   See, for example, the report in the *Clifton and Redland Free Press* for October 30, 1891 (p.3), on her talk in Bristol where Edwards made this case. Her lecture, said the anonymous reporter, might be read as a call to 'stretch out the hand of recognition across the chasm of the centuries, to acknowledge our common humanity'.

36   *Pharaohs, Fellahs*, p. 139.

37   *Pharaohs, Fellahs*, p. 142.

38   *Pharaohs, Fellahs*, pp. 89–91.

39   *Pharaohs, Fellahs*, p. 97.

40   *Pharaohs, Fellahs*, p. 147.

41   *Pharaohs, Fellahs*, p. 165.

42   *Pharaohs, Fellahs*, p. 84.

43   *Pharaohs, Fellahs*, p. 196.

44   *Pharaohs, Fellahs*, p. 221.

45   *Pharaohs, Fellahs*, p. 222.

46   *Pharaohs, Fellahs*, pp. 223, 225.

47   *Pharaohs, Fellahs*, p. 226.

48   *Pharaohs, Fellahs*, pp. 226–7.

49   Cairo Ostracon 25218. From John L. Foster, *Love Songs of the New Kingdom*. Austin: University of Texas Press, 1992. 'All you need is love: Modern themes in ancient Egyptian love poems': https://garstangmuseum.wordpress.com/2018/02/07/all-you-need-is-love-modern-themes-in-ancient-egyptian-love-poems/ Accessed September 2019.

50   At Firth College near Sheffield in 1890, she delivered the talk to a packed hall, to 'frequent and loud applause'. Reported in *Sheffield Daily Telegraph*: 'Lecture on Egyptology', December 6, 1890.

51   *Pharaohs, Fellahs*, p. 268.

52   *Pharaohs, Fellahs*, p. 281.

53   *Pharaohs, Fellahs*, p. 261.

54   For a different perspective on the British invasion, see Chapter 10 of the present work: 'A Quiet Activist'.

55   *A Thousand Miles Up the Nile*, p. 847.

56   *Pharaohs, Fellahs*, p. 856.

57   *Pharaohs, Fellahs*, p. 848.

58   *Pharaohs, Fellahs*, p. 858.

59   *Pharaohs, Fellahs*, p. 856.

60   *Pharaohs, Fellahs*, p. 149.

Chapter 6

1   See also Chapter 4 of the present work: 'The Nile'.

2   Letter, Samuel Birch to Edwards, January 28, 1880, Egypt Exploration Society (EES III. j. 3).

3   I should like to see an international scheme free of all jealousies': EES III. j. 3I.

4   Henry Villiers Stuart to Edwards, EES III. j. 6.

5   Ernest Wallis Budge to Edwards, EES III. J. 1.

6   Ernst de Bunsen (1819–1903): speculative religious thinker (who entertained some dubious, and potentially racist, views). Letter, de Bunsen to Edwards, EES III. j. 2.

7   Stuart Poole to Edwards, EES IV. a. 1; SCO Edwards 565, no.5.

8   Note added by Edwards to a press cutting taken from *The Academy*: SCO Edwards 565, no. 29.

9   On June 19, 1880, a report appeared in *The Academy*, vol. 17, p. 455.

10   Letter, Howarth to Edwards, August 6, 1880: SCO Edwards.

11   Actually erected in the reign of Thutmose III (1479–1425 BC), the obelisk was given to the British government in 1819 by Egypt's ruler Mohamed Ali, to commemorate Lord Nelson's victory at the Battle of the Nile. The obelisk remained in Egypt for 58 years thereafter, because no one wanted to cover the costs of transporting it to Britain. It took Wilson's initiative, finally to bring the monument to London.

12   *Pharaohs, Fellahs*, p. 232. For Edwards' thoughts on the spiritual significance of ancient Egyptian religious imagery at its beginnings, see *A Thousand Miles Up the Nile*, p. 593.

13   'Notes from John O'Gaunt's Chair', *Preston Herald*, December 13, 1890, p. 5.

14   For a detailed discussion of Victorian religious beliefs in relation to Egyptology, see David Gange, 'Religion and Science in Late Nineteenth-Century British Egyptology'. In *The Historical Journal* 49.4, December 2006, pp. 1083–1103. While Gange's claim for religious motives driving Edwards' own personal enthusiasm for Egyptology at times seems somewhat exaggerated, he gives a good sense of how such motives affected the wider Victorian public. As he suggests, for many Victorians the possibility of finding proofs for the truth of religion, whether of Judaism or Christianity, far outweighed any interest in asserting national pride. (Alice Stevenson, on the other hand, probably overstates the case for Edwards' emotional investment in the British imperial project in Egypt: 'By placing archaeological work beside military success, the EEF secured for its British audience a sense of authority and legitimacy in trenching the site'. (*Scattered Finds: Archaeology, Egyptology and Museums*, UCL Press, 2019, p. 30.) In this connection, see also my observations in Chapter 10 of the present work, regarding Edwards' letter to the press about the 1882 invasion.

15   Edwards writes about this in 'The Story of Tanis', *Harper's New Monthly Magazine* 73.437, October 1886, pp. 710–73.

16   Notice in *The Times*, March 30, 1882, p. 8.

17 'The cities of Egypt', *The Academy* 22, 1882, p. 389.

18 'Was Rameses II the pharaoh of the Exodus?' *Knowledge* 2 (1882), pp. 108–9, 141–2, 192–3, 228–9, 244, 260–61, 291–3, 324–6, 357–8, 387, 450.

19 In 'The Progress of Discovery in Egypt', *The Academy*, April 7, 1883, pp. 246–7.

20 Outreach to artists: EES, Aug 15, 1886, III. a. 19.

21 About 160 subscribers were recruited by Edwards herself. See EES III. B. 74.

22 Letter, Edwards to Flinders Petrie, September 22, 1887, the personal papers of Lisette Petrie (PP) 9. iv. 33.

23 'Lying in State in Cairo', *Harper's New Monthly Magazine* 65.386, July 1882, pp. 185–205, 190.

24 Letter to *The Times* of August 29, 1882. Reprinted in *The Star*, September 2, 1882, p. 4. For a slightly different perspective on the British invasion of Egypt, see Chapter 10 of the present work.

25 'The New Boolak Museum'. Letter from Edwards to *The Morning Post*, April 30, 1880, p. 3.

26 Poole wrote to Amelia about this: 'In order to avoid complicating the affair by introducing M. Mariette, I would advise your first writing to Dr Birch asking if he will undertake to carry on the work for you.' May 7, 1880, EES IV. a. 2.

27 January 4, 1881, BM OA 1868–81.1716. Quoted in Moon, *More Usefully Employed*, p. 166.

28 EES XVI. b.20. See also, Margaret S. Drower, 'Gaston Maspero and the Birth of the Egypt Exploration Fund, 1881–3', *Journal of Egyptian Archaeology* 68 (1982), p. 313.

29 'Ce que M. Maspero ne veut pas, c'est qu'on fouille dans un but mercantile pour trouver des objets et les vendre; toutes les fois qu'il soupçonnera un but de cette espèce, il refusera l'autorization.' Naville to Edwards, April 1882, EES IV. e. 2.

30 See Alice Stevenson, in *Scattered Finds: Archaeology, Egyptology and Museums*, UCL Press, 2019, pp. 217–18. Stevenson is both an academic historian – Associate Professor of Museum Studies at the Institute of Archaeology, University College, London – and a former curator of the Petrie Museum of Egyptian Archaeology. As she points out, successive Egyptian governments have worked to control the exportation and dispersal of antiquities from Egypt, culminating in a total ban in 2010. For a useful table of such legislation, beginning with a decree by Mohamed Ali Pasha in 1835, see *Scattered Finds*, Appendix A, pp. 259–60.

31 'Edwards gave in': Letter to Poole, November 13, 1883, EES IV. D.114.

32 Stevenson, in *Scattered Finds*, pp. 218–19.

33 'The Story of Tanis', *Harper's New Monthly Magazine* 73.437, October 1886, pp. 710–73, p. 719.

34 Told in *The Graphic*, June 20, 1877, p. 1.

35 Letter from Maspero, April 15, 1882. SCO Edwards 165.

36 See Margaret S. Drower, *Flinders Petrie: A Life in Archaeology*, 1985. Wisconsin UP, 1995, pp. 62, 69.

37 Quoted in Stevenson, *Scattered Finds*, p. 35.

38 Quoted in Drower, *Flinders Petrie*, p. 93.

39 Kate Bradbury, PP. 10. iv. 6, quoted in Moon, *More Usefully Employed*, p. 240.

40 *Pharaohs, Fellahs, Explorers*, p. 41.

41 *Pharaohs, Fellahs*, pp. 21–22.

42 Letter, Edwards to a neighbour, April 4, 1883, UCL Mss Add 181/4. (Quoted in Moon, p. 185.)

43 Letter, Edwards to Barclay Head, August 25, 1886, EES III. a. 27.

44 See, 'Lecture to the Tamworth Natural History Society, "The Buried Cities of Ancient Egypt"', *Tamworth Herald*, December 10, 1887, p. 8.

45 Letter, May 5, 1887, EES III. a. 64.

46 Kate Hill, *Women and Museums, 1850–1914: Modernity and the Gendering of Knowledge*. Manchester UP, 2016, pp. 166–7.

47 Erasmus Wilson to Edwards, February 6, 1883, EES XVII. b. 7.

48 *The Graphic*, July 31, 1886, p. 6.

49 *The Morning Post*, February 15, 1877, p. 2.

50 Papyri from Thebes and Fayoum: Her talk was reported in the *London Daily News*, Sept 30, 1886, p. 5.

51 *Manchester Courier and Lancashire General Advertiser*, November 3, 1887, p. 3.

52 Letter to the *Manchester Courier* for January 31, 1888, p. 3.

53 Letter, Edwards to Poole, December 6, 1885, EES III. a. 15.

54 Canon Taylor: Emily Paterson to Poole, June 27, 1889, EES III. a. 68.

55 Letter from Renouf to Edwards, November 2, 1886, EES III. a. 47. From Edwards to Francis Llewellyn Griffith, November 4, 1886, EES III. a. 49.

56 Letter to Edward Poynter, of the Society for Preservation of the Monuments of Ancient Egypt, June 29, 1990, EES VIII. b. 31.

57 She addressed these points in a lecture given on December 7, 1888, at The Priory, Nutfield. Reported in *Illustrated London News*, December 15, 1888, p. 6.

58 Quoted in Rees, *Amelia Edwards: Traveller, Novelist and Egyptologist*, London: Rubicon, 1998, p. 59.

59 'Running through our little capital': Edwards to Poole, February 2, 1885, EES III. a. 9; EES III. a. 8, July 1, 1885.

60 Letter, July 1, 1885, EES III. a. 8.

61 Waste of her energy and time: Letter, Edwards to Barclay Head, August 1886, EES III. a. 20.

62 Letter to Thomas Hayter Lewis, August 2, 1888, EES III. d. 19.

63 Ewards to Poole, October 3, 1888, EES III. a. 64.

64 July 10, 1889, EES III. a. 69.

65 Offer to be acting administrative secretary: Letter, September 8, 1886, EES III.
    a. 35.

66 Letter to Francis Griffith, October 19, 1886, EES III. a. 42.

67 January 12, 1885, EES III. g. 7.

68 Poole to Edwards, December 1, 1886, EES III. g. 140.

69 Flinders Petrie to Edwards, regarding his expenses: July 30, 1886, EES. XVII. c.6.

70 Drower, *Flinders Petrie*, p. 101.

71 August 9, 1886, EES XIX. b. 28.

72 Edwards to Petrie, August 1886, EES III. a. 32; PP 9. iv. 6. (See Moon, *More
    Usefully Employed*, pp. 202–3.)

73 Letter to Petrie, August 23, 1886, PP 9. iv. 6. Quoted in Moon, p. 203.

74 Letter to Petrie, December 30, 1886: PP 9. iv. 18. Quoted in Moon, p. 214.

75 Letter from Naville to Edwards, June 30, 1887, SOC Edwards 319.

76 July 11, 1888, EES VIII. 25.

77 SCO Edwards 440. Emily Paterson's talk, in 1931, at the Egypt Exploration
    Society (as the EEF became known after 1919).

78 Letter to Petrie, September 13, 1887, EES IX. d. 7.

79 EES XVII. c. 73.

80 Edwards to Petrie, June 21, 1888, PP 9. iv. 39.

81 Bradbury to Petrie, PP 10. iv. 6. Quoted in Moon, *More Usefully Employed*, p. 240.

82 Letter to *The Times*, October 15, 1890.

83 Drower, *Flinders Petrie*, p. 123.

Chapter 7

1   See Rees, *Amelia Edwards: Traveller, Novelist and Egyptologist*, p. 100:
    'Amelia Edwards will investigate anything except her own reactions'.

2   The Griffith Institute (GI) II. 3/28. Quoted in Moon, *More Usefully Employed*,
    p. 239.

3   'Literary Memories', *Cornishman*, August 18, 1892, p. 4.

4   May 19, 1885, SCO Edwards 99; September 2, 1885, SCO Edwards 100.

5   October 26, 1885, SCO Edwards 103.

6   Invitation to Edwards to visit him in San Remo: July 14, 1883, SCO Edwards 98.

    **By 1886, Lear was feeling apologetic that he did not write to Lucy Renshaw
    more often.**

7   'Dont je rougis chaque jour', Doré told her in a letter of May 10, 1869. (SCO
    Edwards 443.) He calls it (SCO Edwards 451), 'un défaut sans excuse'; yet
    claims to suffer from 'un maladie', 'qu'on pourrait appeler l'aphase épistolaire
    . . . avec vous, mademoiselle, j'ai déjà été plus d'une fois coupable' (SCO
    Edwards 453).

8 Greetings to the Byrnes: May 10, 1869, SCO Edwards 443. Again, he
   sends greetings to the Byrnes, and hopes they may come to London at
   some time when he's there. February, SCO Edwards 445; June 1871, SCO
   Edwards 446.

9 The Franco-Prussian war, and the Paris Commune: 'Malgré bien des
   souffrances, fatigues, privations de toutes sortes', his family are safe; On his
   working holidays in Scotland and Switzerland – 'je reviendrai avec une ample
   moisson d'études et de projets de tableaux'. On what he expects of her book
   about the Nile: 'Je suis sûr que nous allons voir éclore prochainement un livre
   qui vous fera honneur'. He welcomes her back from Egypt: she will have 'des
   grandes et vives impressions dont votre esprit de poète se trouve enrichi et
   renouvelé'. He envies her experience of travel – as he does that of all who have
   seen 'tout ce que contient de beau la planète que nous habitons'. (SCO
   Edwards 451; August 23, 1872, SCO Edwards 448.) He again welcomes her
   home from Egypt: February 17, 1876, SCO Edwards 450.

10 Painting out of doors: See Annie Renonciat, Maurice Rheims, *La vie et oeuvre
   de Gustave Doré*. Paris: ACR,1983, p. 228. Not yet ready to publish . . . critics:
   'je ne suis pas encore prêt de rien publier', for fear of 'les assauts de la critique'.
   For Doré's plans to exhibit in London – the Moses painting, and the Dante's
   Inferno – 'avec laquelle je vais troubler peut-être un peu fort les paisibles
   visiteurs de Bond Street': SCO Edwards 452, 1877; SCO Edwards 453,
   1879.

11 Edwards, 'Gustave Doré: Personal recollections of the artist and his works',
   The Art Journal, 1883, pp. 391–2.

12 Edwards' letter to Doré on the death of his mother: 'les traits si nobles et le
   sourire si doucement sympathique d'elle qui je pleure'. Monday, May 1, 1881,
   SCO Edwards 454.

13 'j'ai entendu d'un peu bien du monde que votre roman publié dans le Graphic
   avait eu un success retentissant.' June 1881, SCO Edwards 455.

14 *Art Journal*, 1883, pp. 391–2.

15 See Chapter 2 of the present work, for Edwards' own account of her
   depression while staying in Rome, in the winter of 1871–2.

16 Draft autobiography for Edward Abbott, editor of *The Literary World*: SCO
   Edwards W22.

17 'My Home Life', *Arena* 4, 1891, pp. 299–310.

18 'My Home Life', p. 299.

19 'My Home Life', pp. 304–10.

20 Matilda Bentham Edwards, 'Amelia B. Edwards, Her Childhood and Early
   Life', *New England Magazine* 7.5, January 1893, p. 563.

21 For some of her activities in Bristol during the late 1880s, see Chapter 10 of
   the present work.

22 Letter, Edwards to Poole, May 7, 1883, EES III. a. 4.

23 SCO Edwards 351.

24 PP 10. iv. 2. Quoted in Moon, *More Usefully Employed*, p. 237.

Chapter 8

1 'That I shall sin again in the way of storytelling I do not doubt, but I venture to think that, for the present, I am more usefully employed.' Edwards, SCO 565.13.

2 *My Brother's Wife*: All references in the present work are to the edition published in New York by Harper and Brothers, 1865.

3 *My Brother's Wife*, p. 112.

4 *My Brother's Wife*, pp. 49, 90.

5 *My Brother's Wife*, p. 64.

6 *The Ladder of Life: A Heart-History*. 1856. London: Routledge, 1857, p. 168.

7 *Ladder of Life*, pp. 149, 155.

8 *Ladder of Life*, p. 249.

9 *Ladder of Life*, pp. 305, 112, 228.

10 *Ladder of Life*, pp. 175, 197.

11 *Ladder of Life*, p. 210.

12 *Ladder of Life*, p. 210.

13 The story is told in Matilda's *Reminiscences*. (London: George Redway, 1898, pp. 153–5.) Matilda B. Edwards' novel, *Dr Jacob* was published by Hurst and Blackett (London, 1864).

14 *Hand and Glove*, London: J. and C. Brown, 1858. All references here are to the Tauchnitz edition, published in Leipzig in 1865.

15 *Hand and Glove*, pp. 89–93.

16 *Hand and Glove*, p. 87.

17 *Hand and Glove*, pp. 219, 144.

18 *Hand and Glove*, p. 315.

19 *Hand and Glove*, p. 61.

20 *Hand and Glove*, pp. 154–5.

21 *Hand and Glove*, p. 102.

22 *Hand and Glove*, pp. 173–4.

23 The novel would be the main topic of an assessment of Edwards' fiction by Katharine Macquoid, herself a prolific novelist. See Mrs Macquoid, 'Amelia Blandford Edwards', in Mrs Oliphant et al, *Women Novelists of Queen Victoria's Reign: A Book of Appreciations*. London: Hurst and Blackett, 1897, pp. 251–74. The review in *The Times* was quoted in *Dublin Evening Mail*, April 1, 1864.

24 *London Daily News*, January 5, 1864, p. 2.

25 'Barbara's History', *The Spectator*, January 23, 1864, p. 23.

26 The *Morning Post*, January 13, 1864, p. 6.

27 *Barbara's History*, vol. 3, p. 195.

28 *Barbara's History*, vol. 1, p. 10.

29 *Barbara's History*, vol. 1, p. 32.

30 *Barbara's History*, vol. 1, p. 15.

31 *Barbara's History*, vol. 1, p. 48.

32 *Barbara's History*, vol. 2, pp. 59–60.

33 *Barbara's History*, vol. 3, p. 226.

34 Edwards' *Miss Carew* (published by Hurst and Blackett in the same year as *Half a Million of Money*), is not included here, as it is essentially a collection of short stories, some of them previously published elsewhere, strung together by a flimsy romantic narrative.

35 *Half a Million of Money*. London: Tinsley, 1866, vol. 2, p. 272. The novel, which first appeared as a serial in Dickens' magazine, *All the Year Round*, (No. 312, April 22, 1865), and in *Harper's Weekly* in America, was republished five times in English between 1865 and 1892, and translated into French, as *L'Héritage de Jacob Trefalden*.

36 *Half a Million*, vol. 2, p. 179; vol. 3, p. 20.

37 *Half a Million*, vol. 3, p. 312.

38 *Half a Million*, vol. 3, pp. 55–57.

39 'Word paintings' of Palermo and Mount Etna: *Half a Million*, vol. 3, pp. 204, 89.

40 *Half a Million*, vol. 2, p. 86; vol. 2, p. 285.

41 *Half a Million*, vol. 2, p. 296.

42 *Half a Million*, vol. 3, p. 232.

43 'Poverty . . . a crime': *Half a Million*, vol. 2, p. 93; Liberty . . . 'a vulgar institution': *Half a Million*, vol.2, p. 102.

44 *Half a Million*, vol. 3, pp. 1–2.

45 *Half a Million*, vol. 2, p. 258.

46 *Half a Million*, vol. 2, p. 239.

47 *Half a Million*, vol. 3, p. 386.

48 *Half a Million*, vol.3, p. 375.

49 His novels move us, Edwards observed, because his characters were 'absolutely real to him'. Herein lies 'the inmost secret of the art of the novelist'. (See, 'A Tribute to Thackeray', a talk reproduced in the *Dublin Evening Telegraph*, Sept. 15, 1894, p. 4.) Thackeray was not, as he is often described, a cynic, Edwards contends; but 'the most human of humanists', who had 'infinite sympathy with all that is best . . . in his erring fellow men'.

50 *Half a Million*, vol. 3, p. 398.

51 *L'Héritage de Jacob Trefalden*. Paris: Hachette, 1881.

52 '. . . parades his money': *Illustrated London News*, December 16, 1865, p. 19; *London Evening Standard*, January 26, 1866, p. 8.

53 Browning, letter to 'Isa', April 19, 1869, pp. 313–15. In *Dearest Isa: Robert Browning's Letters to Isabella Blagdon*, ed. Edward C. McAleer, University of Texas Press, 1951, pp. 313–15; Letter, Browning to Edwards, March 27, 1871, SCO Edwards 17.

54 *Debenham's Vow*. London: Hurst and Blackett, 1870, vol. 1, p. 22.

55 *Debenham's Vow*, vol. 1, p. 252.

56 *Debenham's Vow*, vol. 2, p. 17.

57 Edwards' thoughts on the art of fiction were published in 1894, as 'A Lady Novelist on Historical Novels', in the *Cheltenham Chronicle* for August 4. *The Last Days of Pompeii*, by Edward Bulwer-Lytton, appeared in 1834. Other popular historical fiction was by Walter Scott (for example, his *Ivanhoe*, published in 1819, but still enjoyed by Victorians). In Edwards' lifetime, Charles Kingsley published *Hereward the Wake* (1866), a novel about a Saxon leader's resistance to the Norman conquest.

58 *Debenham's Vow*, vol. 2, p. 189; vol. 2, p. 59.

59 *Debenham's Vow*, vol.2, p. 98. On New Year's Eve, 1862, a mass meeting of Manchester mill hands and their liberal supporters, knowing that it would mean deprivation and hunger for their families, passed a motion in support of the abolition of slavery, and of support for the Union blockade. In a letter of January 19, 1863, President Lincoln wrote in person to praise their 'sublime Christian heroism', and their sacrifice.

60 *Debenham's Vow*, vol. 2, p. 123.

61 The weight of the average American cotton bale: *Debenham's Vow*, vol. 2, p. 51; Cotton prices in the first years of the American Civil War, *Debenham's Vow*, vol.2, p. 121; Beacons in Charleston Harbour, *Debenham's Vow*, vol. 2, p. 55; Adapting a regular cargo ship for blockade-running: vol. 2, p. 59 of the novel.

62 *Debenham's Vow*, vol. 2, pp. 244–9.

63 *Debenham's Vow*, vol. 2, p. 277.

64 *Debenham's Vow*, vol. 3, p. 31.

65 'cricket ball': *Debenham's Vow*, vol.1, p. 62; 'a fine statue': *Debenham's Vow*, vol. 3, p. 80.

66 *Debenham's Vow*, vol. 3, p. 78.

67 *Debenham's Vow*, vol. 3, p. 94; vol.3, p. 95.

68 *Debenham's Vow*, vol. 3, p. 131.

69 *Debenham's Vow*, vol.3, pp. 188–9, vol. 3, p. 197.

70 Rees (p.76) describes Debenham as 'falling prey to what would now be diagnosed as a psychosomatic illness'. She thinks this alleged development destroys credibility in Debenham as a character. In fact, Edwards makes clear that Debenham's collapse is due to overwork, and to the re-opening of a recent stab wound received during a fight on shipboard.

71 *Debenham's Vow*, vol. 3, p. 276.

72 *Debenham's Vow*, vol. 3, p. 275.

73 Letter, Browning to Edwards, March 27, 1871, SCO Edwards17.

74 Letter, Trollope to Edwards, December 9, 1869, SCO Edwards 318.

75 *The Examiner* found Debenham a 'most improbable, unlifelike hero'. (December 25, 1869, p. 4.) Unable to depict male characters successfully: *Pall*

Mall Gazette, December 10, 1869, p. 11. The *Gazette* reviewer also refused to believe that the sudden change in Debenham's life goals could be brought about by the 'paltry accident' of learning about his ancestry. Others disagreed, finding all the novel's characters 'sympathetically and vividly drawn'; adding that the scenes of action showed 'rare dramatic power'. (See, for example, the *Northwich Guardian*, January 9, 1869, p. 2.) *The Examiner* praised the blockade-running scenes. One reviewer added that Edwards showed a rare 'female proficiency in masculine studies'. ('New Light Literature', *Cambridge Independent Press*, November 27, 1869, p. 5.) The *Sunday Times* was content with calling *Debenham's Vow* 'a noble work'. (Quoted in the *Morning Post*, November 23, 1869.)

76 *In the Days of My Youth*. London: Hurst and Blackett, 1873.

77 *Days of My Youth*, vol. 2, pp. 98–108.

78 *Illustrated London News*, March 1, 1873, p. 11.

79 *Days of My Youth*, vol. 2, pp. 291–5.

80 *Days of My Youth*, vol.1, p. 71.

81 *Lord Brackenbury*. London: Hurst and Blackett, 1880.

82 See Edwards' complaint about being unable to find time to fulfil more novel contracts: 'Founding the Fund', Chapter 6 in the present work.

83 Lancelot . . . social conscience. See Moon, *More Usefully Employed*, p. 306.

84 *Lord Brackenbury*, vol. 3, p. 332.

85 The letter about Cuthbert rescuing someone from the burning house is dated simply, 'Saturday'. The queries about Biddulph Moor and the engagement ring, are in a letter of January 14, 1880. (SCO Edwards.)

86 Marianne North to Edwards: SCO Edwards, 256, May 9, 1881. Edward Lear: October 18, 1885, SCO Edwards 102.

87 *London Daily News*, September 21, 1880, p. 3.

88 For quotation from this episode in *Lord Brackenbury*, see Chapter 3 of the present work.

89 I have not included *Miss Carew* or *Monsieur Maurice* as 'novels'. Both are, in essence, collections of short stories.

90 *Chelsea News*, March 9, 1867, p. 7.

91 See Maspero's observations on Egyptology as a practice of the art of fiction, in Chapter 5 of the present work.

Chapter 9

1 Letter to Petrie, April 19, 1888, PP 9. iv. 38, quoted in Moon, *More Usefully Employed*, p. 221.

2 Letter to Petrie, April 19, 1888, PP 9. iv. 38.

3 'a thoroughly good time': *Royal Cornwall Gazette*, Dec 5, 1889, p. 6. In a short snippet of gossip in the comic paper *Ally Sloper's Half Holiday*, Edwards

was said to be 'enjoying a holiday', while observing American 'men and manners'. (March 29, 1890, p. 6.)

4   Letter from Winslow, May 3, 1886, EES II. d. 103. For the honorary degree for Winslow from St Andrews: January 17, 1887, EES II. D. 138.

5   'More Honours for Women', *Dublin Daily Express*, July 26, 1886, p. 5. In Britain, a woman could be awarded the honorary higher degree of 'Legum Doctor' (LLD); but was not eligible for a PhD, honorary or otherwise. A writer in the *Pall Mall Gazette* complained that no honorary degree was available to women in England, other than 'this highly inappropriate LLD'. *Pall Mall Gazette*, reproduced in *Aberdeen Evening Express*, July 19, 1886, p. 2.

6   Reported in the *Brooklyn Eagle*, November 13, 1889.

7   For Edwards' liking for Americans, see, for example, *A Thousand Miles Up the Nile*, p. 600.

8   Kate Bradbury, private Journal, November 3, 1889, p. 5; GI, Bradbury Mss. i, 1–2.

9   Kate Bradbury, November 11, 1889; February 19, 1890. Charles Dickens, visiting America in 1842, had complained of the overheating of buildings there. 'The heat and closeness are quite insupportable. But this is the characteristic of all the public institutions, chapels, theatres and prisons . . . their effect upon an Englishman is briefly told. He is always very sick and very faint, and has an intolerable headache, morning, noon and night.' In *The Letters of Charles Dickens*, vol. 3, eds. M. House et al. Oxford: Clarendon Press, 1965, p. 100.

10 'A Famous Woman', *Detroit Free Press*, February 25, 1890, p. 3; Bradbury, February 24, p. 284.

11 Bradbury, November 11, 1889, p. 23; February 19, 1890, p. 270.

12 Bradbury, November 3–5, pp. 11–12.

13 Bradbury, November 13, p. 28.

14 Bradbury, November 15, p. 29.

15 SCO Edwards 350.

16 SCO Edwards 528.

17 Bradbury, December 1, pp. 67, 70.

18 Rees, *Amelia Edwards: Traveller, Novelist and Egyptologist*, p. 63.

19 'It is cruelly hard for me to bear, and I feel she does not realize it.' Winslow to Edwards' secretary, Emily Paterson, December 2, 1889, EES II. e. 25; Letter, Winslow to Edwards, on receiving her photograph: April 20, 1886, EES II. d. 95.

20 Matilda B. Edwards, 'Amelia B. Edwards, Her Childhood and Early Life', p. 550.

21 *Boston Daily Globe*, November 21, 1889.

22 In *Boston Saturday Evening Gazette*, December 7, 1889.

23 'An Intellectual Treat', *Newhaven Morning News*, November 12, 1889; 'Honors to a Talented Lady', *Boston Herald*, November 30, 1889.

24 Kate Bradbury, Journal, November 16, p. 33.

25 Twain and Warner co-authored a novel, *The Gilded Age* (1873). A satire on greed and corruption in America, it gave its name to the final decades of the nineteenth century.

26 A phrase originally coined by Wordsworth, in a sonnet of 1802 – 'O Friend! I know not which way I must look' – in which the poet lamented, 'Plain living and high thinking are no more'. On Edwards' preference for a little more 'high living', see Bradbury's Journal, January 4, 1890, p. 148.

27 Bradbury, November 20, 1889, p. 38.

28 Bradbury, December 8, p. 83.

29 Bradbury, December 9, p. 90.

30 According to the *Buffalo Commercial*, in 'Ancient Egypt: A Brief Talk with Miss Edwards, the Secretary of the Exploration Fund', January 31, 1890, p. 3.

31 Bradbury, January 26, 1890, p. 200.

32 Mount Holyoke: Bradbury, January 30, p. 220.

33 'miss the train to Boston': Bradbury, December 31, 1889, p. 137; Aurora, Michigan: Bradbury, February 18, 1890, p. 265.

34 Bradbury, February 9, 1890, p. 239; February 14, p. 265; *Macon Telegraph*, March 10, 1890, p. 1.

35 Bradbury, February 24, p. 284; February 5, p. 231.

36 Bradbury, February 6, p. 236; February 26, p. 289.

37 Bradbury, February 14, p. 255.

38 Bradbury, January 24, p. 198.

39 She would be remembered in the honour roll of women's achievements in the main hall of the Woman's Building at the World's Columbian Exposition, held in Chicago in 1893. A frieze in gold lettering bore the names of famous women of the nineteenth century: Queen Victoria, Christina Rossetti, Florence Nightingale, Elizabeth Barrett Browning, Amelia Edwards. Reported in the *Dundee Evening Telegraph*, May 5, 1893, p. 4. (See also Chapter 11 of the present work.)

40 *Sheffield Independent*, January 31, 1890, p. 4. The Municipal Franchise Act of 1869 had given single women who paid property taxes (rates) the right to vote in local elections. It was not, however, until 1894, that all women, single or married, owning property or not, were able to vote in local polls.

41 Quoted in Moon, *More Usefully Employed*, p. 232.

42 The *Kansas City Star* (Kansas City, Missouri), March 22, 1890, p. 4.

43 Benjamin Harrison, a Republican, was president of the United States from March 1889 until March 1893. He is best remembered for his advocacy of African-American voting rights, and of the extension of educational opportunities for Blacks. He was also a supporter of the Egyptian Exploration Fund. He lost popularity owing to his policy of raising interstate tariffs to fund increased government spending and was voted out after a single term in office.

44 The reception was reported in the *Derby Daily Telegraph* for April 12, 1890; the *Eastern Daily Press*, for February 3, 1890 (p.8); the *Worcestershire Chronicle* of April 12; and the *Northern Whig* (April 21, 1890, p. 6).

45 'a little trying to German members': Bradbury, March 9, p. 332; 'Opportunities
    . . . American girls': *Worcestershire Chronicle*, April 12, 1890, p. 3. For
    Edwards' comments on the sexism of the British university system, see *The
    Hartford Courant*, March 20, 1890, p. 7.

46 'Amelia B. Edwards', *Brooklyn Daily Eagle*, Wednesday March 19, 1890, p. 4.

47 *Northern Whig*, April 28, 1890, p. 6.

Chapter 10

1   'The Late Miss Amelia Edwards', *Bristol Mercury*, April 25, 1892, p. 6. The
    view was taken up by Joan Rees: 'She did not campaign openly for women's
    suffrage'. (*Amelia Edwards: Traveller, Novelist and Egyptologist*, p. 79.)

2   SCO Edwards 440.

3   In June 1881, along with William Morris, Lord Houghton, and six other
    notables, she addressed the Society for the Protection of Ancient Buildings.
    London Daily News, June 25, 1881, p. 4.

4   'I trust I shall be able to avail myself of your kind invitation.' Letter from Louis
    Blanc, August 1854, SCO Edwards.

5   'Amelia Blandford Edwards', in *Mid-Victorian Memories*. London; John
    Murray, 1919, pp. 110–18, p. 118.

6   'Amelia B. Edwards', *Boston Daily Globe*, April 28, 1890, p. 8.

7   Letter to Lucy Stone, written in Amherst, January 16, 1890, declining an invitation
    to attend the 20th annual meeting of the Massachusetts Woman Suffrage
    Association. Reproduced in the *Boston Daily Globe*, January 29, 1890, p. 2.

8   *Boston Sunday Herald*, March 30, 1890.

9   *York Herald* obituary, April 23, 1892, p. 9.

10 'The Rights of Women', *Hereford Times*, March 8, 1856, p. 13.

11 'The Rights of Women', in the *Wiltshire Independent*, March 6, 1856, p. 2.

12 For the full list of names on the suffrage petition of 1866, see https://www.
    parliament.uk/documents/parliamentary-archives/1866SuffragePetitionNames
    WebFeb18.pdf

13 'Fifty Years Ago', in *The Western Daily Press*, March 27, 1937, p. 7.

14 For her petition request to the Poole family, see her letter of May 1887, EES IX.
    c. 22.

15 See Moon, *More Usefully Employed*, p. 217; PP 9. iv. 27.

16 *Bristol Mercury*, January 30, 1888, p. 8.

17 The Bristol meeting was reported in the *Bath Chronicle* (February 16, 1888,
    p. 2). Between 1867 and 1889, no less than thirteen bills proposing legislation
    for the extension of the suffrage to women were brought before Parliament. In
    1888, 169 MPs had signed a statement urging Parliament to make time in the
    next session, for a new debate on the subject. https://www.parliament.uk/
    about/living-heritage/transformingsociety/electionsvoting/womenvote/case-
    studies-women-parliament/suffragettes-in-trousers/peter-mclagan/

18 For Edwards' letter to the Boston suffrage convention, see Chapter 9 of the present work: 'America'.

19 See 'A Thousand Miles Up the Nile'; and 'Inventing Egypt' in the present work.

20 See also the detailed discussion of the provisions made in Edwards' will, in the final chapter of this book, 'Reputation'.

21 In 'Metropolitan Gossip', Belfast News-Letter, October 27, 1877, p. 4.

22 In the Morning Post, January 26, 1878, p. 6.

23 Paddington Times, August 1, 1877; Moon, More Usefully Employed, pp. 156–7.

24 Letter, May 3, 1878, to Kate Field: Boston PL MS KF 1080. Quoted in Moon, More Usefully Employed, p. 156. (Moon also cites an angry letter from a dissatisfied customer of the laundry. Whether, though, the failure of the business was due to the work being of an unsatisfactory standard generally, or whether this was an isolated incident, is unknown.)

25 'A Challenge', Woman's Signal, February 22, 1894, p. 3.

26 Letter, Edwards to Cobbe, January 7, 1888. Frances Power Cobbe correspondence, 1855–1904, mss CB 1–854.

27 Edwards to Cobbe, December 3, 1889; December 7, 1889.

28 Her coming participation in the anti-vivisection debate was announced in the Western Daily Press for March 2, 1889, p. 6.

29 The petition was printed in a number of national and regional newspapers, including the Western Daily Press for November 5, 1891.

30 In A Thousand Miles Up the Nile, p. 470; 'butchery', A Thousand Miles, p. 527.

31 Matilda B. Edwards, in 'Childhood', p. 563.

32 'A Lady's Appeal', the Western Daily Press, March 17, 1886, p. 6. In the winter of 1879, she sent a similar appeal to The Times. (Reprod. in Taunton Courier, January 8, 1879, p. 5.)

33 From the Hon. Secretary, Mrs Robert F. Sturge, in the Western Daily Press, April 23, 1892, p. 8.

34 Western Daily Press, April 19, 1892, p. 5; Clifton Society, April 21, 1892, p. 8.

35 Morning Post, April 30, 1880, p. 3.

36 'The Seat of War in Egypt', in The Star, September 2, 1882, p. 4, quoting Edwards' letter to The Times of August 29. 'Cities . . . captivity: 'The land of Goshen', London Daily News, August 17, 1882, p. 6; reprod. in Wiltshire and Gloucestershire Standard, August 19, 1882, p. 8.

37 Casper Andersen, British Engineers and Africa, 1875–1914. 2011. London and New York: Routledge, 2016, pp. 147–53.

38 Debenham's Vow, vol. 3, p. 223.

Chapter 11

1 Pall Mall Gazette, March 5, 1890, p. 6; Bradford Daily Telegraph, March 5, 1890, p. 4; Croydon Chronicle and East Surrey Advertiser, March 22, 1890,

p. 7; *Derby Daily Telegraph*, April 12, 1890, p. 2; *The Globe*, March 22, 1890, p. 6.

2 *Croydon Chronicle and East Surrey Advertiser*, March 22, 1890, p. 7; 'From our Lady Correspondent', *Sheffield Daily Telegraph*, February 20, 1891, p. 4.

3 *Belfast News-Letter*, August 20, 1872, p. 2.

4 'Mrs Freund': *Dundee Courier*, November 14, 1871, p. 3; 'Amelia Lewis': *Chester Chronicle*, November 18, 1871, p. 5.

5 *The Academy*, June 19, 1880.

6 Reported in *The Star*, September 16, 1870, p. 12.

7 According to *Lloyds Weekly Newspaper*, December 10, 1871, p. 5.

8 *Croydon Chronicle and East Surrey Advertiser*, March 22, 1890, p. 7.

9 *Aberdeen Press and Journal*, January 6, 1892, p. 6.

10 'Clever stories': 'Books of the Week', in *The Examiner,* May 15, 1858, p. 5. *Debenham's Vow* – 'decidedly a clever book': *Morning Advertiser*, Dec 22, 1869, p. 8; 'When she lectured on ancient Egypt, she was "the clever lady"': 'A String of Chinese Peach Stones', *Western Daily Press*, March 7, 1896, p. 3; The 'learned lady' (report on an Egyptology lecture at Birkbeck Institute): *Sheffield Daily Telegraph*, February 20, 1891, p. 4; 'powerful sketches of character', and 'clever artistic touches', *Liverpool Mercury*, January 10, 1873, p. 7. There are 'clever, incisive sayings' in *Half a Million of Money: London Evening Standard*, Jan 26, 1866, p. 8.

11 'Literature and Art', *Nottingham Evening Post*, December 4, 1890, p. 2.

12 *Western Daily Post*, November 9, 1891, p. 7.

13 *Western Daily Press,* March 7, 1896: 'A String of Chinese Peach Stones'.

14 'all the better. . .America': *Sheffield Daily Telegraph*, February 20, 1891, p. 4. 'It stops my work': Letter from Edwards to Petrie, May 1, 1890, PP. 9. iv. 52, quoted in Moon, *More Usefully Employed*, p. 233.

15 See also J.W. Pye, 'Painful last days of the queen of Egyptology', in *KMT: A Modern Journal of Ancient Egypt* 5.4, 1995, pp. 77–78.

16 *Manchester Times*, August 8, 1890, p. 6.

17 PP. 9. iv. 2, quoted in Moon, *More Usefully Employed*, p. 236.

18 Reported in *York Herald,* April 23, 1892, p. 9. Balfour at that time was Secretary for Ireland in the Conservative cabinet.

19 SCO Edwards 459.

20 *Glasgow Evening Post*, Júly 13, 1892, p. 4; *Kinross-shire Advertiser*, June 4, 1892, p. 3.

21 The 'best claim . . . for a Civil List pension': *Montgomeryshire Echo*, July 23, 1892, p. 3. A West Country paper: 'Literary Jottings', *Warminster and Westbury Journal*, July 30, 1892, p. 7; 'painstaking and conscientious work', *Norwich Mercury*, January 9, 1892, p. 4.

22 In Pye. 'Painful last days', p. 80.

23 October 14, 1891, EES I. b. 2.

24 Published by Osgood, McIlvaine in London, and by Harper in New York.

25 Letter to Griffith, December 23, 1891, EES III. d.49.

26 January 10, 1892, PP. 10. iv. 3. Quoted in Moon, *More Usefully Employed*, p. 240.

27 *Glasgow Herald*, February 6, 1892, p. 7.

28 Musical knowledge: *St James' Gazette*, April 18, 1892, p. 12; Ernest Budge, tribute: Obituary in *Saturday Review*, April 1892; 'Everything to make her happy': Matilda B. Edwards, 'The Late Miss Amelia Edwards', *Bristol Mercury*, April 25, 1892, p. 6.

29 Letter from Kate Bradbury to Petrie, in personal papers of Miss Lisette Petrie, PP. 10. iv. 8. Quoted in Moon, *More Usefully Employed*, p. 242.

30 'The Funeral of Miss Amelia B. Edwards', *Pall Mall Gazette*, April 22, 1892, p. 6.

31 Other inscriptions on the monument are to Sarah Braysher, 'who died in Paris in the flower of her age' on the 25th of June 1864; and to 'Ellen Drew Braysher, widow of John Braysher Esq. and for some thirty years of her ninety years the beloved companion of Amelia B. Edwards'.

32 *Western Gazette*, May 13, 1892, p. 8.

33 *York Herald*, April 19, 1892, p. 5.

34 'Mrs Macquoid', 'Amelia Blandford Edwards', in Mrs Oliphant, *Women Novelists of Queen Victoria's Reign: A Book of Appreciations*, p. 251.

35 'She was in truth a model contributor': Matilda Betham Edwards, quoting the editor of *The Academy*. In, 'Amelia B. Edwards, Her Childhood and Early Life', p. 549.

36 'Her best work . . . given to Egypt': *Western Morning News*, April 18, 1892, p. 5; 'one of its most devoted students': *Shields Daily Gazette*, April 23, 1892, p. 4.

37 Reported in *Dundee Evening Telegraph*, May 5, 1893, p. 4.

38 See obituaries in the *Journal of Egyptian Archaeology*, Vol. 88, 2002, pp. vii-xiii.

39 'favourite writer of women's stories': *Paisley and Renfrewshire Gazette*, December 1, 1892, p. 4.

40 The *Western Daily Press*, January 24, 1924, p. 5.

41 The *Western Daily Press*, July 20, 1915, p. 5.

42 https://historicengland.org.uk/listing/the-list/list-entry/1439170 Accessed November 2019.

43 https://historicengland.org.uk/listing/the-list/list-entry/1439170 Published September 23, 2016; accessed November 2019.

44 Verdi, *Aida,* 2012, Royal Albert Hall. The production, with set design by Isabella Bywater, was twice reviewed in *The Guardian* online (on February 26 and February 28, 2012, respectively).

BIBLIOGRAPHY

Works by Amelia Edwards

Novels and Short stories

'The Painter of Pisa', *Illustrated Magazine of Art* 1, 1853, pp. 330–31.
'The Château Regnier', *Eliza Cook's Journal* 8.207, April 16, 1853, pp. 387–90.
'Annette', *Chambers' Edinburgh Journal* 20.511, October 15, 1853; and 21.512, October 22, 1853.
My Brother's Wife: A Life-History. London: Hurst and Blackett, 1855. (All references in the present work are to the edition published in New York by Harper and Brothers, 1865.)
The Ladder of Life: A Heart-History. 1856. London: Routledge, 1857.
Barbara's History: A Novel. New York: Harper, 1864.
Hand and Glove. 1858. Leipzig: Tauchnitz, 1865.
Miss Carew. London: Hurst and Blackett, 1865.
Half a Million of Money. London: Tinsley, 1866.
Debenham's Vow. London: Hurst and Blackett, 1870.
Il Guanto Fatale. Milan: Emilio Croce, 1872. (Translation of *Hand and Glove*.)
In the Days of My Youth. London: Hurst and Blackett, 1873.
Monsieur Maurice, and Other Tales. London: Hurst and Blackett, 1873.
Lord Brackenbury. London: Hurst and Blackett, 1880.
L'Héritage de Jacob Trefalden. Paris: Hachette, 1881. (Translation of *Half a Million of Money*.)

Travel and Egyptology (books)

Untrodden Peaks and Unfrequented Valleys: A midsummer ramble in the Dolomites. London: Longmans, Green, 1873. (Second edition: London: Routledge, 1890.)
A Thousand Miles Up the Nile. London: Longmans, Green, 1877.
Egyptian Archaeology, by G. Maspero. (Translation from the French, by Amelia Edwards.) London: Grevel, 1887.
Pharaohs, Fellahs and Explorers. New York: Harper and Brothers, Franklin Square, 1891.

Articles

'Bubastis: An Historical Study', *The Graphic*, January 11, 1890, p. 10.

'The Cities of Egypt', *The Academy* 22, 1882, p. 389.

'The Doré Gallery', *Morning Post*, May 4, 1869.

'The Land of Goshen', *London Daily News*, August 17, 1882, p. 6; reprod. in *Wiltshire and Gloucestershire Standard*, August 19, 1882, p. 8.

'Lying in State in Cairo', *Harper's New Monthly Magazine* 65.386, July 1882, pp. 185–205.

'My Home life', *Arena* 4, 1891, pp. 299–310.

'The New Boolak Museum'. Letter from Edwards to *The Morning Post*, April 30, 1880, p. 3.

'The Progress of Discovery in Egypt', *The Academy*, April 7, 1883, pp. 246–7.

'The Seat of War in Egypt', *The Star*, September 2, 1882, p. 4.

'The Story of Tanis', *Harper's New Monthly Magazine* 73.437, October 1886, pp. 710–73.

'A Tribute to Thackeray'. Lecture by Amelia Edwards, reproduced in the *Dublin Evening Telegraph*, September 15, 1894, p. 4.

'Was Rameses II the Pharaoh of the Exodus?' *Knowledge* 2 (1882), pp. 108–9, 141–2, 192–3, 228–9, 244, 260–61, 291–3, 324–6, 357–8, 387, 450.

Minor works of nonfiction

Etiquette for Gentlemen: being a manual of minor social ethics and customary observances. London: Knight, 1857.

A History of France from the Conquest of Gaul by the Romans to the Peace of 1856. London: Routledge, 1858.

A Lady's Captivity among Chinese pirates in the Chinese seas. (Fanny Loviot, transl. Amelia B. Edwards.) London: Routledge, 1858.

Sights and Stories: being some account of a holiday tour through the north of Belgium. London: Victoria Press, 1862.

The Story of Cervantes. London: Routledge, 1862.

Ballads. London: Tinsley, 1865.

Manuscript sources

BM: The British Museum.

CB: mss CB, Frances Power Cobbe correspondence, The Huntington Library, San Marino, California.

EES: Egypt Exploration Society. (In 1919, the Egypt Exploration Fund changed its name to Exploration Society.)

GI: The Griffith Institute, University of Oxford.

Gerald N Wachs Collection, University of Chicago.

KB: Kate Bradbury's American journal, in the Griffith Institute collections as Bradbury Mss. i, 1–2.

Library Company of Philadelphia, Anne Hampton Brewster correspondence, 1.17.

PP: Personal papers (of Lisette Petrie).

SCO: Somerville College Library, Oxford.
UCL: University College London Special Collections.

Secondary sources in print

Andersen, Casper. *British Engineers and Africa, 1875–1914. 2011.* London and New York: Routledge, 2016, pp. 147–53.

Asbury, Beth L. 'Pitt-Rivers, the Painter and the Palaeolithic Period', Pitt-Rivers Museum, University of Oxford. *Birmingham Egyptology Journal,* 2014.

Asbury, Beth L. '*Barbara's History'*, review in *The Spectator,* January 23, 1864, p. 23.

Asbury, Beth L. 'Books of Eastern and Colonial Life: Egypt and its Explorers', *The Graphic,* April 9, 1892, p. 22.

Asbury, Beth L. 'Books of the Week', review *in The Examiner,* May 15, 1858, p. 5.

Boyle, Alan and Susan. *Spirits of the Dolomites.* London: Leannta, 2018.

Brady, Sean (ed.). 'The Correspondence of John Addington Symonds and Havelock Ellis on the project of sexual inversion'. *John Addington Symonds and Homosexuality: A critical edition of sources.* London: Palgrave Macmillan, 2012, pp. 239–41.

Drower, Margaret S. *Flinders Petrie: A Life in Archaeology.* 1985. Wisconsin UP, 1995.

Drower, Margaret S. 'Gaston Maspero and the Birth of the Egypt Exploration Fund, 1881–3'. *Journal of Egyptian Archaeology* 68 (1982), pp. 299–317.

Edwards, Matilda B. 'Amelia B. Edwards, Her Childhood and Early Life'. *New England Magazine* 7.5, January 1893, pp. 549–64.

Edwards, Matilda B. 'Amelia Blandford Edwards', in *Mid-Victorian Memories.* London; John Murray, 1919, pp. 110-18.

Edwards, Matilda B. *Dr Jacob.* London: Hurst and Blackett, 1864.

Edwards, Matilda B. 'The Late Miss Amelia Edwards', *Bristol Mercury,* April 25, 1892, p. 6.

Edwards, Matilda B. 'The Two Dromias', in *Reminiscences,* London: George Redway, 1898, p. 128.

Edwards, Matilda B. 'Fifty Years Ago', in *Western Daily Press,* March 27, 1937, p. 7.

Foster, John L. *Love Songs of the New Kingdom.* Austin: University of Texas Press, 1992.

Foster, John L. 'From our Lady Correspondent', *Sheffield Daily Telegraph,* February 20, 1891, p. 4.

Gange, David. 'Religion and Science in Late Nineteenth-Century British Egyptology'. *The Historical Journal* 49.4, December 2006, pp. 1083–1103.

Gange, David. 'Grand Amateur Concerts at Westbury-on-Trym', *Bristol Daily Post,* December 16, 1870, p. 3.

Hill, Kate. *Women and Museums, 1850–1914: Modernity and the Gendering of Knowledge.* Manchester University Press, 2016.

House, M., et al. *The Letters of Charles Dickens,* vol. 3, eds. M. House et al. Oxford: Clarendon Press, 1965.

Keay, Julia. *With Passport and Parasol: The Adventures of Seven Victorian Ladies.* London: BBC Books, 1989.

Keay, Julia. 'A Lady's Appeal', *Western Daily Press*, March 17, 1886, p. 6.

Keay, Julia. *'Lecture on Egyptology', Sheffield Daily Telegraph*, December. 6, 1890.

Linton, Eliza Lynn. *My Literary Life*. Ed. Beatrice Harraden. London: Hodder and Stoughton, 1899.

Linton, Eliza Lynn. 'Literary Memories', *Cornishman*, August 18, 1892, p. 4.

Linton, Eliza Lynn. *'Lord Brackenbury'*, review in *Pall Mall Gazette*, September 14, 1880, p. 12.

McAleer, Edward C., ed. *Dearest Isa: Robert Browning's Letters to Isabella Blagdon*. Austin: University of Texas Press, 1951.

Macquoid, Mrs [Katharine]. 'Amelia Blandford Edwards', in Mrs Oliphant et al, *Women Novelists of Queen Victoria's Reign: A Book of Appreciations*. London: Hurst and Blackett, 1897, pp. 251–74.

Moon, Brenda. *More Usefully Employed: Amelia B Edwards, Writer, Traveller and Campaigner for Ancient Egypt*. London: Egypt Exploration Society, 2006.

'Notes from John O'Gaunt's Chair', *Preston Herald*, December 13, 1890, p. 5.

Pye, J.W. 'Painful last days of the Queen of Egyptology'. *KMT: A Modern Journal of Ancient Egypt 5.4*, 1995, pp. 77–78.

Rees, Joan. *Amelia Edwards: Traveller, Novelist and Egyptologist*. London: Rubicon, 1998.

Renonciat, Annie, and Maurice Rheims. *La vie et oeuvre de Gustave Doré*. Paris: ACR, 1983.

Stevenson, Alice. *Scattered Finds: Archaeology, Egyptology and Museums*. UCL Press, 2019.

Stevenson, Alice. 'A String of Chinese Peach Stones', *The Western Daily Press*, March 7, 1896, p. 3.

Sturge, Mrs Robert F. 'From the Hon. Secretary', *The Western Daily Press*, April 23, 1892, p. 8.

Twain, Mark, and Warner, Charles Dudley. *The Gilded Age: A Tale of Today*. 1873. New York: Penguin Random House, 2001.

Wilkinson, John Gardner. *Manners and Customs of the Ancient Egyptians*. London: John Murray, 1837. (6 volumes, 1837–41.)

Websites

Egypt Exploration Society, www.ees.ac.uk

Garstang Museum, 'All you need is love: Modern themes in ancient Egyptian love poems'. https://garstangmuseum.wordpress.com/2018/02/07/all-you-need-is-love-modern-themes-in-ancient-egyptian-love-poems/

Historic England (Amelia Edwards' grave), https://historicengland.org.uk/listing/the-list/list-entry/1439170

Parliamentary archives, https://www.parliament.uk/documents/parliamentary-archives/1866SuffragePetitionNamesWebFeb18.pdf, https://www.parliament.uk/about/living-heritage/transformingsociety/electionsvoting/womenvote/case-studies-women-parliament/suffragettes-in-trousers/peter-mclagan/

Other periodicals consulted for untitled articles not listed in secondary sources

Magazines and journals

The Academy
Ally Sloper's Half Holiday
Arena
The Century
All the Year Round
The Art Journal
The Athenaeum
Good Words
Harper's New Monthly Magazine
The Historical Journal
Knowledge
Woman's Signal
The Young Woman

London-based and national

Bell's Weekly Messenger
The Examiner
Freeman's Journal
The Guardian
The Globe
The Graphic
Illustrated London News
Lloyds Weekly Newspaper
London Daily News
London Evening Standard
Morning Advertiser
Morning Post
Paddington Times
Pall Mall Gazette
Saturday Review
The Star
St James' Gazette
Sunday Times
The Times
The World

Regional newspapers, England and Wales

Bradford Daily Telegraph
Cambridge Independent Press

Chelsea News
Cheltenham Chronicle
Chester Chronicle
Croydon Chronicle and Surrey Advertiser
Derby Daily Telegraph
Eastern Daily Press
Liverpool Mercury
Manchester Courier and Lancashire General Advertiser
Manchester Times
Montgomeryshire Echo
Northern Whig
North London News
Northwich Guardian
Norwich Mercury
Norwood News
Nottingham Evening Post
Preston Herald
Sheffield Daily Telegraph
Sheffield Independent
Shields Daily Gazette
Tamworth Herald
Worcestershire Chronicle
York Herald

West Country
Bath Chronicle
Bristol Daily Post
Bristol Mercury
Bristol Times and Mirror
Clifton and Redland Free Press
Clifton Society
Cornishman
Royal Cornwall Gazette
Taunton Courier
Warminster and Westbury Journal
Western Daily Press
Western Gazette
Western Morning News
Wiltshire and Gloucestershire Standard

Regional newspapers, Ireland

Belfast News-Letter
Dublin Daily Express
Dublin Evening Mail

Regional newspapers, Scotland

Aberdeen Evening Express
Aberdeen Press and Journal
Dundee Courier
Dundee Evening Telegraph
Dundee, Perth and Cupor Advertiser
Glasgow Evening Post
Glasgow Herald
Kinross-shire Advertiser
Paisley and Renfrewshire Gazette
The Scotsman

American Newspapers

Boston Daily Globe
Boston Herald
Boston Saturday Evening Gazette
Brooklyn Daily Eagle
Buffalo Commercial
Detroit Free Press
Hartford Courant
Kansas City Star
Macon Telegraph
Newhaven Morning News

INDEX